Jonathan Michie

Macroeconomic Reforms, Growth, and Stability

Macroeconomic Reforms, Growth, and Stability

B.B. Bhattacharya
Sabyasachi Kar

OXFORD
UNIVERSITY PRESS

OXFORD
UNIVERSITY PRESS

YMCA Library Building, Jai Singh Road, New Delhi 110001

Oxford University Press is a department of the University of Oxford.
It furthers the University's objective of excellence in research, scholarship, and education by publishing worldwide in

Oxford New York
Auckland Cape Town Dar es Salaam Hong Kong Karachi
Kuala Lumpur Madrid Melbourne Mexico City Nairobi
New Delhi Shanghai Taipei Toronto

With offices in
Argentina Austria Brazil Chile Czech Republic France Greece
Guatemala Hungary Italy Japan Poland Portugal Singapore
South Korea Switzerland Thailand Turkey Ukraine Vietnam

Published in India
by Oxford University Press

First published 2007

ISBN-13: 978-0-19-568419-3
ISBN-10: 0-19-568419-2

Typeset in AGaramond 11/13
by Archetype, New Delhi 110002
Printed in India by Pauls Press, New Delhi 110020
Published by Oxford University Press
YMCA Library Building, Jai Singh Road, New Delhi 110001

Dedicated to our parents

CONTENTS

FOREWORD

This volume is being published as part of the IEG series on 'Studies in Economic and Social Development' (Number 67 of the Series earlier called the Studies in Economic Development and Planning), being the outcome of research work undertaken by its authors at the Institute of Economic Growth. The first publication to be brought out under the new name has the stated objective of 'analysing the past and throwing light on the future of the Indian economy', using a macroeconomic perspective. Such a perspective provides a backdrop for examining several aspects of economic and social development.

In the last quarter of a century, the Indian economy has undergone a silent revolution in terms of breaking the shackles of the 'Hindu Rate of Growth' and sustaining about 6 per cent growth rate for the 1980s and the 1990s. Although this was a significant feat by international standards, it was probably just the beginning of the Indian growth story. As the performance of recent years seems to indicate, the economy has shifted gear to an even higher growth trajectory in the new millennium. In this backdrop, the academician as well as the policy maker is confronted with two sets of questions. The first set seeks an explanation of the sustained performance in the past. The second set wants to know what we can expect in the future. This volume deals with both and answers them on the basis of a rigorous econometric modelling exercise, which carries forward the tradition of the IEG-DSE macro-econometric model for Project Link. The different components of the model, its validation, and the different simulations are described in detail to testify its underlying robustness. This constitutes one of the major strengths of the book.

The volume analyses the past performance of the economy in terms of the two decades of growth—the 1980s and the 1990s. It maintains that one of the important factors that influenced the performance of the economy during these decades was the structural reforms—partial in the 1980s and more substantial during the 1990s. Of course there were other natural and policy induced factors as well. Comparing and analysing the impact of all these factors, the study concludes that the overall growth shows no significant upturn during the 1990s as a result of reforms. However, the reforms played a very important role of containing inflation and macro imbalances during this period. Further, several simulations performed for the 1990s with the counterfactual scenarios studied shed light on the factors that promoted and constrained growth in the 1990s.

The volume then shifts its focus to the future of the economy, both in term of problems and prospects. Perhaps the greatest challenge that the economy will face in the future will be from domestic and external shocks. Whether they are in the form of droughts, oil price shocks, or capital flights, these shocks have wrecked havoc on the performance of the economy in the past. An important finding that emerges from this study is that the economy has become more resilient to these shocks over time, in particular rainfall shocks. The optimist would, of course, be interested to know how the economy will perform in the absence of any such shocks. The authors use a modified smaller model to examine this hypothesis with reference to shocks from rising oil prices, rate of growth of world imports, and capital flow shocks. An interesting finding is that they find that there is no instability in the long run from fiscal or external sectors, though short run impacts may exist.

The last part of the study looks into the future and postulates that a sustainable high growth rate shall have to depend on higher growth rates in agriculture and industry, even while the tertiary sector has become the engine of growth. In this context, the study finds that the economy has indeed moved on to a higher growth trajectory with a growth rate of around 7 per cent. Other issues relating to the external sector and oil prices are also highlighted, issues that are at present casting their shadows on the near-term future as well.

For the speedy elimination of poverty and to join the middle-income economies in the near future, the economy needs to grow at about 8 per cent or more. The important policy implication of this study is that such a target can be realized only with significant increases in both public investment and the productivity of capital in agriculture and industry.

There is enough in this volume for experts to ponder over, sufficient for policy makers to take account of, and a great deal for researchers and students of macroeconomics to learn from. I am certain that it shall add to both an understanding of the changing structure of the Indian economy and to public debate on appropriate policy directions to take.

October 2006
Delhi

Kanchan Chopra
Director,
Institute of Economic Growth

Preface and Acknowledgements

This book emerged from a macroeconometric modelling and forecasting exercise at the Development Planning Centre (DPC) of the Institute of Economic Growth. The objective of the exercise was to help the Indian Planning Commission with periodic assessment of the macroeconomic behaviour of the economy and provide forecasts of the key macroeconomic variables such as GDP growth rate, saving and investment rate, inflation rate, and money growth rate. Initially the exercise was done through simple relationships observed among various macroeconomic variables. The results of these exercises were presented at various seminars in India and abroad. Based on the feedback received at these seminars a comprehensive model was built not only to analyse the macroeconomic behaviour of the Indian economy but also to analyse the impact of various policy reforms initiated from time to time. In particular, the focus was on an evolution of the impact of the structural reforms initiated in India since 1991on the long-run growth and stability of the economy. In this respect this could be the first comprehensive quantitative exercise to evaluate the impact of structural reform in India.

Although the focus of attention in this book is statistical analysis, the book covers both theoretical and empirical aspects of model building. We have analysed the behaviour of different sectors of the economy—agriculture, industry, services, and public administration—in relation to known macro theories. It is observed that no particular theoretical model can adequately cover all features of the Indian economy. We have therefore followed an eclectic approach linking elements of Keynesian, Classical, and Structuralist theories of macro behaviour.

The modelling and forecasting exercise at the DPC was initiated through a project financed by the Netherlands Bureau for Economic Policy Analysis at the Hague, through Erasmus University, Rotterdam, and the Indian Planning Commission, New Delhi. Arjun Sengupta, the then Member Secretary of the Indian Planning Commission and George Wardenburg of the Erasmus University at Rotterdam played key roles in steering this project. Eugene Verkade of the Netherlands Bureau for Economic Policy Analysis and Manmohan Agarwal of the Jawaharlal Nehru University collaborated on the preliminary forecasting exercises in the early stages. This book however emerged out of the joint efforts of the present authors, based on our own version of the model of the Indian economy. We, however, thank Eugene Verkade and Manmohan Agarwal for their collaboration in preparation of various working papers based on the earlier versions of the model. We are also grateful to Pranob Sen, Principal Adviser to the Indian Planning Commission for continuous interaction and suggestions. We have also benefited from discussions at various seminars and conferences in both India and abroad at different stages of the model building exercise. However, the responsibility for all errors is ours.

A number of research and statistical assistants have helped us in data analysis and computation of the model from time to time. In particular we would like to thank Sachikant Mishra, Sarina Johnson, and Mahua Paul for their dedicated services. We also gratefully acknowledge comments and suggestions given by members, advisers, and officials of the Planning Commission in various seminars presented on the model. We gratefully acknowledge the staff of the library and the computer unit at the Institute of Economic Growth for providing us all materials and computational assistance. We would also like to thank the Director and the faculty of the Institute for their valuable comments and suggestions. Most of all, we would like to thank our wives, Swapna and Shaon, for their constant support and encouragement, without which the book would not have been possible.

October 2006
Delhi

B.B. Bhattacharya
Sabyasachi Kar

Tables and Figures

Tables

Figures

Abbreviations

AR(1)	Autoregressive Transformation
CAB	Current Account Balance
CPB	Central Planning Bureau
CPI	Consumer Price Index
CRR	Cash Reserve Ratio
CSO	Central Statistical Organization
DGCIS	Directorate General of Commercial Intelligence and Statistics
DPC	Development Planning Centre
DSE	Delhi School of Economics
FDI	Foreign Direct Investment
FERA	Foreign Exchange Regulation Act
GDP	Gross Domestic Product
ICOR	Incremental Capital–Output Ratio
IEG	Institute of Economic Growth
IEG-DSE	A joint project of Institute of Economic Growth and Delhi School of Economics
IMF	International Monetary Fund
LDC	Less Developed Countries
LIBOR	London Interbank Offered Rate
MAE	Mean Absolute Error
MAPE	Mean Absolute Percentage Error
MRTP	Monopolies and Restrictive Trade Practices
NCAER	National Council for Applied Economic Research
NSE	National Stock Exchange
OGL	Open General Licences
OLS	Ordinary Least Squares Regression
QR	Quantity Restrictions
R&D	Research & Development
RBI	Reserve Bank of India

RMSE	Root Mean Square Error
SEBI	Securities and Exchange Board of India
TIS	Theil's Inequality Statistics
TSLS	Two Stage Least Squares Regression
VAR	Vector Autoregression
WPI	Wholesale Price Index

1

INTRODUCTION

The performance of the Indian economy during the last quarter of a century has brought it to the forefront of discussions on development economics. Barring China, no other country has evoked as much interest in its growth performance, particularly in the context of its adopting market friendly reforms since the 1990s. Part of this interest is due to the fact that even after growing at a fast rate to become one of the largest economies in the world, the Indian economy still has large reserves of untapped human resources and productivity-enhancing capabilities to grow even faster and in a sustained manner. The crucial issue is whether the economy is on track to achieve such growth rates in the future. This book is an attempt to explore this issue. To this end, we systematically analyse the performance of the Indian economy in the post-independence period and provide some predictions about the future based on this analysis of the past.

The strength of this book lies in the fact that it is based on a detailed macromodel of the Indian economy (the DPC–IEG model) that has been tried and tested for its power of explaining Indian economic performance over the last few years. Till recently, there had been no long-standing models of the Indian economy that could be used repeatedly for projections and policy analysis, with regular updating. Along the lines of such efforts in industrialized countries, there was a need for a model that could be revised periodically, taking into account changing economic realities, revisions in data, and new theoretical developments. Initiatives in this direction were taken in the 1990s when the National Council for Applied Economic Research (NCAER) and a joint project by Institute of Economic Growth and Delhi School of Economics (IEG–DSE) started institutionalized model building for the Indian economy. In 1997, the Development Planning Centre

(DPC) of the IEG started work on the construction of the DPC–IEG model, which is the basis of this book. The strength of this model is that it combines a number of characteristics, which gives it an edge over other models in literature. These characteristics are as follows.

- This model is based on a continuous macroeconometric exercise that 'learns from experience' rather than a one-time modelling exercise. This is a characteristic that the model shares with only one or two other similar models.
- Significant time series data belonging to the post-reform period allow this model to analyse the post-reform changes in the economy.
- The post-reform data (generated during a period of significantly less state intervention than before) also make it possible to test for various theories about different parts of the economy that are based on the assumption of a market-oriented economy.
- The theoretical model has adopted a significantly market-oriented structure (even though the 1970s and early 1980s adopted significant state interventions) enabling it to give better forecasts for the future when recent market orientations are expected to continue.

The final version of the model is a result of several experiments carried out during the last few years of the model building process. In the early stages, the exercise continuously tested the robustness of the model—by comparing the short-run forecasts with the observed data — and made suitable changes to the model. As a result, the final version of the model is quite different from the earlier versions that were presented at various seminars during the development of the model.

The structure of the book can be described in terms of three distinct but related parts. The first part covering Chapters 2 and 3 is mostly descriptive, and provides a thorough analysis of the macroeconomic trends and interlinkages in the Indian economy. The second part covers Chapters 4 and 5. Based on the structure of the economy described in the first part, it presents and discusses various aspects of the DPC–IEG macro model. The third part—Chapters 6 and 7—uses the model presented in the second part to analyse the past, and to forecast the future performance of the Indian economy. It may be useful, at this point, to describe in some detail the objectives and findings of each of the chapters in the book.

The first step in the construction of a macromodel involves gaining an understanding of the various facets of the economy. The focus of Chapter 2 is to fulfil this requirement by scrutinizing the trends and changes in the economy during the period that is relevant to our study. Accordingly, it gives an analytical account of the economy in the post-independence period, although the stress is on the last three decades, which is the sample period for our model. Broadly, this chapter can be divided into two parts. In the first part, the chapter details the changing economic paradigms that strongly influenced the policy framework in each period as well as the performance of the economy during these periods. It starts with the period immediately following independence, when the policy-paradigm in India was strongly influenced by the 'Development Consensus'. This school of thought stressed on the path of industrialization in order to get rid of the problems of underdevelopment and advocated temporary protection to domestic industry from international competition. Over time, however, the chronic problems in the external sector made the policy makers feel that foreign exchange was becoming a very scarce commodity and hence every effort must be made to save it from use in non-priority areas. Thus, by the 1970s, the development consensus gave way to what the chapter terms as the 'Structuralist Perspective'. According to this view, if there is any rigidity or stickiness in the relative prices in an economy, then trade restrictions are justified purely to conserve foreign exchange. This led to a strategy of 'development through planning and controls' during the 1970s. In terms of performance, the low rates of industrial growth that the economy experienced during the late 1960s continued through the 1970s. Ultimately, the policy makers in India were convinced that the control regime was responsible for this and some changes towards liberalization started taking shape during the 1980s. The economy performed remarkably well during the 1980s. Ironically—as the chapter points out—it is in the period immediately following this decade that the Indian economy experienced a big external balance crisis. The Gulf war precipitated the crisis by increasing the oil import bill on the one hand, and slowing down remittances on the other. In order to break out of this critical balance of payments situation, India took a substantial loan from the International Monetary Fund (IMF) in 1991 and also adopted its programme of stabilization and structural reforms. Interestingly, the economy put up a mixed performance during the post-crisis period in the 1990s, with high growth rates during the fast half and slowdown during the second half of the decade.

The second part of Chapter 2 describes the trends in the important macroeconomic variables over the relevant period. This gives a clearer understanding of where the economy is headed in the future. It also helps in identifying important trend breaks that have taken place in the past. These breaks, whether due to policy changes or due to structural changes, have been incorporated into the macromodel in order to get more accurate simulation results.

The construction of a macromodel is also based on the choice of an appropriate theoretical framework. Choosing a particular framework has to be based on scrutinizing the alternative frameworks that can be and have been used for this purpose. In Chapter 3, these issues are dealt with in great detail by surveying the literature on macromodelling in general and the Indian macromodels in particular. The chapter starts by describing the chronological development of the macromodelling literature in the US and Europe. It describes the contributions of Quesnay, Walras, and Kalecki, and finally the Keynesian revolution. The pioneering attempt at large-scale model building was associated with Tinbergen in Europe and Klein in the US. For many years, macroeconometric models have been constructed as empirical counterparts to the Keynesian system. In recent years, however, econometric models based on alternative paradigms have also appeared in the literature.

The chapter also brings up certain methodological issues. Macromodelling is based primarily on the 'structural macromodelling' methodology associated with the Cowles Commission. The important steps involved in such an exercise include: (i) constructing a theoretical model, (ii) acquiring data, (iii) estimating the behavioural equations, (iv) simulating the model, (v) validating the model, and (vi) forecasting and counterfactual simulations. Model builders are faced with alternative paradigms such as the Walrasian, the Keynesian, and the Structuralist paradigms and most of them combine elements from some or all of these.

Next, the chapter describes the development of the literature in the Indian context, dividing the period into four phases. The first phase started with Narasimham's pioneering work in 1956 and covered the 1960s. Models developed during this phase were aggregative, simple, medium-sized, and all of them were undertaken as doctoral dissertations. The second phase covered the 1970s and most models developed in this period were also undertaken as doctoral dissertations. However, they were more disaggregated and better focused on policy issues. In the third phase, covering the 1980s and the early 1990s, considerable progress was made in modelling the Indian economy. These models were much more disaggregated than the earlier ones and focused on policy issues. The fourth phase covering the late 1990s has ushered in much larger models that are comparable to those in developed countries. These models are maintained by reputed institutions on an ongoing basis and are regularly used for forecasting. Finally, the chapter gives a detailed description of the treatment of the various sectors in the existing literature on the Indian economy.

Chapter 4 presents the macroeconometric model that is the basis of all subsequent analysis of the economy in this study. It starts by detailing the objectives of building the model and describes the chronological development of the model over the last few years. Next, it details the different parts of the model, the sources of data, and statistical procedures that have been used to estimate the behavioural equations in the model. Finally, there is a detailed description of the structural identities and behavioural equations from the six parts of the model, that is, aggregate supply, aggregate demand, prices, monetary sector, fiscal sector, and external sector. The description includes the theoretical underpinnings of the identities and behavioural equations. Moreover, in the case of behavioural equations, the results of the estimations are presented together with the corresponding regression statistics. From these estimated equations, the important explanatory variables are highlighted and the implications of these results are discussed. These discussions reveal a number of important aspects of the economy and provide inputs into our analysis of the economy in subsequent chapters.

The detailed description of the macromodel in this chapter starts with the framework of the model that is based on an eclectic approach. Thus it is Keynesian in outlook but combines elements of neoclassical and structuralist views as well. The model is broadly classified into four blocks namely, the production, fiscal, monetary, and external sectors. The production block determines output, aggregate demand, and price variables. Output is in real terms and disaggregated into four sectors—agriculture, industry, service, and public administration. Aggregate demand, on the other hand, is estimated in nominal terms as the sum of consumption, investment, and net exports. The aggregate price level is determined as the variable that equilibrates aggregate nominal demand and aggregate real output. Apart from the aggregate price, the model also estimates four sectoral prices, as well as the consumption and investment deflators. In the monetary sector, the model determines money supply and interest rates. Money supply is a function of reserve money and the money multiplier. The rate of interest equilibrates the demand for and the supply of money. The fiscal sector has a detailed and disaggregated representation of the revenue earned and the expenditure carried out by the government. This sector determines the revenue and the fiscal deficit. The external block deals with trade and external transactions. There are separate behavioural equations for exports of goods, exports of services, imports of oil and non-oil groups, and imports of services. Separate equations are specified for net current transfers and capital transactions. The exchange rate is the equilibrating variable in this sector.

In order to understand how a macromodel works, it is important to focus on the important transmission mechanisms of the model. Furthermore, it is important to test how well the model performs in simulating the real economy. Chapter 5 deals with both these issues. The first part deals with the mechanics of the model. This includes a description of how the important macro variables are determined in the model and how the policy variables and other exogenous factors affect these important macro variables through various channels. It starts with the determination of aggregate output, which is the sum of agricultural output, industrial output, output from the service sector, and the output from public administration. In the first three sectors, the output is the product of the capital stock and the output-to-capital ratios. In the fourth sector, that is, public administration, the sectoral output is determined by the salaries and wages paid by the government. This implies that the first three sectors of our models are capital constrained, and so, we have estimated investment functions for the sectors separately. The various prices in the model are determined by different mechanisms. The macromodel has well-specified monetary, fiscal, and the external sectors. In the monetary sector, the monetary base broadly consists of the outstanding Reserve Bank of India (RBI) credit to the government and the foreign exchange reserves. In this sector, we also have the deposit rate, the lending rate, the rate of return on government securities, and the average rate of interest on public debt. These four interest rates interact with each other to give the interest rate structure. The fiscal sector has a significant impact on various components of the economy through policy choices that are implemented in different parts of this sector. These parts are the expenditures of the government, the revenue earned by the government, and the deficit incurred by the government. In the external sector, the volume of imports determines the industrial and total output, while the net exports affect aggregate demand and price through the open economy multiplier.

Next, the chapter describes a number of trade-offs built into the model. An increase in the average tariff rate can lead to lower fiscal deficit and prime lending rate and hence higher output. On the other hand, it may lead to lower output due to lower imports and industrial output. An increase in the employment in public administration may lead to an increase in output by increasing the gross domestic product (GDP) from public administration. However, an increase in the employment in public administration may lead to higher fiscal deficits and prime lending rates bringing down investments and output. The model also manifests the growth–inflation trade-off that is well known in the macroeconomic literature.

The second part of Chapter 5 deals with the validation of the model. This section starts by listing the sources of errors that are built into the model. Next, there is a comparison of the performance of the various sectors in replicating the real economy. This is done using standard tests of validation. Finally, there is a validation of the performance of all the important variables in each of the sectors.

The performance of the various sectors of the economy at any given point of time depends on a number of factors acting simultaneously on the economy. A macromodelling exercise allows us to distinguish between these by carrying out a counterfactual simulation of each of these factors separately. Chapter 6 presents some such simulations that study the impact of the important policies and other exogenous shocks on the economy. This exercise is carried out separately for the 1980s and the 1990s. The section on the 1980s presents five simulations examining the impact of monetized deficits, droughts, monetary policy, government employment, and fertilizer subsidies on the performance of the economy. The economic performance during the 1980s had two significant characteristics, that is, it exhibited high rates of growth and ended up with large fiscal imbalances. The simulations for the 1980s focus particularly on these two issues.

The model simulations for the 1980s show that the high levels of monetized borrowings definitely played a role in the high growth rates, largely through the public investments that it financed, and marginally through the government's consumption and overhead expenditures. The drought played only a marginal role in bringing down growth rates during the 1980s, as the agricultural sector seems to have become resilient to such shocks in the long run. However, there was some spillover effect of the drought on the industrial and services sector. The high interest rates during this period definitely dampened the growth impetus. Moreover, they were quite unnecessary as part of a tight monetary policy as lower interest rates would not have been inflationary in this context. As far as fiscal deficits are concerned, the high rates of monetized borrowings that financed the high rates of government expenditure did lead to greater fiscal imbalance. Lowering the growth rate of government employment would have reduced the fiscal imbalance but it would have also brought down the growth rate due to the current national accounting practice of imputing the value added in public administration based on the employment in this sector. Similarly, a lower fertilizer subsidy would have brought down the fiscal deficit but at the cost of the agricultural and aggregate growth rates.

During the 1990s, the most significant economic events were the crisis of 1991, the high growth during the first half of the decade, the slowdown during the second half, and the final imbalances during the end of the decade. The section on the 1990s presents seven simulations that focus on the impact of exogenous shocks, monetized borrowing, drought, monetary policy, procurement prices, tax rate, and implementation of the Fifth Pay Commission for government salary and wages on shaping some of these important events during the 1990s. We find that the oil price hike and the drought at the beginning of the decade did not have any significant impact on the growth rates, inflation rates, or the fiscal deficit. This again underlines the resilience of the economy to such shocks. Next we study the impact of the regime change and adoption of market friendly reforms on the performance of the economy. The overall growth showed no significant upturn during the 1990s as a result of reforms. However, it has been very successful in keeping a check on inflation rates and the fiscal and external deficits. The slowdown during the second half of the decade has sometimes been associated with the reduction in borrowing from the RBI, the poor rains during the end of the decade, or the high interest rates during this period. The simulations indicate that in the absence of the reduction in borrowing from RBI, the growth rate would have been higher, particularly if it had financed higher public investments. Poor rainfall also had a role to play in the slowdown, as did a high interest rate regime. Significantly, a lower interest rate regime would not have been inflationary in this case. The fiscal balances, as we have already mentioned, was kept in check by the reforms. However a higher rate of growth of procurement prices, reduction in tax rates, and a hike in salaries by the Fifth Pay Commission have all resulted in a rising fiscal deficit although in all these cases, these factors have also had a small but positive impact on growth rates.

Given the good performance of the Indian economy in the past, there is a lot of optimism about what it can achieve in the future. Simultaneously, there are some misgivings about how resilient the economy has become to various kinds of shocks. Chapter 7 deals with these two issues. It starts by describing some modifications that have been made to the original model in order to make it more useful for simulations and forecasts. The efficacy of the modified model is tested on the basis of ex-post forecasts. It is shown that although the economy underwent significant structural changes during the period after 1994 due to liberalization of the economy, the model takes care of these changes and represents the economy quite accurately.

The second part of the chapter studies the effect of five shocks that affect the growth of the Indian economy. These include two domestic shocks (rainfall shortfall and fiscal profligacy) and three external shocks (oil price hike, world trade shock, and capital flow shock). Shocks can have an impact on various aspects of the growth process. These aspects include the magnitude of the impact on growth rates, the pervasiveness of the shocks in the long run, the capability of the shock to give rise to stagflationary situations, and the capability of the shock to give rise to instability in the fiscal or external sectors.

What are the inferences that we draw from these simulations? First, any shock that affects the supply side, such as the rainfall shock, will have a big impact on GDP growth. The impact is pervasive because rainfall deficiency not only reduces agricultural output but also non-agricultural output via sectoral interlinkages. The long run impact of this shock depends on the magnitude of the accelerator. However, since rainfall moves in cycles, it has a tendency to restore balance in the long run and hence the long run impact is more muted than the short run impact. Second, the shocks affecting the demand side lowers the output first in the industrial sector (which is demand constrained) and then the tertiary sector through intersectoral linkages. The long run impact of demand-induced shocks again depends on the accelerator. Third, the fiscal profligacy shock affects both aggregate demand and supply. A rise in government expenditure may stimulate the industrial demand in the short run but has a marginal effect in the long run. However, a cut in public investment operates perversely through both aggregate demand and supply and thereby leads to a lasting long run impact. Fourth, in the case of the trade shock, the long run impact is neutralized by the exchange rate adjustment and hence this results in a marginal change in long run growth corresponding to this shock. Clearly, the deregulation of exchange rate has introduced a built-in stability in the operation of this multiplier. To sum up, it is fair to say that realistic rainfall and fiscal profligacy shocks have a stronger growth-retarding effect compared to realistic scenarios of the other three shocks, both in the short as well as the long run. We also find that the oil price hike, the capital flow shock, and fiscal profligacy show strong pervasiveness, while the economy is much more resilient to the rainfall shock and the world trade shock in the long run. The rainfall shock and fiscal profligacy is stagflationary in the long run, while the oil price hike, capital flow shock, and world trade shocks are not stagflationary in the long run. Finally, we find from our study that the oil shock, world trade shock, and the capital flow shocks (that is, the external shocks) give rise to some instability in the external sector in the short run. Similarly, the fiscal profligacy shock and the world trade shock give rise to some short run instability in the fiscal sector. However, in the long run we find that none of the shocks have any significant negative impact on either the fiscal deficit or the external reserves.

The last part of this chapter presents some forecasts for the Tenth Plan as well as the Eleventh Plan period in the absence of any shocks. The first simulation here is for the short run, which focuses on the Tenth Plan period (2002–3 to 2006–7). It is clear that even in the absence of any shock, the 8 per cent growth rate targeted in the Tenth Plan is unattainable under current conditions, as it is significantly higher than the 6.78 per cent growth rate forecast for the period. This is partly due to the fact that the targeted investment rates are also very high and are unattainable during the Tenth Plan period. The tertiary sector has become the engine of growth with remarkably high growth rates, but the other sectors—particularly agriculture—are not doing that well. Any attempt at higher growth rates will be possible only if the agricultural and industrial sectors grow at a higher rate. Another issue that is of some concern is the fall in public investment rate. Any growth-oriented strategy will have to focus on greater public investments, especially in sectors like infrastructure, etc.

The final simulation in this chapter is the long-run simulation that focuses on the Eleventh Plan period. The forecasts indicate that the economy is moving to a high growth trajectory of about 7 per cent growth rate per annum. Moreover, the economy will achieve this with a low rate of inflation and manageable levels of fiscal deficit. The only cause of worry for the Eleventh Plan period is the external sector. It may be noted that the forecast for the Eleventh Plan is based upon high international oil prices prevailing during 2004–5. The forecasts indicate a sharp deterioration in the external balances during the Eleventh Plan period. This negative current account balance is inspite of the optimistic assumptions regarding private transfers and capital flows. The broad conclusion that emerges is that unless the capital balance remains robust, the economy may not be able to sustain high oil prices in the long run.

2

The Development Experience

After some sluggish growth, at about 3.5 per cent per annum, in the first three decades of the post-independence period, the Indian economy attained an impressive growth rate of about 5.6 per cent in the last two decades. Furthermore, during the mid-1990s, the economy grew by more than 7 per cent per annum. This has given rise to a vision of attaining even higher growth rates and joining the club of 'Asian Miracle' economies. Perhaps the strongest manifestation of this vision lies in the Planning Commission's ambitious growth target of 8 per cent for the Tenth Five Year Plan. How does one explain this wide variation in the performance of the Indian economy over the past decades? In this chapter, we attempt to look for some answers by analysing the policies pursued, the performance, and the structural changes in the Indian economy, particularly during the last three decades. This will not only motivate the important issues discussed in the latter sections of the book, but also corroborate the assumptions made about the Indian economy in the econometric model that is the basis of our work.

The issue of achieving high growth rates has been of great interest to economists, particularly theoreticians, right from the days when the subject was in its formative years. In recent times, however, empiricists and policy analysts have also taken an active interest in the subject. It is easy to understand this interest, since achieving a high rate of growth is an important objective for any country, as it enables them to reach higher levels of per capita income within a shorter time period. For a developing country, there is an even more pressing reason to increase the growth rates as much as possible. Higher growth rates enable these countries to reduce poverty and unemployment, allowing them to attain greater prosperity in a more equitable manner. It is in this perspective that we need to assess the potential of the Indian economy for attaining high growth rates in the future. Of course, any such assessment would have to be in the context of the past growth performance of the economy. In the Indian case, the post-independence period provides an ideal backdrop against which we can contrast the likely policies and performance of the future.

THE EARLY PHASE OF DEVELOPMENT

Economic policy in post-independence India was strongly influenced by the set of ideas popularly known as the development consensus. This school of thought stressed the fact that underdevelopment was closely related to the lack of industrialization of an economy. A number of empirical studies also supported this view by showing that there is a high degree of correlation between the extent of industrialization in an economy and its growth rate. A natural corollary to this idea was that developing countries must embark on a path of industrialization in order to get rid of their economic problems. The propounders of these ideas, however, realized quite early that this would not be an easy task for these countries. The reason for this lies in the scale economies exhibited by the industrialization process. As economists right from Adam Smith to Kaldor were well aware, the dynamic nature of these economies of scale implied that industries or economies that had an early start would be able to take advantage of these scale economies, thereby ensuring that they had more competitive cost structures compared to those who started later. In effect, this implied that industries in developing economies would never be able to compete with those from the developed ones. The only way through which these industries could develop involved a process of providing them with temporary protection from international competition. This is the crux of the policy of import substitution that was an integral part of the development consensus and a cornerstone of indian economic policy after independence.

The Indian approach to development in fact consisted of three components one of which was the policy of import substitution. The other two components were the focus on the public sector and the centrality of the planning process. The primacy of the public sector was based on the idea that certain key sections of the industrial sector constituted the 'commanding heights' of the economy and hence the state must actively participate in the production process in these particular industries. The development of industries such as railways, telecommunications, electricity was thus left to the public sector. This sector also included the production of important industrial raw materials, such as steel, petroleum, heavy machinery. Together with import substituting trade policies, the active encouragement of domestic industries through the public sector was supposed to give a 'big push' to the domestic industry. However, the success of this process depended critically on the correct allocation of resources to the various sectors of the economy. This correct allocation of resources was sought to be achieved through the planning process.

It is evident that, at least in the initial stages, the inward looking policies pursued by the Indian policy makers were primarily motivated by the wish to provide Indian industries with an opportunity to become competitive in the world market. This is the classic infant industry argument. Over time, however, the chronic problems in the external sector led to significant changes in this viewpoint. In the face of balance of payments problems, the policy makers started feeling that foreign exchange was becoming a very scarce commodity and hence every effort must be made to save it from use in non-priority areas. This, of course, led to an even more protectionist strategy with across-the-board protection, irrespective of whether the individual cases qualified as infant industries or not. Thus, by the 1970s, the development consensus gave way to what is popularly known as the 'Structuralist Perspective'.

THE 1970s : GROWTH AND INSTABILITY

According to the structuralist view, if there is any rigidity or stickiness in the relative prices in an economy, then trade restrictions are justified purely to conserve foreign exchange. Over the 1950s and 1960s, slowly but surely, it is this motivation rather than the longer run technological and infant-industry considerations, that became the guiding spirit of Indian policy makers. Moreover, controlling the use of foreign exchange involved not only trade policy but industrial policy as well, with industrial licensing being used to substitute domestic goods for importables. In fact, controls in the industrial and trade sectors were a part of an overall approach towards a controlled and planned development process, the manifestations of which were evident in other sectors as well. By the 1970s, these controls was quite well entrenched and a number of studies—following Little, Scitovsky, and Scott

(1970)—had started analysing their effects on the Indian economy. The salient features of the control regime during the 1970s were the following.

- Industrial licensing policy: The scale, technology, and location of an investment project were regulated through the licence requirements. Any plan to expand, relocate, and change the output or input mixes needed prior permission from the government.
- Import control policy: Imports were controlled through the distribution of import licences as well as tariffs and quantity restrictions. The foreign exchange that was needed for payments against imports was made available only to importers who had licences to import.
- Foreign exchange control: In order to ensure that the foreign exchange was used only for approved imports, the government made it mandatory for all exporters to surrender their foreign exchange earnings to the RBI at the official exchange rate. These became part of the foreign exchange reserves and were allocated to the importers through import licensing processes.
- Foreign exchange rate control: The exchange rate regime followed a fixed rather than a market-determined exchange rate. During the first half of the 1970s, the rupee was first pegged to the US dollar and then to the pound sterling. Since 1975, the RBI started pegging the rupee to a basket of currencies belonging to India's trading partners.
- Capital market control: The private sector's access to domestic equity markets as well as debt markets was tightly controlled.
- Price control: The prices of some of the vital consumption goods such as foodgrains, sugar, and vegetable oil were controlled by the government. Important inputs such as irrigation, fertilizer, and electricity prices also came under price controls by the government.
- Controls in the banking sector: Together with the nationalization of banks in 1969, this sector was subjected to a number of controls. The deposit and lending rates were fixed by the government at levels lower than market clearing rates. A large portion of the

loanable funds went to the government through the enforcement of the reserve ratios. There were direct and selective credit controls over the use of rest of the loanable funds as well, particularly through the enforcement of priority lending.

The performance of the economy during this decade was quite poor. The agricultural performance fluctuated wildly between positive and negative growth rates throughout the 1970s. This erratic behaviour is sharply brought out by the fact that within this decade, five years experienced negative growth rates (most significantly in 1979 when the agricultural growth rate went down to – 12.77 per cent) while there was more than 5 per cent growth in three years. Due to this erratic behaviour, the average agricultural growth rate for the decade was an abysmally low figure of 0.6 per cent. The industrial performance during this decade can be divided into three parts. The industrial growth rates remained at significantly low levels till 1974. During the next four years, the growth rates rose to around 7 per cent. 1979–80 saw a dramatic fall in industrial growth as it touched – 3.08 per cent. On an average, the industrial growth rate for this decade was a low 3.98 per cent. The performance of the service sector mirrors the experience in the industrial sector. Thus the initial years exhibit low growth rates, followed by higher growth rates during 1975–6, and a significant slump in 1979. The average rate of growth for this sector for the decade was 4.27 per cent. As a result of the poor performance of the agricultural and industrial sectors, the aggregate economy did poorly as well. Except for 1975 and 1977, when both the agricultural and industrial sectors performed well, the rate of growth of the economy remained quite low with a decadal average of 2.63 per cent. This however includes 1979 when the growth rate of the economy fell sharply to – 5.22 per cent, partly due to the second oil price hike and partly due to severe crop failure during that year. If 1979 is dropped from the sample, then the decadal average rises to 3.61 per cent. This is very close to what was popularly called the 'Hindu rate of growth'. As far as prices are concerned, the 1970s again present a very erratic picture. Inflation rates rose sharply in the initial years, reaching a peak of 17.29 per cent in 1973, fell very sharply in 1975 to – 2.89 per cent, and then exhibited a strong rising trend for the rest of the decade reaching 15.13 per cent in 1979. The average for the decade was about 8.53 per cent.

The aggregate fiscal stance during this period was quite conservative. The revenue deficit was negative for most of this period, that is, there was a surplus on the revenue account. This surplus kept increasing till 1975 after which it exhibited a declining trend. The fiscal deficit also exhibited a similar trend with a downward tendency during the first half of the decade and a rising trend in the second half. The decadal average for the revenue deficit to GDP ratio was – 0.88 per cent and for the fiscal deficit to GDP ratio was 4.71 per cent. The negative value of the revenue deficit implies that a portion of the revenue was financing capital expenditure during this period. As far as the external balances are concerned, the decade experienced significant fluctuations in both trade balances as well as current account balances. The trade balance (that is, exports minus imports) to GDP ratio fluctuated around – 1 per cent till 1976 but fell sharply after that. This fall in the trade balance was due to a simultaneous increase in imports and decrease in exports during this period. The average trade balance to GDP ratio for the decade was – 0.81. The current account balance also exhibited fluctuations during this period with the current account deficit to GDP ratio showing a decadal average of – 0.10.

THE 1980s: UNSUSTAINABLE ACCELERATION OF GROWTH

The strategy of 'development through planning and controls' that was adopted by the policy makers during the 1950s and 1960s continued in full sway during the 1970s. However, the low rates of industrial growth that the economy experienced during the late 1960s continued through the 1970s and this led to a number of studies that criticized the effectiveness of these policies. Little, Scitvsky, and Scott (1970) was one of the pioneering studies in this context that suggested that these policies were responsible for choking off growth in developing economies. Later, the Mackinon and Shaw hypothesis suggested that financial markets repressed by these policies were responsible for low savings and inefficient use of capital in these economies. Krueger and others contributed to the rent seeking literature, which dealt with the loss of resources due to corrupt practices involved in the licensing system. All these critiques of the then existing system of controls felt that there was a need to move towards a market-led economy and this would ensure higher growth rates. The planners and policy makers in

India were also influenced by some of these ideas and some changes towards liberalization had started taking shape even during the 1970s. However, these moves towards a market-led economy really gained momentum in the 1980s. A new Industrial Policy Statement was framed in 1980 that removed the division between small and large scale industries, liberalized licensing for large scale industries, regularized the installation of excess capacity by these industries, and allowed automatic expansion of capacity to some of them. By 1985 the growing irrelevance of the existing Monopolies and Restrictive Trade Practices Act (MRTP) was recognized and a number of industries were exempted from this act. A scheme for automatic endorsement for the expansion of capacity was also initiated. A concept of broad banding was introduced which ensured greater flexibility to the manufacturers to determine their product mix. In 1986, another group of industries was delicensed from MRTP and Foreign Exchange Regulation Act (FERA). The threshold asset limit for FERA was also raised. Further liberalization of industrial licensing was undertaken in 1988 with some projects being exempted from the requirement of such licences. The reforms were not limited to the industrial policy only. Another area that underwent changes in policy during the 1980s was the external sector. In 1985 a trade policy was announced that attempted to give more flexibility to the exporters. It reduced the number of canalized imports and also simplified the related procedures. The system of automatic licences was abolished and most of the goods under this scheme were moved to the open general licences (OGL). Hence, a definite attempt was being made during the 1980s to remove some of the complexities of the control system even though these attempts were at best only partially successful in doing so.

Two important and related policy changes in the 1980s were taking place simultaneously in the fiscal sector. The first was the adoption of an expansionary fiscal policy involving high levels of government expenditures. More significantly, it was the revenue expenditure (as a proportion of GDP) that rose to very high levels during this period while capital expenditure (as a proportion of GDP) stagnated and, started falling during the second half of the 1980s. The overall government expenditure to GDP ratio was significantly higher in the 1980s compared to the 1970s. The second change that was taking place involved the method of financing these high levels of government expenditures. During the 1980s, there was a perceptible shift from a tax-financed expenditure programme to a debt-financed expenditure programme. Tax receipts as a proportion of total expenditure fell during the 1980s while fiscal deficit as a proportion of total expenditure rose during the same period. The two changes together led to a sharp increase in the fiscal deficit to GDP ratio during the 1980s.

The economy performed remarkably well during this decade. The agricultural sector continued to exhibit fluctuating growth rates in the 1980s, although the average performance was significantly better compared to the 1970s. There were only three years that had negative growth rates and even these negative rates were small in comparison to those experienced in the 1970s. The decadal average growth rate for the sector was 4.42 per cent, the highest amongst the last three decades. The industrial sector experienced a revival after the stagnation of the 1960s and 1970s with positive and high growth rates throughout the decade. The industrial growth rate fluctuated around 6 per cent during the first half of the decade and maintained a rising trend during the second half, culminating with a high 10.33 per cent in 1989. The decadal average growth rate for the industrial sector was 6.80 per cent, that is, almost double that of the 1970s. The services sector also performed very well during this decade with the growth rate showing an increasing trend throughout the period. The services growth rate, which was a reasonable 4.15 per cent in 1980 went up to 9.03 per cent in 1989 and this ensured that the decadal average growth rate for this sector remained at a high 6.58 per cent. The improved performance in the agricultural, industrial, and services sectors during the decade resulted in a high rate of growth for the economy as a whole. In particular, 1980, 1983, and 1988 achieved very high growth rates as both agriculture and industry did particularly well in these years. The decadal average growth rate for the economy as a whole was 5.85 per cent, again almost double that of the 1970s. Moving next to prices, the economy experienced a steady rate of inflation throughout the decade. The inflation rate during the decade was at its highest at 10.94 per cent in 1980 and at its lowest at 6.82 per cent in 1986, with the decadal average equal to 8.58 per cent. As we have already mentioned, the fiscal stance during the decade was expansionary in nature. The revenue deficit to GDP ratio was negative (implying a surplus) in 1981 and positive for the rest of the decade, with an increasing trend throughout the period. This increasing trend ensured that the decade had an average revenue deficit to GDP ratio of 1.6 per cent, a far cry from the revenue surplus in the 1970s. As a result of the rising trend in revenue deficits, the fiscal deficits also increased significantly at least in the first half of the decade. There was a diminishing tendency in the fiscal deficit to GDP ratio after 1986 but in the face of rising revenue deficits, this simply implied a fall in the government's capital expenditures. The decadal average for the fiscal deficit to GDP ratio was a high 8.14 per cent, nearly twice as much as that in the 1970s. The external balances, particularly the trade balance was in a very bad shape at the beginning of the decade. The trade balance to GDP ratio was less than – 4 per cent in 1980. Subsequently, it improved significantly throughout the decade to reach –1.53 per cent in 1989. The decadal average for the trade balance to GDP ratio was – 2.61 per cent. Interestingly, while the trade balance improved throughout the decade, the current account balance deteriorated over the same period. The current account to GDP ratio was less than – 2 per cent during the first half of the decade but fell significantly after 1984. This deterioration of the current account in the face of improvements in the trade balance was due to a sharp decline in net invisible flows during this decade. The decadal average of the current account to GDP ratio was –1.84 per cent.

THE 1990s: REFORM AND STRUCTURAL CHANGES

The 1980s were a significant decade for the Indian economy as it successfully broke out of the shackles of the 'Hindu rate of growth' and grew at rates much higher than ever before. Ironically, it is in the period immediately following this decade that the Indian economy experienced the biggest crisis in all of its post-independence existence. It is, of course, without a doubt that a number of external factors had a significant role to play in precipitating the crisis. However, it was some of the policies followed during the 1980s that had actually given rise to (what was widely perceived as) a potentially critical situation. In particular, the shift from the tax-financed expenditure programme to the debt-financed expenditure programme had led to a steady increase in both the domestic as well as the external debt to GDP ratios. By the end of the 1980s, they had reached such high levels that there was a genuine worry of India slipping into a debt trap. It is in such circumstances that the economy was subjected to a number of external shocks that catalyzed the potential crisis into an actual one. The most significant shock was the Gulf war and this led to an increase in the oil import bill on the one hand, and a slowdown in remittances on the other. This put severe pressure on the balance of payments situation. The political turmoil in the country—with four governments in a span of two years—also gave rise to a situation rife with uncertainty. The precarious situation in the external sector, the possibility of getting into a debt trap, and the political uncertainties together resulted in a complete loss of investor confidence in the Indian economy. This further aggravated the problem by cutting off international credit lines from private and commercial sources. The result of all these was a steep fall in foreign exchange reserves which reached such low levels in January 1991 that there was a chance of India defaulting on her international obligations.

In order to break out of this critical balance of payments situation, India took a substantial loan from the IMF in 1991 and also adopted its programme of stabilization and structural reforms. The pro-market philosophy behind these reforms was, of course, consistent with the earlier attempts towards liberalization undertaken during the 1980s. In fact, the policy makers were convinced that it was the rigidities in the economic system inherent in a controlled regime that were responsible for the crisis and that the time was ripe for a drastic change in policy approach towards the liberalization of the economy. This approach resulted in the adoption of a number of pro-market policies.

- The capital market reforms: This involved setting up institutions such as the Securities and Exchange Board of India (SEBI), National Stock Exchange (NSE), and so on that could provide more transparency to the transaction and ensure that the agents in the stock market did not indulge in unscrupulous practices. Mutual funds were allowed to enter the market so that small investors could enter the market without going through brokers and middlemen. The most significant change in policy regarding this sector was the decision to allow foreign institutional investors to enter these markets.
- Foreign exchange reforms: The foreign exchange rate regime shifted from the practice of pegging to a basket of currencies to a managed float in 1993. Simultaneously, the RBI started regulating the market by the purchase and sale of foreign exchange. The

government also moved to convertibility for transactions in the current account.

- Interest rates and banking reforms: The interest rate is now determined in consonance with the market forces and there is no attempt made to deliberately keep them pegged at a low level. Statutory liquidity ratios have been brought down. Prudential norms and capital adequacy norms have been laid down to ensure that the quantum of bad loan and non-performing assets remain within limits.
- Tax reforms: There has been significant reduction in direct and indirect tax rates in order to maintain them at international levels. A number of schemes including the famous 'one by six' criteria have been introduced to expand the tax base and increase tax revenues.
- Autonomy of the RBI: The practice of automatic monetization of the fiscal deficit through the issue of short period treasury bills to the RBI has been discontinued. The volume of Reserve Bank credit to the government is determined by the apex bank while the government now falls back on its market borrowings to balance its budget.
- Abolition of the licence system: The licensing requirement for domestic production and imports was the most important component of the control regime. This system has been largely abolished as a tool of industrial and trade policy.
- Reforms in the external sector: The government started lifting quantity restrictions (QRs) on imports from the mid-1980s and substituting them with tariffs. During the 1990s, QRs were largely abolished and tariffs rates were also brought down significantly.

The performance of the economy in the 1990s can be analytically divided into two parts—the situation leading up to the crisis in 1991 and the subsequent performance of the economy. We have described previously some aspects of the situation that led to the crisis, particularly the fiscal and balance of payments situations. The crisis manifested itself in the real sectors as well. The agricultural and industrial growth rates were both negative in 1991 while the services sector growth rate was significantly lower than that in the 1980s. All these resulted in the economy growing at 1.3 per cent in 1991 compared to 10.47 per cent in 1988. The fiscal deficit to GDP ratio shot up to 9.39 per cent in 1990 coming down somewhat to 7 per cent in 1991. The current account balance to GDP ratio reached a peak of –3.05 per cent in 1990. It was in these circumstances that the balance of payments crisis broke out and led to the initiation of significant market-oriented reforms in the economy throughout the 1990s.

The economy has put up a mixed performance during the post-crisis period. The agricultural sector experienced more stable growth in the post-1991 period with the growth rates varying within a smaller band compared to the 1970s and the 1980s. However, the average growth performance was relatively poor with a decadal average growth rate of 2.87 per cent, almost a third lower than that in the 1980s. The industrial sector exhibited a strong revival in the first half of the decade following the 1991 crisis. The industrial growth rate shot up from – 0.55 per cent in 1991 to 11.80 per cent in 1995. However, in the second half of the decade, the industrial sector slipped into a recession with an average growth rate of about 5.5 per cent. The average industrial growth rate for the decade was 5.87 per cent, while that for the post-1991 period was 6.38 per cent. The services sector, like in the previous decades, followed a pattern very similar to the industrial sector. Thus, there was a significant fall in growth rates in 1990 and 1991, followed by a sharp increase till 1995, and then a significant fall in growth rates in the second half of the decade. The decadal average growth rate for this sector was 7.48 per cent, higher than both the 1970s and the 1980s. In fact, this decadal average growth rate has exhibited a continuous rise in the last three decades, indicating a strong upward trend in the growth rates of this sector. The performance of the overall economy in the post-1991 period has been quite stable with the aggregate growth rate varying between 5 per cent and 7.5 per cent. However, the initial period (up to 1996) exhibited an increase in growth rates, while the period after that showed a steady decline in the same. The average growth rate for the period 1990 to 2000 was 5.74 per cent, while that for the post-1991 period was 6.25 per cent. The economy exhibited steadily declining inflation rates throughout the decade, particularly in the post-1991 period. The inflation rates shot up during the crisis, reaching 13.82 per cent in 1991, but fell steadily after that, reaching a low of 3.93 per cent in 1999. The decadal average inflation was 8.46 per cent, almost identical to that during the

1970s and the 1980s. The fiscal policy following the crisis was focused at keeping the government's deficits within control and this endeavour was successful in the initial years. In the second half of the decade, however, this trend was reversed and the deficits went up significantly. The revenue deficit to GDP ratio hovered around 3.5 per cent till 1996 but rose to 6.65 per cent in 1999. The fiscal deficit to GDP ratio actually fell from 9.39 per cent in 1990 to 6.43 per cent in 1996, but again went up to 8.90 per cent in 1996. These figures clearly indicate that initial attempts to bring down the governments deficits failed during the second half of the decade. The average revenue deficit to GDP ratio during the decade was 4.36 per cent, that is, almost three times that of the 1980s. Interestingly, the fiscal deficit to GDP ratio for the decade is 7.54 per cent, that is, lower than that of the 1980s. This strongly implies a significant cut in capital expenditures during the 1990s. The trade balance registered some improvement in the first few years with the trade balance to GDP ratio going up from – 1.86 per cent in 1990 to – 0.77 per cent in 1994. Subsequently, this trend was reversed and the trade balance to GDP ratio fell continuously, reaching – 2.85 per cent in 1999. This deterioration of the trade balance in the second half of the decade was mainly due to a fall in the exports to GDP ratio in the same period. The current account balance improved significantly during the decade compared to the 1980s. The average current account balance to GDP ratio for this period was – 1.17 per cent, almost a third less than that of the 1980s. This improvement was mainly due to a marked increase in the net invisibles inflow.

OVERVIEW OF MACROECONOMIC PERFORMANCE

We shall start our assessment with the sources of growth in the Indian economy. This will be followed up by a discussion of the nature of the growth and its consequences in terms of the changes in the sectoral compositions. We shall also discuss the inflationary trends and the performance of the economy in the monetary, fiscal, and external sectors. In the theoretical literature, a large volume of work has focussed on the sources of economic growth, right from the post-war years. It started with the 'Harrod–Domar' formulation, which demonstrated that with fixed capital–output ratios, steady state growth was proportional to investment ratios. This framework provided the greatest impetus to policies of 'investment-led growth'. Soon afterwards however, the

'Harrod–Domar' formulation was challenged by the 'Solow model'. According to Solow, higher investments can contribute to per capita growth only in the transitional periods (that is, before the steady state is reached). In the steady state, investments have no impact and only 'technical progress' can give rise to per capita growth. Subsequent work on growth during this period was mostly based on variants of the Solow model. For a long time however, the idea of 'technical progress' was a black box and there was no satisfactory theoretical analysis of the factors causing it. This situation changed significantly during the late 1980s and the 1990s, with the emergence of the theories of 'endogenous growth'. According to these theories, technical progress could depend on a whole range of factors, such as human capital formation, research and development (R&D) expenditures, government expenditure, especially on infrastructure, and these could generate steady state growth of per capita income. In recent years these ideas have strongly influenced policy makers, and strategies of growth have focused more and more on these issues.

It is important to note at this juncture that both the Solow model as well as the endogenous growth models are crucially dependent on the assumption of full employment of labour. This makes the framework of these models somewhat unsuitable for the Indian economy, with its huge reserves of unemployed labour. In fact, right from the inception of the planning process in India, it was understood that the 'Harrod–Domar' framework, with its focus on capital formation and the capital–output ratio, was a more suitable construct for the Indian economy. Within this framework, the growth rate in India can be increased either by increasing investment or bringing down the capital–output ratio. Furthermore, the capital–output ratio can be decreased by either using up unutilized capacity, or more efficient use of existing capacity, or adopting better technology. Here, the first case corresponds to a demand-constrained system, while the second and third correspond to supply-constrained systems. Interestingly, even within this 'Harrod–Domar' framework, the ideas thrown up by the endogenous growth literature are relevant in the case of the supply-constrained systems. This is due to the fact that factors like human capital, R&D activity, infrastructure, etc., can increase labour's productivity as well as capital's efficiency and technological capabilities. Thus, apart from the investment ratio, factors influencing the efficiency of capital are also important determinants of the growth in the Indian economy. Let us now look at some of these factors in the light of their behaviour in the Indian economy in the last three decades up to the present.

Savings, Investments, and the Incremental Capital–Output Ratios

In a capital constrained economy like India, growth is determined by aggregate saving and investment behaviour. As far as savings are concerned, the economy has performed remarkably well during 1970–2000. The gross saving rate, which was 14.56 per cent in 1970 jumped to a peak of 25.1 per cent in 1995 and slowed down thereafter to reach 22.26 per cent in 1999. This aggregate saving behaviour however, does not reveal the significant differences at the sectoral level. The biggest component of aggregate saving is the savings in the household sector. This component has been the pivot of the Indian savings behaviour, and the significant increases in the saving rate can be largely attributed to increased savings in this sector. The household saving rate was 10.15 per cent in 1970, and has increased steadily throughout the period to reach 19.77 per cent in 1999. The second component of aggregate saving is corporate saving. This component remained relatively stagnant during the 1970s and the early 1980s, but increased significantly in the early phase of economic liberalization in the 1990s to reach a peak of 4.93 per cent in 1995, after which it has fallen continuously. The final component of aggregate saving is that in the public sector, and it is here that the performance has been very poor. This is especially true during the 1980s and the 1990s, when it came down from 4.55 per cent in 1978 to – 1.19 per cent in 1999. It should be clear from these trends that the savings in the household sector is quite high and may have already reached its peak, given the low levels of per capita income of the economy. Another problem associated with increasing the household saving is the turmoil in the financial sector. The conclusion of all this is that any significant increase in the aggregate saving rate has to come primarily from the corporate and the public sectors. The aggregate and sectoral saving rates over the last three decades are presented in Figure 2.1.

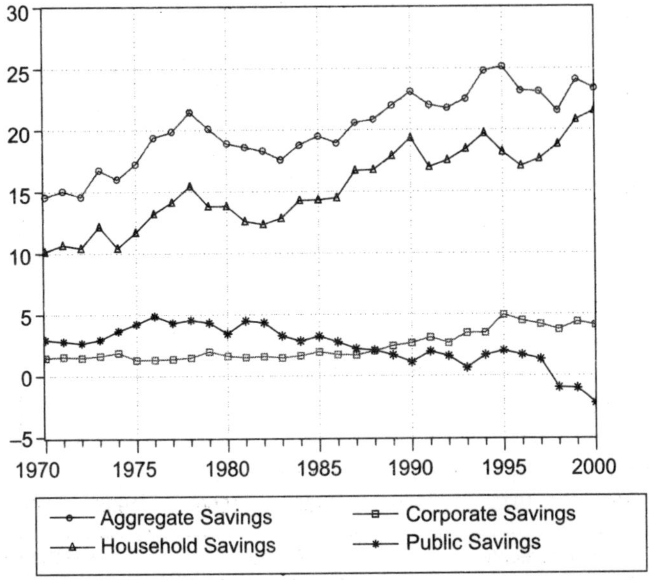

Figure 2.1 Aggregate and Sectoral Savings Ratios as a Percentage to GDP, 1970–2000.

Source: Computed from RBI's Handbook of Statistics on Indian Economy (*www.rbi.org.in/scripts/statistics.aspx*).

The aggregate investment behaviour has mirrored the aggregate savings behaviour during 1970–2000. It increased from 15.42 per cent in 1970 to a peak of 26.85 per cent in 1995, before coming down to 23.26 in 1999. At the sectoral level, private investment rose steadily throughout this period, going up from 9.43 per cent in 1970 to 15.65 per cent in 1999. Public investment, which was 6.39 per cent of GDP in 1970, increased to 11.17 in 1986, after which it has fallen continuously to as low as 7.06 per cent in 1999. The aggregate and sectoral investment rates over the last three decades are presented in Figure 2.2. One way to increase investment rate would be to augment domestic savings with foreign investment. Of course, foreign investment is a double-edged sword as there are problems associated with servicing this investment. The capability to service these investments would in the long run depend on the performance of the external sector.

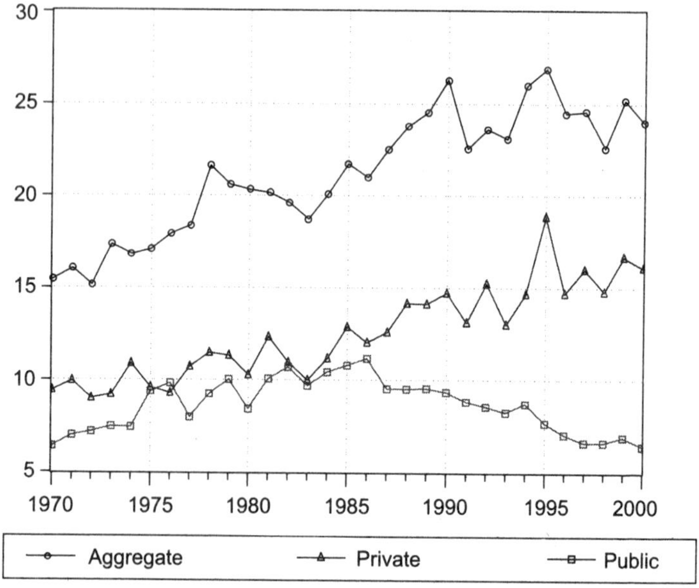

Figure 2.2 Aggregate and Sectoral Investment Ratios as a Percentage to GDP, 1970–2000.

Source: Same as for Figure 2.1.

Savings and investment lead to growth through the accumulation of capital. The efficiency of capital is, of course, the other important factor determining growth. The efficiency of capital is inversely related to the incremental capital–output ratio (ICOR). Let us now look at the behaviour of the aggregate and sectoral ICORs in the last three decades. A close look at these shows that for the aggregate as well as the agricultural and industrial sectors, the ICORs have maintained a steady value. Interestingly, in the services sector, the ICOR has exhibited a steady decrease over the period indicating an increase in the efficiency of capital in this sector. The ICOR for aggregate GDP and for the agricultural, industrial, and services sectors over the period 1970–2000 are presented in Figures 2.3, 2.4, 2.5, and 2.6, respectively. The lack of any decline in the ICOR for aggregate GDP, as well as those for the agricultural and industrial sectors, even after the liberalization of private investment in 1991, indicates that there has been no corresponding rise in the productivity of capital.

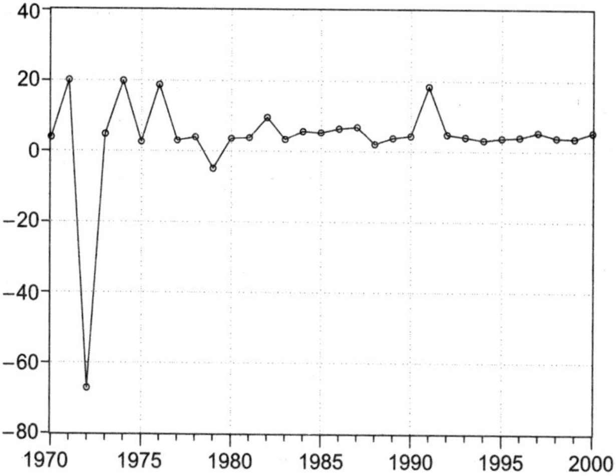

Figure 2.3 Incremental Capital–Output Ratio in Aggregate GDP, 1970–2000.

Sources: Computed from (i) RBI's Handbook of Statistics on Indian Economy (*www.rbi.org.in/soripts/Statistics.aspx*).

(ii) CSO's Statistical Abstract India (various issues).

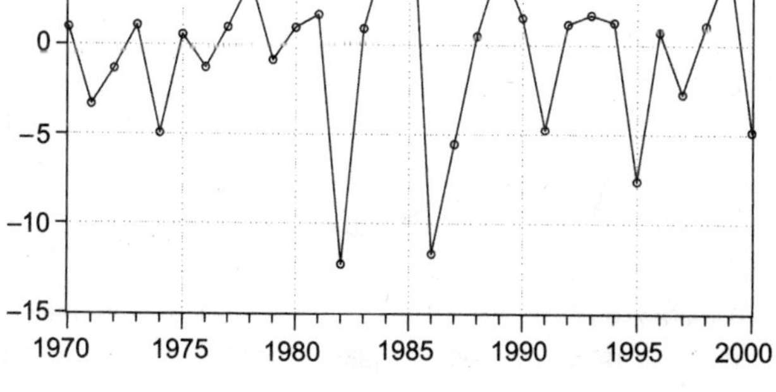

Figure 2.4 Incremental Capital–Output Ratio in Agricultural Sector, 1970–2000.

Sources: Same as for Figure 2.3.

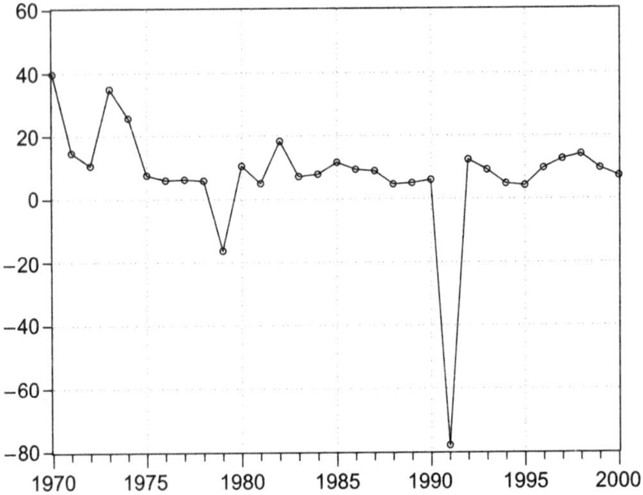

Figure 2.5 Incremental Capital–Output Ratio in Industrial Sector, 1970–2000.

Sources: Same as for Figure 2.3.

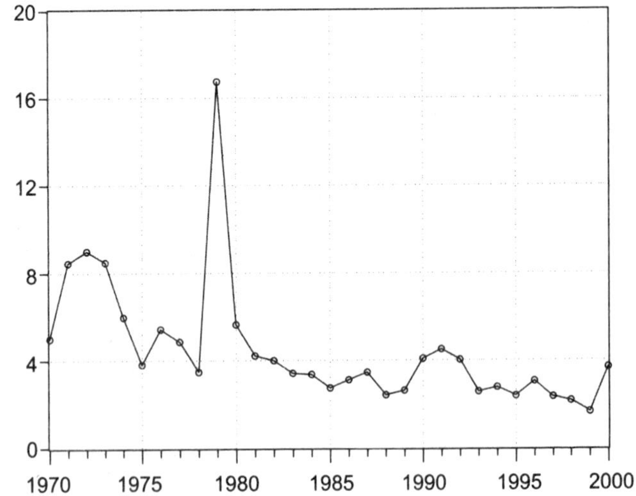

Figure 2.6 Incremental Capital–Output Ratio in Services (except Public Administration), 1970–2000.

Sources: Same as for Figure 2.3.

Aggregate and Sectoral Growth

Let us now look at the nature of the growth process in the Indian economy for the past three decades. In 1970, the real GDP of the indian economy (base year 1993–4) was Rs 296,278 crore. Over the next three decades, the economy grew at an average rate of 4.8 per cent, which led to the real GDP reaching Rs 1,193,922 crore by the year 2000. In other words, there has been a four-fold increase in the real GDP in these three decades. This growth has not been uniform of course. In fact the 1970s could only achieve a poor 3.15 per cent rate of growth, while the 1980s and the 1990s attained a much more healthy 5.63 per cent and 5.6 per cent, respectively. The aggregate growth rates over the last three decades are presented in Figure 2.7. From this it is clear that in the last two decades, the Indian economy has broken free from the shackles of the infamous 'Hindu rate of growth'. The distribution of growth has been uneven not only across decades but also across the various sectors of the economy. The agricultural sector, by far the biggest in 1970, grew at a low average rate of 2.69 per cent during 1970–2000, while the industrial and services sector (excluding public administration) grew at much higher rates of 5.61 and 6.24 per cent, respectively, over the same period. The growth rates for the agricultural, industrial, and services sectors over the last three decades are presented in Figures 2.8, 2.9 and 2.10 respectively.

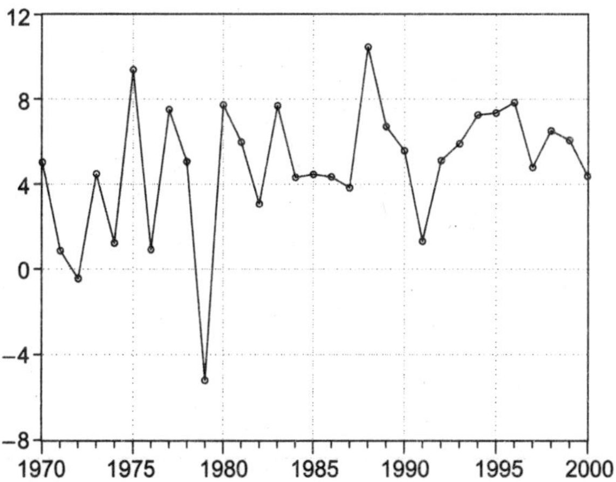

Figure 2.7 Aggregate GDP Growth Rate, 1970–2000.
Source: Same as for Figure 2.1.

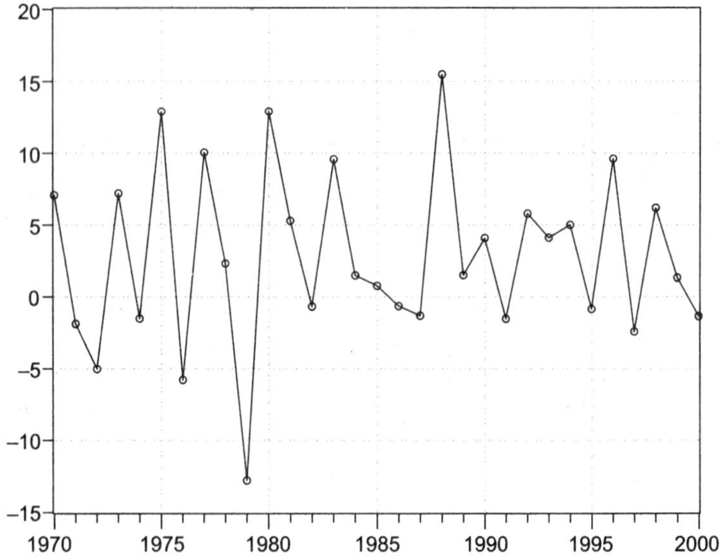

Figure 2.8 Agriculture Sector Growth Rate, 1970–2000.
Source: Same as for Figure 2.1.

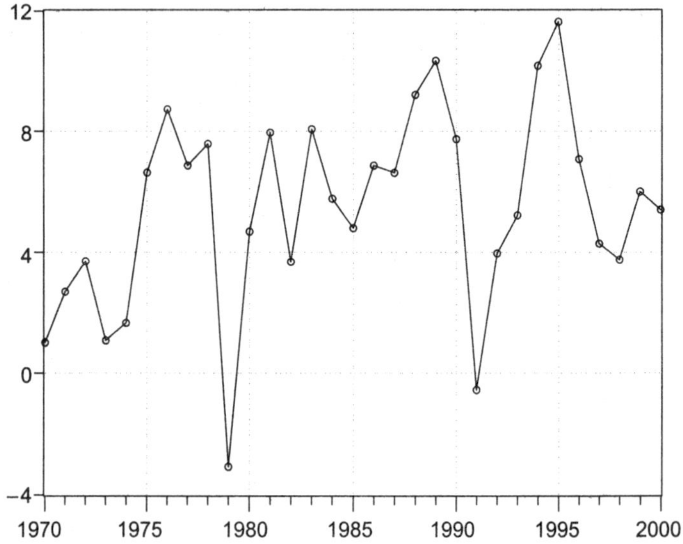

Figure 2.9 Industrial Sector Growth Rate, 1970–2000.
Source: Same as for Figure 2.1.

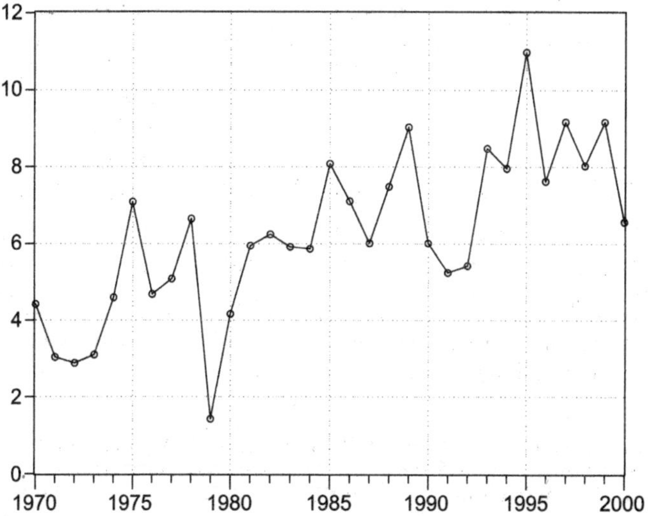

Figure 2.10 Service Sector (excluding Public Administration) Growth Rate, 1970–2000.

Source: Same as for Figure 2.1.

Changes In Sectoral Composition

The aggregate and sectoral GDP growth rates for the three decades and for the whole period are presented in Table 2.1. The differential growth rates across the sectors have resulted in significant changes in the sectoral composition of output. The agricultural sector has lost its pre-eminent position with its share in GDP coming down from 46 per cent in 1970 to 24 per cent in 2000. Consequently all the other sectors have gained in terms of their share in the GDP. The share of industry has gone up steadily from about 22 per cent in 1970 to 28 per cent in 2000, while the share of public administration and defence has increased from 4 per cent to 6 per cent in the same period. However, it is the services sector that has shown the most remarkable result, increasing its share from about 28 per cent in 1970 to about 42 per cent in 2000. If we add the GDP from public administration and defence to the services sector we get the tertiary sector, whose share in GDP in 2000 has reached close to 50 per cent. The sectoral composition of output at different points of time during the three decades is presented in Table 2.2.

Table 2.1 Long Run Growth Rates. *(per cent per annum)*

	Agriculture	Industry	Services	Public Adminis-tration and Defence	Aggregate GDP
1971–80	1.83	4.05	4.26	5.38	3.15
1981–90	3.54	7.10	6.76	6.49	5.63
1991–2000	2.69	5.68	7.69	6.64	5.60
1971–2000	2.69	5.61	6.24	6.15	4.80

Source: Computed from Handbook of Statistics on Indian Economy (*www.rbi.org.in/scripts/statistics.aspa*).

Table 2.2 Percentage Share of Different Sectors in Aggregate GDP.

Year	Agriculture	Industry	Services	Public Administration and Defence
1970	46	22	28	4
1980	40	24	31	5
1990	32	27	35	6
2000	24	28	42	6

Source: Same as Table 2.1.

Clearly, the Indian growth experience has been quite varied during 1970–2000. The average growth rate in the post-independence period up to the 1970s was a poor 3.6 per cent per annum, giving rise to the term the 'Hindu rate of growth'. In the last two decades, however, the economy broke the shackles of the 'Hindu rate' and grew at a healthy rate of 5.7 per cent per annum. The growth was particularly high after the post-1991 crisis, averaging about 6.3 per cent per annum.

Prices and Inflation

There are a number of indices used to define prices and inflation rates for an economy. In the Indian context, the three most important indices are the GDP deflator, the consumer price index (CPI), and the wholesale price index (WPI). Over the three decades, the GDP deflator has increased by almost 1025 per cent, while the CPI and WPI have increased by about 1060 per cent and 985 per cent, respectively. The decadal averages of the inflation rates have shown remarkable stability. Thus, for example, the inflation rate based on the WPI has been 9 per cent, 8.81 per cent, and 8 per cent for the three decades respectively. This similarity in the decadal averages seems to indicate an upper limit to the psychologically acceptable inflation rates for the Indian economy. Of course, the volatility around the average inflation rate has been very different for the three decades. Thus the 1970s witnessed major fluctuations in the inflation rates while there has been more stability during the 1980s and the 1990s. The 1990s have also exhibited a marked downward trend in inflation rates. This phenomenon is probably related to the competition from the external sector as well as the slowdown during the second half of the decade. The inflation rates for the period 1970 to 2000 are presented in Figure 2.11.

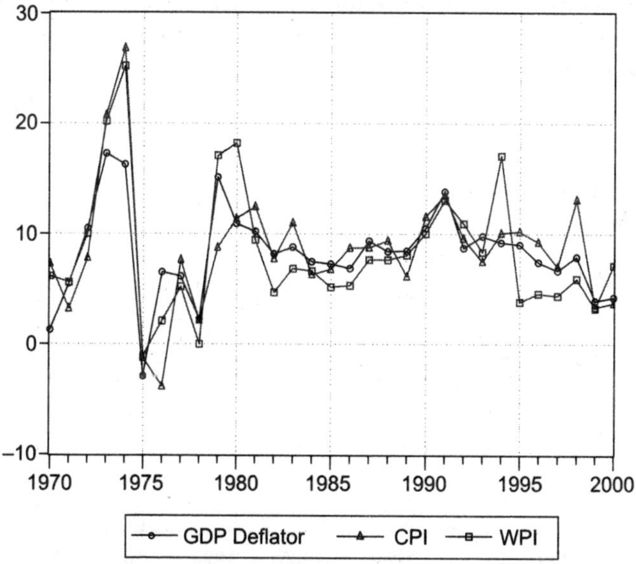

Figure 2.11 Inflation Rates, 1970–2000.
Source: Same as for Figure 2.1.

The Monetary Sector

Over the three decades, the reserve money rose from 4823 crore to 303,311 crore, that is, it increased more than sixty-two times its original value. This increase was made possible by an annual average growth rate in excess of 14 per cent. During this period, there has also been a significant change in the composition of reserve money. The reserve money is largely composed of RBI credit to the government and the rupee value of our foreign exchange reserves. We find that the proportion of RBI credit fell from about 76 per cent in 1970 to about 48 per cent in 2000, while the proportion of foreign exchange reserves went up from about 15 per cent in 1970 to about 65 per cent in 2000. Thus the reserve money is now largely determined by the performance of the external sector.

Corresponding to the growth in the reserve money, the money supply has also grown from 11,020 crore in 1970 to 1,313,220 crore in 2000, that is, it increased more than 119 times. This increase was due to an annual average growth rate of about 17.3 per cent. It may be noted that the money supply has grown at a faster rate than the reserve money indicating an increase in the money multiplier. This is largely due to financial innovations and institutional changes in the financial sector. The growth rates of reserve money and money supply are presented in Figure 2.12.

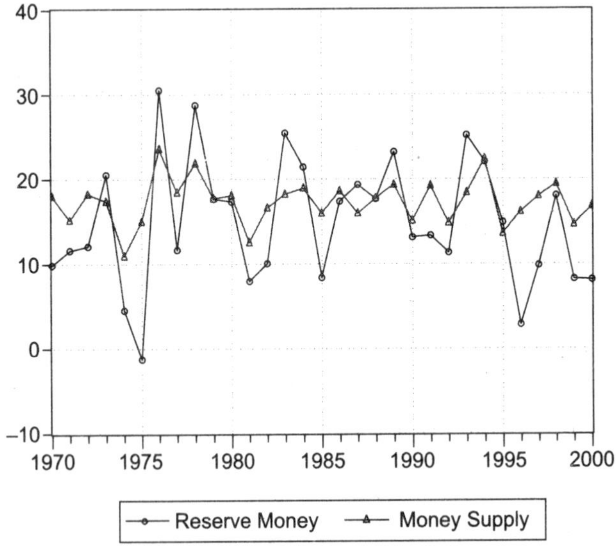

Figure 2.12 Reserve Money and Money Supply Growth Rates, 1970–2000.
Source: Same as for Figure 2.1.

The interest rate regime has also seen significant changes during this period. During the 1970s and the 1980s, interest rates were fixed by the RBI. This system was changed with the deregulation of the interest rates during the early 1990s, and the banks were given the freedom to determine their own interest rates. However, the RBI still continues to influence these rates by suitably modifying the bank rate and the cash reserve ratio (CRR). The trends in the interest rates have also been significantly different for the three decades. The 1970s experienced a relatively low and rising interest rate regime. During the 1980s, the interest rates as well as the spread between the deposit and lending rates were high. This trend continued till the early 1990s, after which there has been a downward trend in both interest rates and the spread. These trends in the interest rates are presented in Figure 2.13.

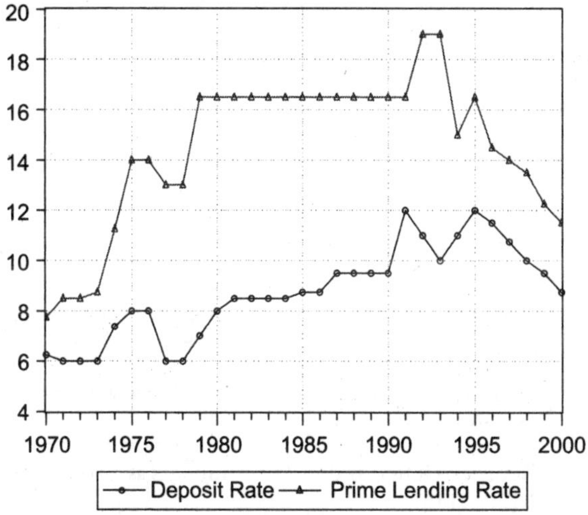

Figure 2.13 Interest Rates, 1970–2000.
Source: Same as for Figure 2.1.

The Fiscal Sector

The fiscal sector consists of the income, expenditure, and deficits of the government. As far as the income, expenditure, and deficits in the revenue accounts are concerned, there have been very significant changes over the years 1970 to 2000. Both the revenue income and expenditure (as a percentage to GDP) exhibited increasing trends till the mid-1980s, after which they kept falling for the next ten years or so, and have again shown an upward trend after the mid-1990s. Another notable aspect is that till the mid-1980s, the revenue income and expenditure approximately moved together and this resulted in very low (and sometimes negative) values of the revenue deficit. After the mid-1980s, however, the expenditure has been significantly higher than the income leading to high and increasing revenue deficits during this period. The revenue deficit and its determinants are presented in Figure 2.14.

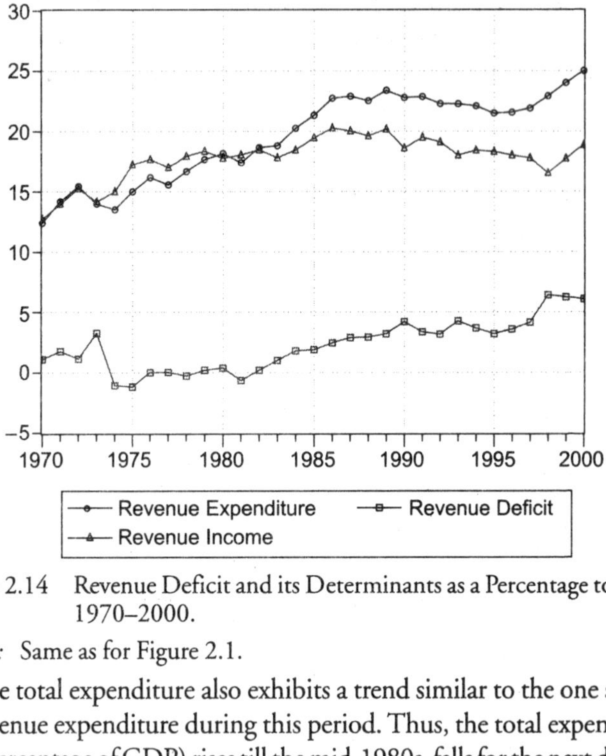

Figure 2.14 Revenue Deficit and its Determinants as a Percentage to GDP, 1970–2000.

Source: Same as for Figure 2.1.

The total expenditure also exhibits a trend similar to the one shown by revenue expenditure during this period. Thus, the total expenditure (as a percentage of GDP) rises till the mid-1980s, falls for the next decade, and rises again after the mid-1990s. However, the fall after the mid-1980s is much sharper than that for the revenue expenditure, clearly implying a sharp fall in the capital expenditure during this period. This is also clear from Figure 2.15 that plots revenue and capital expenditure (as a ratio of total expenditure) during this period. As a result of the sharp decline in capital expenditure, the fiscal deficit shows a downward trend during this period. However, this trend is reversed in the latter half of the 1990s, as total expenditure rises steeply during this period. The fiscal deficit and its determinants are presented in Figure 2.16.

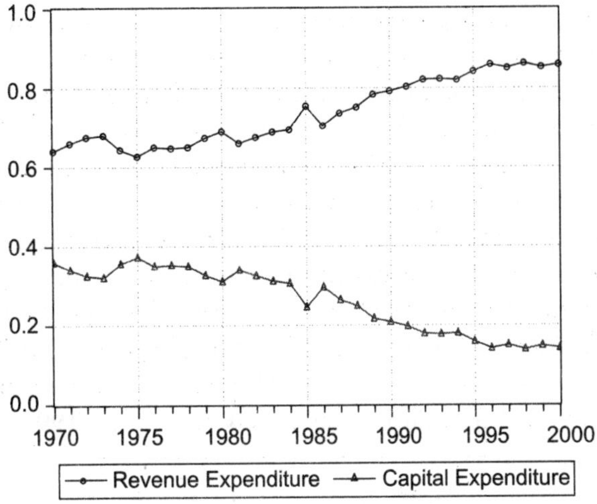

Figure 2.15 Revenue and Capital Expenditure as a Ratio to Total Expenditure, 1970–2000.

Source: Same as for Figure 2.1.

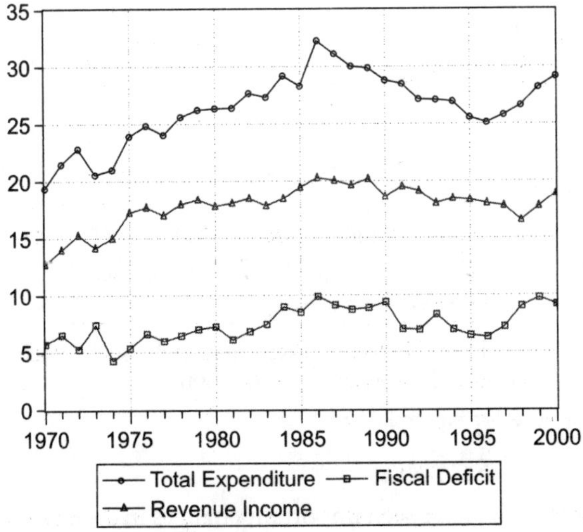

Figure 2.16 Fiscal Deficit and its Determinants as a Percentage to GDP, 1970–2000.

Source: Same as for Figure 2.1.

Another aspect of the fiscal scenario that has exhibited changing patterns is the mode of financing of the total expenditure. At an aggregate level, the total expenditure can be either financed by revenue income (tax and non-tax revenue) or else contributes to the fiscal deficit. The share of total expenditure that is financed by tax revenue, non-tax revenue, and the fiscal deficit is depicted in Figure 2.17. From this figure, it is clear that from the mid-1970s, there is a downward trend in the tax financed proportion of total expenditure and a corresponding upward trend in the proportion of total expenditure that is covered by the fiscal deficit. As we have pointed out earlier, this amounted to a debt financed growth strategy during the 1980s and resulted in high levels of debt-to-GDP ratios. This trend was reversed during the first half of the 1990s but there seems to be a return to the high deficit syndrome during the last few years of the 1990s.

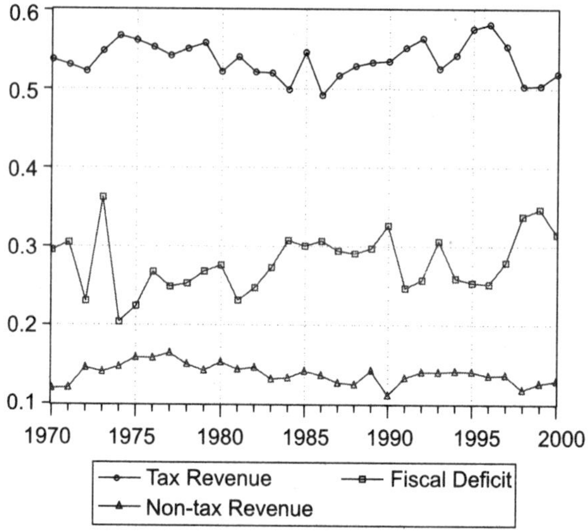

Figure 2.17 Tax Revenue, Non-tax Revenue, and Fiscal Deficit as a Ratio to Total Expenditure, 1970–2000.

Source: Same as for Figure 2.1.

The External Sector

The three decades have seen important changes in the external sector. The economy has become more globalized with the export to GDP ratio going up from 3.33 per cent in 1970 to 9.95 per cent in 2000, while the import to GDP ratio rose from 3.55 per cent to 11.28 per cent over the same period. The export ratio exhibited an increasing trend till 1976, fell for the next nine years, showed an increasing trend from 1985 onwards, stagnating a little after 1995 but came up sharply after 1998. The import ratio rose very sharply throughout the 1970s, particularly due to the oil shocks. After 1980, the import ratio performed similar to the export ratio, with a downward trend till the mid-1980s and an upward trend thereafter (following the policies of imports liberalization) stagnating a little after 1995 but coming up sharply after 1998. The comparative performance in the exports and the imports sectors determines the trade balance of the economy. The sharp increase in imports during the second half of the 1970s in the face of falling exports ratio led to a dramatic increase in the trade deficits during this period. The trade deficit declined during the 1980s and the first half of the 1990s due to some good performance in the exports sector. However, the closing years of the 1990s have seen some stagnation in exports and this has resulted in an increase in the trade deficits during this period. The export, import, and trade balance ratios over the last three decades are presented in Figure 2.18.

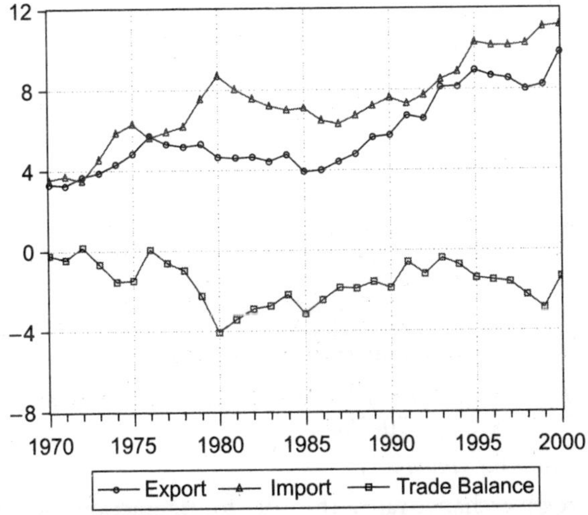

Figure 2.18 Trade Balance and its Determinants as a Percentage to GDP, 1970–2000.

Source: Same as for Figure 2.1.

The current account balance (CAB) is determined by the trade balance (merchandise) and the flow of net invisibles. The flow of net invisibles exhibited an increasing trend during the 1970s, a falling trend during the 1980s, and a rising trend during the 1990s. However, the rise during the 1970s was not enough to counter the sharp fall in the trade balance (merchandise) during the same period and this led to deterioration in the current account balance (as a percentage of GDP). This deterioration in CAB continued during the 1980s due to the falling trend in the net invisibles in this period. During the 1990s, the upward trend in the net invisibles and the downward trend in the trade balance have more or less countered each other, leading to the CAB (as a percentage of GDP) maintaining a value between 0 and 2 per cent during this period. The CAB and its determinants (all as percentages of GDP) are presented in Figure 2.19.

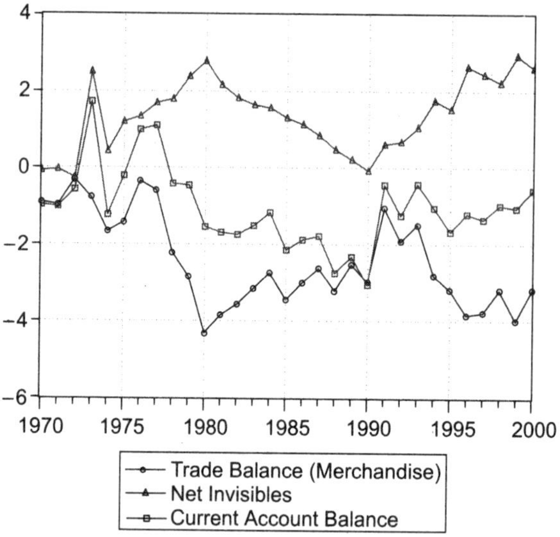

Figure 2.19 Current Account Balance and its Determinants as a Percentage to GDP, 1970–2000.

Source: Same as for Figure 2.1.

The foreign exchange rate is the price for transactions in the foreign exchange market. India had adopted a fixed exchange rate regime till 1973 after which it switched to a regime of managed float of the currency. Finally in 1993, the economy moved to a system of market-determined exchange rates. Under the managed float regime, the exchange rate maintained a steady value of around Rs/US$ 8 during the 1970s. The currency depreciated steadily during the 1980s reaching around Rs/US$ 18 by 1990. The foreign exchange crisis in the early

1990s forced a steep depreciation in 1991 when the exchange rate grew by about 36 per cent from about Rs/US$ 18 to about Rs/US$ 24.5. Subsequently in 1993, the move towards market-determined rates again led to a substantial depreciation. The exchange rate continued to rise significantly throughout the 1990s reaching a value of Rs/US$ 46.6 in 2000. The exchange rate for the three decades is given in Figure 2.20.

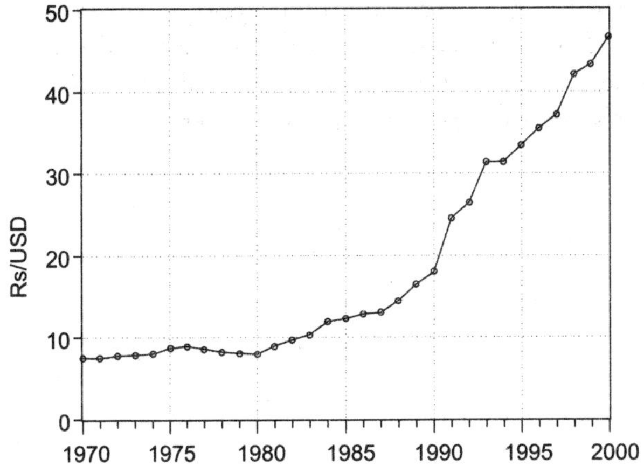

Figure 2.20 Exchange Rate, 1970–2000.
Source: Same as for Figure 2.1.

CONCLUDING REMARKS

Till now we have described the economic regimes, the resultant performances, and the broad trends in the important macroeconomic aggregates of the Indian economy in the post-independence period. It may be pointed out at this juncture that in a market economy, macroeconomic aggregates such as growth rates, inflation rates, fiscal deficits, etc. are determined through a complex process that involves the interaction between the various sectors of the economy. They also depend on exogenous factors such as international price of petroleum, rainfall, volume of world trade, etc. Thus, any discussion of the actual and potential performance of the economy has to take all these points into account. More specifically, it is of interest to ask whether the economy could have performed differently in the past and whether it can perform well in the future given its interlinked structure and the expected trends in the exogenous factors. An answer to this question can be provided only by a macromodelling exercise that explicitly incorporates the interlinkages between the various sectors of the economy. In this book, we have attempted to do this on the basis of a macromodelling exercise that we have carried out at the IEG for the past few years. In this model, we have incorporated the important interlinkages between the production, fiscal, monetary, and external sectors and generated the sectoral and aggregate growth rates of the economy. The interlinkages and the detailed sector-wise behaviour of the economy have been culled from the evidence of the past three decades that we have described in this chapter.

3

MACROMODELLING OF THE INDIAN ECONOMY

The market-oriented reforms carried out during the 1990s have greatly enhanced the importance of macroeconomic policies. In view of the greater role assigned to the markets, appropriate policies that provide the right market signals are likely to play a more critical role than in the past, when various economic variables were regulated directly. In this context, macromodels and their forecasts have assumed great importance as they examine the relationships between various macro aggregates and provide estimates of the direction as well as the magnitude of the effect of policies on the economy. In this chapter, we shall present a survey of the macroeconometric modelling literature, with special emphasis on the contributions to the modelling of the Indian economy. In the next section, we start by outlining the historical background of the macromodelling literature. This is followed by a section on the development of the literature, mostly in the Netherlands and in the United States of America. The third section describes the methodology used to construct macromodels. The fourth section deals with some of the broad methodological issues that have emerged as a result of the development of the macromodelling literature. The fifth section outlines the chronological development of the literature in the Indian context. The final section presents a detailed discussion of the similarities and differences in the treatment of the Indian economy, in terms of the models identified in the fifth section. The objective of this chapter is two-fold. First, it gives a detailed yet simple introduction to the various issues related to macromodelling. Second, by giving a thorough survey of the existing models and their characteristics, it attempts to explain where our model (described in detail in the next two chapters) stands with respect to the existing literature.

MACROECONOMETRIC MODELLING: ANTECEDENTS

There have been a number of early contributions in theoretical and applied economics that foreshadowed the arrival of econometric models in general and macroeconometric models in particular. Perhaps the earliest example of this is Francois Quesnay's *Tableau Economique*, a classic analysis that can reasonably be regarded as the first stylized macroeconomic model. Later on, the Walrasian General Equilibrium system became an inspiration for several generations of econometricians, as they attempted to find empirical counterparts to his abstract system of equations. Walras himself considered the possibility of an empirical implementation of his system. Thus, in his *Elements d'economic politique pure*, he speaks of relating the rational and rigorously exact equations of exchange and production to the empirical and approximate equation of sales written as a function of price. However, in the modern literature, the focus of macroeconomic models has shifted from the Walrasian system as it was increasingly felt that this system did not accurately describe the real world. In particular, the great depression of the late 1930s shifted the focus from the Walrasian to the Keynesian framework and most subsequent macroeconometric models were largely influenced by the Keynesian analytical structure. However, there were a couple of other important contributions to the subject during this period that helped lay the groundwork for the construction of the early econometric models. Among these, the two most important were those by Ragnar Frisch (1933) and Michal Kalecki (1935). Frisch's 'Propagation problems and impulse problems in dynamic economic', presented a simple dynamic model of the business cycle. From this model, Frisch obtained a system of mixed difference-differential equations and showed that if 'reasonable values' for the structural parameters are substituted, the solution paths are all damped cycles. However, Frisch also recognized that the use of reasonable values is no substitute of rigorous econometric work and he added, 'I think, indeed, the statistical determination of such structural parameters will be one of the main objectives of the economic cycle analysis of the future'. A similar model was published by Kalecki (1935) in *Econometrica.* This model could also be reduced to a difference-differential equation, though the generation of cyclical behaviour depended on certain parametric values.

Kalecki used statistical data of the United States for crude estimates of the parameters of his system and found these values generated cycles.

These contributions were, however, completely overshadowed by the Keynesian revolution, which profoundly influenced all subsequent developments in macroeconomic model building. There is no doubt that Keynes has contributed more than any other economist in encouraging the systematic estimation of national accounts magnitudes and the construction of econometric models. Keynes' theorizing completed the steps that other economists including Pareto, Frisch, and Kalecki had taken away from microeconomic analysis of Walras, allowing researchers to deal with concepts and quantities that were much easier to measure in practice. This in turn permitted a return to aggregative concepts, which were used in Quesnay's Tableau, with a much higher degree of precision. This aspect of the Keynesian revolution opened the field to macroeconometric model building. Indeed, it may be noted that for many years macroeconometric models have been constructed as empirical counterparts to the Keynesian system. It is only in recent years that econometric models based on alternative paradigms have appeared in the literature.

A BRIEF HISTORY OF MODEL BUILDING

The pioneering attempt at large-scale model building was primarily associated with the studies in the 1930s by Jan Tinbergen. In his seminal contribution, 'Business Cycles in the United States of America 1919–1932' that was published in 1939, Tinbergen constructed an annual model of the US economy fitted by ordinary least squares (OLS) to data for the period 1919–32. There were 31 behavioural equations and 17 identities for a total of 48 equations. All the relationships were linear and Tinbergen used fractional lags as approximation of distributed lags. However, there were very few exogenous variables (in fact, there were five), which reflected a Walrasian tradition of a largely closed or internally contained model. In the mid-1940s, the Cowles Commission for research in economics, USA, initiated a programme of structured model building within the framework of a complete system of national accounts. Within this programme, Klein developed models that were principally used for hypothesis testing and giving a description of the economy. In addition, the models were used to calculate expenditure multipliers and analysing the cyclical nature of the economy. Interestingly, they were not used for policy simulation or forecasting.

It was only in the 1950s that serious and sustained macromodelling activity was initiated by Klein (1950) and Klein and Goldberger (1955). During the same period, the Dutch Central Planning Bureau (CPB), under the guidance of Tinbergen, developed a number of models for the Dutch economy. The model for 1955 is one of those early models that was used by the CPB for forecasting and policy analysis. This model was strictly linear. It placed heavy stress on exports and imports in keeping with the open nature of Dutch economy. There were twelve identities, four institutional equations, and eleven behavioural equations for a total of twenty-seven equations. The behavioural equations were fitted to a sample of inter-war and post-war years combined, by a variety of methods. This model was used extensively for macroeconomic policy formulation in the Netherlands during the decade following its construction and publication.

Over the 1960s, macroeconometric research become an integral part of the research agenda for economists. The early 1970s, however, witnessed the decline of Keynesianism as a dominant paradigm amongst both policy makers as well as academicians in the United States and with it, macromodelling—at least in the Keynes–Klein tradition—ceased to be on the research agenda. In Europe, however, Keynesian economics and macromodelling remained a serious subject. In recent years, there have been new developments that have resulted in a variety of alternative models. One such development is the increasing importance assigned to such issues as information, expectation, and contracts. Another important development is the increasing use of micro-theoretic foundations as the building blocks of an overall macromodel. These developments have had far reaching implications for both policy formulation and modelling methodology. Macromodelling has attained a new stage of evolution drawing upon the new paradigms in macroeconomic theory, emergence of more refined methodology, and renaissance of market economy.

METHODOLOGY OF MODELLING

Macromodelling is based primarily on the 'structural macromodelling' methodology associated with the Cowles Commission. Almost all the models are estimated using annual observations. In general, the equations are estimated separately using the OLS method. In case of serial correlation, the equations are estimated with autoregressive transformations AR(1). The simultaneous estimation of the equations is not feasible as the number of observations is usually not sufficiently large. Most time series variables exhibit non-stationarity. To deal with this problem, behavioural equations are estimated in growth rates or first differences rather than in levels. The performance of the model is assessed through simulation. Simulation provides estimates of changes in different variables with changes in certain exogenous variables. An exogenous change in one part of the model gets translated to the other parts through a number of channels. In some cases, the same change may lead to opposite effects through different channels and these give rise to trade-offs between these opposing effects. The net result in these cases depends on the relative strength of these effects. The simulation results therefore depend upon how accurately the model is specified in terms of interlinkages between different variables. This in turn requires validation of the model. The validity of the model depends upon how well it is capable of reproducing the observed data. Most models therefore report the results of the validation. Validation tests include estimation of the root mean square error (RMSE) and Theil's inequality statistics for the endogenous variables. The methodology adopted in macroeconometric exercises may be summed up in terms of the following steps.

1. Constructing a theoretical model of the macroeconomy on the basis of an appropriate framework, with the chosen degree of disagregation and appropriate closure rules.
2. Acquiring time series data for all the variables (endogenous as well as exogenous) for the period to be studied.
3. Estimating the behavioural equations on the basis of the a priori theories and the time series data. Usually OLS or TSLS estimating methods are used in the literature. Suitable changes can be made to the behavioural equations during the course of this exercise.
4. The whole model including the technical equations, identities, and the behavioural equations are solved (simulated) using the Gauss–Seidel method in order to generate the predicted values of the endogenous variables.

5. The model is validated by examining the behaviour of the errors (difference between the forecasted and the actual values of endogenous variables) in terms of statistical measures like RMSE and Theil's inequality statistics.
6. The validated model can be used to forecast out of sample values of the endogenous variables or analyse counterfactual policy stimulations.

With new developments in macroeconomic theories, the methodology described above has also came under attack. It has been argued that structural models are not well specified insofar as few parameter restrictions are imposed across equations. This has implications for the identification of structural parameters. As an alternative to this, Sims proposed a new alternative methodology known as Vector Auto Regression (VAR) modelling. This debate over appropriate methodology is however far from over.

METHODOLOGICAL ISSUES IN THE MODELLING LITERATURE

In order to analyse the literature on macromodelling, it is important to look at the models in terms of issues such as analytical framework, the level of disaggregation of the model, and the adjustment processes for transmission from one equilibrium to another.

Analytical Framework

The choice of the analytical framework depends on an understanding of some important and interrelated characteristics of the economy. These include the role played by the price system in bringing about equilibrium (that is, the extent to which economic agents may respond in terms of price rather than quantity adjustments), the organizational structure of markets, and the severity of various constraints on the performance of the economy. Till recently, model builders were faced with two alternative paradigms depending on the role that is assigned to prices and on how markets function. These are the Walrasian and the Keynesian paradigms. The former draws its basic elements from the General Equilibrium Theory of Walras, later vintages of which are the Neoclassical Theory and the more recent New Classical Economics (Tobin 1980). The latter, on the other hand, includes several vintages and extensions of the basic theory expounded in Keynes' General

Theory. For simplification, these two broad alternative paradigms are labelled as the Classical and Keynesian. The basic premises of the classical theory are that price is the sole equilibrating variable and that market clearing is necessary for equilibrium. These assumptions of the classical theory ensure that all resources are fully employed, which in turn means that firms are producing what they intend to produce though they may leave some capacity unused intentionally. Furthermore, money is only a veil having no influence on the real variables like output, investment, or employment. Keynesianism departed from the classical theory in many directions. Three major aspects of the Keynesian paradigm are: (i) money wage rigidities, (ii) liquidity preference, and (iii) the consumption function. Contrary to the classical theory, Keynesian theory assigns an important role to aggregate demand and this leaves scope for less than full capacity utilization. Given the price ineffectiveness, it emphasizes on quantitative adjustment in production to ensure equilibrium in the markets. Until about the early 1970s, a widely shared consensus seemed to be that the Keynesian methodology was not of much relevance to less developed countries (LDCs). It was argued that the main production sector is the agricultural sector, and this sector is not demand constrained. Rather, capital is the binding constraint, making these economies supply determined. However, subsequently many of these stylized facts about LDCs were thought to be exaggerated. It came to be recognized that the Keynesian model is more flexible and comprehensive and that the functioning of LDCs is quite likely to be along Keynesian lines (Chakravarty 1979; Pandit 1977; Rakshit 1982). It was argued that one of the most important characteristics of these economies is the segmentation of commercial activities and the related market imperfections. This tends to erode the capability of the price system as an equilibrating force. Consequently economic agents are prone to rely more on quantity than on price adjustments. However, there are few instances of a pure Keynesian model for these economies with most modellers arguing for a mix of the classical and Keynesian frameworks.

During the 1960s, debates on economic policy in the context of developing countries gave rise to the structuralist school of thought. Structuralist economists maintained that the less developed countries have complex structural dynamics and that their functioning is conditioned by a large number of socio-political parameters, such as skewed income distribution, imperfect markets for capital, labour, and trade, dependence on imports, and such other factors. These characteristics imply that any policy implication based on oversimplified economic models may be counter-productive. Some of the basic arguments of the structuralists are: (i) savings and foreign exchange reserves are effective constraints on development, (ii) sectoral imbalances initiate the process of inflation with money supply being passive or endogenous to the economic system, (iii) public investment is complementary to private investment, and (iv) quantitative adjustments predominate over price adjustment due to price rigidities. Some authors have argued that while many elements of structuralism are universal to LDCs in varying degrees, some of them are quite special to the Latin American economies. Consequently, they felt that the structuralist approach has only limited relevance to developing countries like India. However, Klein (1984) observed that certain salient features of the developing countries need to be incorporated in macroeconomic modelling. For instance, the governments in most developing countries predominate as producer, investor, and consumer. Their activities are constrained in several ways. Therefore, their behaviour is neither fully exogenous nor market oriented. Besides, most developing countries are infected by resource constraints. These supply bottlenecks may arise from inadequate infrastructure, shortage of imported inputs, poor harvests due to natural factors, and capital shortage. The model should make allowance for resource-constrained output. At the same time, demand factors should also be assigned a role.

In addition to the structuralist view, another important development in macroeconomics has been the increasing emphasis on issues such as information, expectation, and contracts. With this development, the central theme of the two paradigms, classical and Keynesian, also came to be interpreted in terms of the role and treatment assigned to such issues. For instance, the current interpretation of the central theme in the Keynesian theory is that information is imperfect and costly to acquire. As regards contracts, it assumes that macroeconomic adjustments are governed by contracts, which cannot be redrawn in the short run. The theory treats expectations exogenously. On the contrary, the new classical theory asserts that expectations are endogenous and are formed rationally. These assumptions have important policy implications.

To sum up, the applicability of any particular theory is unwarranted on both analytical and empirical grounds. Thus most models combine the elements of the neoclassical and Keynesian formats with Structuralist views and new theoretical developments.

Level of Disaggregation

There are a number of considerations that determine the level of disaggregation a model should adopt. The first consideration is the availability of data. A second consideration is the extent to which prices and quantities are meaningfully conceptualized and measured corresponding to a certain disaggregations. The objective is to divide the economy into sectors which are more or less homogenous as regards the following issues: (i) the concept and statistical measurement of price and output adjustment, (ii) the extent to which the resource constraint may or may not be binding, (iii) the forms of market structure, (iv) the extent to which activities are publicly or privately managed, and (v) the nature of product and organization of production. For instance, agriculture and related activities are differentiated from manufacturing and construction due to highly differentiated characteristics. Output in the agricultural sector is determined largely by the supply side forces particularly rainfall, while prices are market clearing and competitively determined. In the industrial sector, output may be demand constrained and prices may be subject to a mark-up factor. Besides, the former is nearly completely privately controlled while the latter has mixed ownership. Within these broad sectors also, substantial differences exist across sub-sectors. However, manageability of data and availability of data are important considerations that need to be taken into account while deciding on the level of disaggregation.

Adjustment Processes

One of the most important aspects of a macromodel is its transmission mechanism, that is the various modes of adjustments that the model permits for transmission from one equilibrium to another. The individual equations or blocks of equations do not by themselves determine the character of the model until the adjustment modes are specified. Two fundamental adjustments are related to output and prices. There are various other adjustment factors as well, for instance, those related to the money and asset markets, factor pricing, government budget, and external sector response to domestic and external shocks. Depending upon the Keynesian–neoclassical–structuralist mix, these processes differ in different models. However, a current review of literature suggests a broad consensus regarding some of the adjustment mechanisms. For instance, almost all models consider agricultural supply to be weather determined and agricultural prices to be market clearing. Production in the industrial sector in most models is assumed to be resource constrained. The industrial sector is assumed to entail greater quantitative adjustments as it has excess capacity combined with fixed price mechanisms. The Service sector is expected to depend on the activities in other sectors of the economy.

MACROMODELLING IN INDIA

The construction of macroeconometric models of the Indian economy has had a relatively long history, particularly amongst those in the third world. The pioneering exercise in developing a short-term planning model for India was carried out by Narasimham (1956) for his PhD dissertation, under the supervision of L.R. Klein. This was followed by a number of similar attempts. Over the years there has been significant developments in the process of model building in India. In fact we can meaningfully divide the whole period into four distinct phases with each phase exhibiting greater degree of sophistication in the models compared to those in the previous one. In the following discussion, the evolution of macromodelling in India is presented in terms of these four phases.

The First Phase

The first phase started with Narasimham's work in 1956 and covered the 1960s. Models developed during this phase were aggregative, simple, medium-sized, and explanatory. Almost all of them were undertaken as doctoral dissertations. These models were mostly constructed with data taken from a common period. For example, Narasimham (1956), Marwah (1963, 1972), and Chaudhry (1963) took their data from pre-independence as well as post-independence years. On the other hand, both Krishnamurty (1964) and Agarwala (1970) confined themselves to the post-independence period. All the models used annual time series data, which meant that the sample size was small. Estimation was carried out by some single-equation technique, that is, OLS and 2SLS, ratios, percentages, products, logs, and actual values all appeared in the same model, which was linear in nature. Though the models were simple and described the whole economy, some of them had a specific focus. For instance, Marwah (1963) focused on the price behaviour, whereas Krishnamurty (1964) analysed the investment behaviour and endogenous population growth. Chaudhry (1963) and Dutta (1964) were concerned with external trade while Agarwala (1970) examined the growth in a dualistic economy. By and large, these models could be seen as explorations of specification for the economic relationships valid for the Indian economy. Table 3.1 describes some of these models.

Table 3.1 Models Constructed during the First Phase.

Author	Period	Salient Features
Narasimham (1956)	1923–48	First macroeconometric model for India and any developing country; similar to Klein and Goldberger's model
N. K. Chaudhry (1963)	1930–55	Exploring some economic relationships in the external sector
K. Krishnamurty (1964)	1948–61	Endogenously determined population; disaggregation of output into agricultural and non-agricultural output
K. Marwah (1963)	1939–60	Based on an income–expenditure framework; used for policy experiments with respect to deficit financing and broad fiscal policy; analyses inflation in India
T. Mammen (1967)	1948–9 to 1963–4	Specified role of foreign capital; focused on money market
UNCTAD (1968)	1950–1 to 1962–3	Based on two-gap theory; designed to assess trade prospects and capital needs of India

(Contd.)

Table 3.1 (*Contd.*)

Author	Period	Salient Features
K. Marwah (1972)	1939–65	First Indian macromodel to undertake estimation, forecasting, multiplier calculation, and policy simulation
R. Agarwala (1970)	1920–61	Based on Lewis' two-sector (agriculture and industry) growth model

Sources: R.G. Bodkin, L.R. Klein, and K. Marwah (1986); K.L. Krishna, K. Krishnamurty, V. Pandit, and P.D. Sharma (1991); K. Krishnamurty (1992); and V. Pandit (1995).

THE SECOND PHASE

The second phase covered the 1970s and most models developed in this period were also undertaken as doctoral dissertations. However, they were more disaggregated and better focused on policy issues. They allowed for lagged and more complex adjustment processes. Finally, they had an improved database. Some of these models are described in Table 3.2 with their salient features.

Table 3.2 Models Constructed during the Second Phase.

Author	Period	Salient Features
Pandit (1973)	1950–1 to 1965–6	Analysed the role of foodgrain output in growth and price stability
Pani (1977)	1950–1 to 1969–70	Comprehensive analysis of the money market
Sreenivas (1974)	1950–1 to 1965–6	Compares alternative theories of prices
Chakrabarty (1977)	1952–66	Focus on price formation, particularly in the market for cereals and manufactured goods
Ahluwalia (1979)	1951–73	Recognizes duality in Indian production; estimates marketed surplus of foodgrains; undertakes static and dynamic simulations

(*Contd.*)

Table 3.2 (*Contd.*)

Author	Period	Salient Features
Bhattacharya (1975)	1948–9 to 1967–8	Interactions between real and monetary variables
Mammen (1973)	1948–9 to 1963–4	The structure of financial and monetary markets
Gupta (1973)	1948–9 to 1967–8	The structure of financial and monetary markets

Sources: Same as Table 3.1.

The Third Phase

In this phase, covering the 1980s and the early 1990s, considerable progress was made in modelling the Indian economy. Several models were constructed mostly by independent model builders including Ghose, Lahiri, Madhur, and Roy (1983), Pani (1984), Bhattacharya (1982, 1984, 1987), Krishnamurthy (1984), and Pandit (1984, 1985b, 1985c, 1986b, 1986c, 1989). Others included Bhattacharya and Rao (1986), Bhattacharya and Guha (1992), Ahluwalia and Rangarajan (1986), Pandit and Bhattacharya (1987), Panchmukhi and Mehta (1991), and Bhattacharya (1987). Apart from these there are several important sectoral studies. For instance, Rangarajan, Basu, and Jadhav (1989) deals with interaction of government deficit and domestic debt; Kannan (1985) provides analysis of external sector; Marwah (1987) studies the exchange rate; Rangarajan and Singh (1984) focuses on the reserve money multiplier while Pradhan, Ratha, and Sharma (1990) deals with the interrelationship between public and private sector and so on. Many of these were based on the earlier macromodelling experience of the same authors. These models were much more disaggregative and focused on policy issues. Some of these models are described in Table 3.3 with their salient features.

Table 3.3 Model Constructed during the Third Phase.

Author	Period	Salient Features
Ghose, Lahiri, Madhur, and Roy (1983)	1960–78	General model

(*Contd.*)

Table 3.3 (*Contd.*)

Author	Period	Salient Features
Pani (1984)	1969–70 to 1981–2	Output, demand, and prices and their interaction
Bhattacharya (1984)	1951–2 to 1975–6	Public expenditure, inflation, and growth
Krishnamurthy (1984)	1961–2 to 1979–80	Interrelationship between public and private investment and inflation–growth trade-off
Pandit (1984)	1950–1 to 1977–8	General model with focus on output and price
Pandit (1985b)	1950–1 to 1974–5	Macroeconomic structure, stabilization policies, and growth
Pandit (1985c)	1955 to 80	Supply, demand, and monetary policy
Pandit (1986b)	1951 to 80	Test for structural break in the mid 1960s.
Pandit (1986c)	1953–4 to 1980–1	External trade
Bhattacharya and Rao (1986)	1966–7 to 1983–4	Agriculture–industry inter–relationship and public investment.
Ahluwalia and Rangarajan (1986)	1960–1 to 1979–80	Agriculture–industry linkages
Pandit and Bhattacharya (1987)	1960–1 to 1979–80	Resource mobilization, growth, and inflation
Bhattacharya (1987)	1950–1 to 1984–5	Effectiveness of monetary policy
Madhur (1987)	1950–1 to 1984–5	Impacts of fiscal and monetary policy
Chakrabarty (1987)	1962–3 to 1983–4	Linkages among real, fiscal, and monetary sectors

(*Contd.*)

Table 3.3 (*Contd.*)

Author	Period	Salient Features
Krishnamurthy, Pandit, and Sharma (1988)	1961–2 to 1982–3	Growth, productivity, infrastructure, trade, public and private investment, and relative prices
Kannan (1988)	1968–85	Monetary approach to BOP
Panchmukhi and Mehta (1991)	1970–84	Emphasis on trade flows
Mehta and Sinha(1991)	1951–2 to 1984–5	External trade and public sector
Rastogi (1991)	1951–87	Rational expectation model with government budget, external trade, and labour market
Bhattacharya and Guha (1992)	1960–70 to 1988–9	Public debt–domestic and external sector interrelationships

Sources: Same as Table 3.1.

The Fourth Phase

The current fourth phase covering the late 1990s till date has ushered in much larger models that are comparable to those in developed countries. These models are maintained by reputed institutions on an ongoing basis and are regularly used for forecasting. They have a number of advantages over the one-time models as they regularly incorporate new information by way of data, reflect changes in the economic policies, and reflect new developments in theory and quantitative techniques. An effort in this direction was initiated jointly by the IEG and the DSE in the early 1990s. At present, the NCAER model, the IEG model, and the DSE model belong to this category. These models are revised on a continuous basis in order to improve their results. Their structure has been discussed at various fora and results based on them have been presented on a regular basis.

SECTORAL SPECIFICATIONS OF THE INDIAN ECONOMY

In the last section we described the chronological development of macroeconometric models constructed to represent the Indian economy. A survey of these models indicates that while there is consensus on certain aspects of the Indian economy, there are other areas that are less than fully understood. In this section we shall compare and contrast the sectoral specifications of some of these models, bringing out their similarities and differences. For analytical convenience, we have divided this section into five parts, namely, production, aggregate demand, prices, fiscal and monetary sector, and the external sector.

PRODUCTION

Production is at the core of all macroeconometric models. Depending on their objective and focus, different models have adopted different levels of disaggregation at the sectoral levels. Though there are variations, in general, economic activities have been classified into four sectors— agriculture, industry services, and public administration. In recent years, recognizing the importance of infrastructural constraints, some modellers have also considered infrastructure as a separate sector. Intra-sectoral disaggregation levels have also differed from model to model depending on the objective of the model builder. Many model builders, for instance, have disaggregated agriculture into foodgrain and non-foodgrain sector. Ahluwalia and Rangarajan (1986) differentiated between foodgrains and commercial crops. Pani (1977) argued that disaggregation is desirable at the individual crop level due to shiftability in production line given relative price level. In the manufacturing sector, distinction has been made between registered and unregistered manufacturing (Pani 1984) and the consumer goods industries and heavy industries (Ahluwalia and Rangarajan 1986). In the services sector also, important sub-sectors like infrastructure and transport have been analysed separately by many model builders (see for instance, Madhur 1987; Pani 1977). Another important issue is the choice of the dependent variable. Many model builders in the initial phases used the absolute values of the production activity. However, levels of time series observations incorporate strong trend elements and as a result it is often difficult to distinguish between apparent and real relationships. To tackle this problem, some model builders have estimated equations by utilizing data on changes in variables while others have worked with the growth rates or logarithms.

The agricultural sector is the primary supplier of raw material and foodgrains for the Indian economy. In most of the models, agricultural output is taken to be supply determined. The total output in this sector is determined, given technology, by natural resources—particularly land area—water, fertilizer, and capital stock. All these variables are expected to affect production positively. There is a certain consensus that market signals are not important in the short run for the production in the agricultural sector.

Unlike the agricultural sector, the industrial and the services sectors have been treated very differently by different model builders. Four important variants of these treatments are described here.

- The industry is supply constrained. Using the production function approach, some modellers assume output to be constrained by the available resources. Although some of the earlier models included both labour and capital in the production function (Ahluwalia 1979; Bhattacharya 1984 etc.), most models have assumed capital stock to be the binding constraint while labour is implicitly taken to be in excess supply at the prevailing wage rate. Insofar as output in the service sector is directly related to the level of activity in the commodity producing sectors—agriculture and industry—all output in such models is supply constrained. One of the prominent supply-constrained models is Bhattacharya (1984).
- At the other extreme, there are other models that are explicitly demand determined. Most models in the first and the second phase of development described earlier, including Pandit (1973) and Bhattacharya (1975), were Keynesian in their framework. Supply appeared in these models as aggregative production function or as price functions. Earlier models also used the approach of combining the Keynesian expenditure equations with a neoclassical aggregate production function to derive employment. Madhur (1987) adopted a model in which manufacturing as well as service sector output is determined by the real aggregate expenditure, that is, demand. However, since the model does not guarantee that increases in demand will be met

by increases in output, the residual adjustment is brought about by the changes in private stock.

- Some model builders incorporated demand in the service sector while output in the industrial sector is supply constrained. Pani distinguished between registered manufacturing, unregistered manufacturing, transport, and other services. The first three are supply constrained. The overall GDP is demand constrained which implies that the equilibrium between supply and demand is brought out by adjustment in the other output. Thus, notwithstanding the inclusion of three production functions, supply is adjusted to demand. Pandit (1985, 1995) sought to restore balance between the demand and supply sides by matching the two and taking the lower side of the two.
- There are models that have combined both demand and supply side factors in the determination of industrial and service sector output. While doing so, Ahluwalia (1979) and the IEG model have introduced utilization of capacity to capture the effects of demand factors. Ahluwalia sought to determine capacity utilization by imports, raw material availability, and public constraints, public investment represents demand factor. Pani also incorporated an equation on capacity utilization but it was subject to only the supply side factors making the model supply constrained.

Aggregate Demand

Macroeconomic theory confers an important role to aggregate demand in an economy and a significant share of the Indian models reflects this. The consumption functions play a pivotal role in the modelling of demand. The simple Keynesian consumption function was modified and extended during the 1950s and 1960s giving rise to the permanent income hypothesis, life cycle hypothesis, and relative income hypothesis as alternatives to the absolute income hypothesis. The main thrust of these extensions has been to distinguish between expected and unexpected incomes, to introduce new variables like wealth and to take account of demographic characteristics affecting household decisions and to recognize ratchet effects in consumption–saving behaviour. However, the empirical evidence did not find much use for these theories in the Indian case in many early models. It has been argued (Desai 1973; Bhattacharya 1975, 1984; Pandit 1995 etc.) that most of these micro-theoretic hypotheses are derived from assumptions unlikely to hold for countries like India where a predominant proportion of households live at or below the poverty line. At such low levels of income where a majority of the population has practically no assets, the propensity to consume from permanent income may not be substantially different from that of transitory income. In view of this, while modelling demand, most studies have adopted a consumption function based on the absolute income hypothesis. Many recent models have been more ambitions, however. For example, Mammen (1999) captures the permanent income hypothesis while the IEG model is based on the Modigliani consumption function. These studies on aggregate consumer behaviour show that apart from income, various other variables may also affect consumption expenditures significantly. The share of agricultural output in GDP is one such variable. The relevance of this variable is based on the assumption that the marginal propensity to consume of the rural population is higher than that of the urban population. However Pandit (1991) does not find much difference between the two. Money supply is another variable that has been incorporated to capture the real balance effect. Mammen (1999) found that the rate of interest and wealth also have significant impact on consumption. The IEG model also finds consumption to be related to net wealth apart from current income.

Investment behaviour has been hard to model not only in India but also elsewhere (Pandit 1995). Several factors that are difficult to quantify affect it. In the Indian context, it is still harder to model due to the partially controlled nature of the economy. Apart from the analysis of the investment behaviour as a part of the model, there are certain substantive studies on the fixed investment behaviour at the industry level in India (Krishnamuthy and Sastry 1975; Swamy and Rao 1975 etc.). While determining investment, many studies have disaggregated between private corporate and government on the one hand and between fixed and inventory investment on the other. Most studies have taken government investments as exogenously policy determined. Private investment functions are derived using the Keynesian investment function and the accelerator principle. However there are other variables as well. In some recent studies, finance is incorporated along with interest and income variables. Bhattacharya (1984), Pandit (1984, 1985d) found commercial bank credit to be important. This could be due to the fact that till the early 1990s, credit was rationed and interest rates were highly regulated and failed to reflect the forces of demand and supply. Pandit (1983) found that the impact of expected inflation on private corporate investment is significant. Other factors that have been found to be important are the advance rate of commercial banks (Bhattacharya, Barman, and Nag 1994), availability of resources as measured by savings (Krishnamurty and Pandit 1984), institutional credit and public investment expenditures. Some studies have also treated household investment separately. It has been argued that since the household sector (which includes household enterprises, small businesses, and other informal small scale activities) has different objectives compared to the corporate sector, it has to be dealt with separately. One important aspect of their functioning is the limited access of these enterprises to the organized capital and credit markets. This means that they have to depend largely on their own resources to finance investment. Krishnamurty and Pandit (1984) have assumed their investments to be influenced positively by the share of agriculture in total output. Mammen (1999) however, incorporated gross saving of the household sector, real personal disposable income, and government borrowing from domestic sources. While the first two affect household investment positively, the last variable has a negative influence on it. This shows that government borrowing has a crowding out effect on household investments.

So far as inventory accumulation component is concerned, most supply-constrained models assumed it to be the adjusting factors. However, in recent models, inventory accumulation is modelled separately. Bhattacharaya (1984) argued that stock adjustment could not be a long run phenomenon. If output rises or falls continuously then prices rather than stocks will have to change. Besides, the gap between demand and supply would affect prices after a limit. Therefore, in many recent models, price adjustment restored equality between demand and supply and a separate function was devised for inventories. Mammen (1999) used a total inventory behaviour function instead of explaining sectoral inventory investment. He tested and found bank credit to be significant in determining inventory accumulation.

PRICES

It should be noted that the notion of an equilibrium price level in a comparative static context is different from that of inflation rate in a dynamic model. However, most general models have made no distinction and there are price-behaviour specific models, which are exclusively concerned with inflation. Raj (1966) and Chakrabarty (1977) are some of the models dealing with price behaviour. Apart from these studies, almost all models have incorporated inflation as part of the model specification. As in the case of modelling of production activity, price determination has also been modelled in different ways by different modellers. The earlier models were strongly influenced by the neoclassical 'Quantity Theory' of money. The neoclassical framework postulates perfectly flexible prices. Within this framework, real variables are determined in the real sector while prices are determined by money supply. Thus the major explanation of inflation was in terms of growth of money supply, which is considered to be a demand-pull factor. Many studies found a close relationship between money supply and prices in India. Two early attempts to move away from the standard quantity theory framework were those by Weintraub (1965) and Raj (1966). Weintraub used a pure mark-up on wage costs approach while Raj used the inflationary gap framework. By the late 1960s, cost-push factors were being increasingly acknowledged as important sources of inflation in India. Most studies in the 1970s started highlighting the role of cost-push factors without ruling out the importance of the monetary factors. Typically, money supply per unit of real output has been used as a proxy for excess liquidity in the economy and the cost factors include wage rate relative to productivity and administered price of critical inputs. There have also been structuralist influences on some of these models with structural factors like the food sector (Pandit 1973; Ahluwalia 1979; Ahluwalia and Ranganathan 1986; and Chakrabarty 1977), prices of oil and other crucial imports having been emphasized in the determination of prices. In the case of food prices, real per capita income, money supply, and food supply are found to be significant while in the manufacturing sector, cost-push factors (administered prices of various inputs like energy, import prices of domestically produced agricultural raw materials, wage rate, material prices, labour productivity) along with money supply turned out to be the main determinants. The behaviour of prices thus incorporates both monetarist and structuralist viewpoints. The price index for the services sector is mostly determined by the prices in the agricultural and industrial sector, factors influencing labour cost—wage rate and labour productivity—and excess money supply. In the infrastructure sector, prices are explained by the administered input costs.

Some models have stressed the sectoral approach to price formation. Balakrishnan (1991) disaggregates the production sphere of the economy into agricultural and industrial output, and stresses that the trends in aggregate inflation can be understood only by studying the sectoral price behaviour. In his model, he treats agricultural price determination as a market clearing exercise determined by demand and supply, while industrial prices are determined by input costs. Ahluwalia (1979) emphasized the linkages between agricultural and non-agricultural prices. She felt that effect of agricultural prices was postulated in a cost-push framework with little effort being spent on the explanation of the agricultural prices themselves. She captured these linkages by estimating a marketed suplus function of foodgrains. The relative price of foodgrains vis-à-vis manufactures depends on the marketed surplus of foodgrains and non-agricultural income (the supply and demand factors) and also on government distribution of foodgrains and the import price of foodgrains (these are proxies for the government's quality and price interventions in the foodgrain market). The relative price of commercial crops in terms of manufactured goods depends on the value added in manufacturing output of commercial crops, import price of crude material that can substitute commercial crops in the domestic market.

Monetary and Fiscal Sector

The short run determination of the levels of output and prices brings into sharp focus the role of monetary and fiscal policies. Analytically, the main issues have been: (i) impact of these polices on different aspects of the economy, (ii) linkages between the two policies, (iii) channels of causation, and (iv) degree of effectiveness of these policies. The extent to which these issues have been addressed depends on the size of the model and the focus of the model. Some studies are exclusively focused on government finances and related issues. These studies have a detailed model of government receipt and expenditure with most items endogenously determined. In this context, the phenomenon of crowding-in, associated with public investment in India, has attracted the attention of quite a few model builders. This phenomenon has an important implication on the trade-offs between growth and inflation. Bhattacharya (1984) is one of the early studies that analysed the public sector behaviour at a highly disaggregated level. The focus of the analysis is on the interrelationship between public expenditure, resource mobilization, inflation, and growth. The overall behaviour of the public sector is analysed through a single budget constraint identity, linking public sector expenditure to public sector revenue. The behaviour of tax revenue is analysed separately for corporate tax, land revenue, personal tax revenue, excise, sales, import duty, and other indirect taxes. Capital receipts are divided into borrowing from overseas, capital consumption allowances, borrowing from commercial banks, borrowing from the central bank, borrowing from nationalized insurance institutions, etc. On the expenditure side, the public sector's gross fixed inventory investments are treated as exogenous variables while government consumer expenditure on wages, subsidies, transfer payments, and interest payments are treated as endogenous variables. This study showed that many conclusions of the Keynesian theory are altered once a budget constraint is introduced in the analysis. This analysis suggests that there is an inherent dynamism in government revenue and expenditure through the budget constraint and this dynamism is transmitted into aggregate demand via multiplier operations. Many studies followed thereafter focusing on the public investment and its relationship with private sector investment and fiscal operations. Krishnamurty, Pandit, and Sharma (1989) analysed the public sector investment and its interrelationships with private investments and relative prices. Madhur (1987) examined the macro impacts of monetary and fiscal policy changes. Rangarajan, Basu, and Jadhav (1989) dealt with dynamic interaction of government deficits and domestic debt. Pradhan, Ratha, and Sharma (1990) presented an analysis of interlinkages between public and private investment and its implications for income distribution through an input–output based model. Mammen (1999) investigated interlinkages between the foreign and government sectors.

Most models have assumed public sector investment as a policy-determined exogenous variable. However, in his 1992 model, Mammen has endogenized public sector investment also. He observed that public sector investments are largely financed through borrowing. His results show that over 90 per cent variations in government investment are accounted for by market borrowing. He also analysed the interlinkages between the government sector and the foreign sector. For this, he included exchange rate in the tax revenue equations. His argument was that during inflation, exchange rate depreciates, reducing real imports. This not only reduces custom revenue but also excise revenue collected on the sales of imported goods. The results imply that the budget deficit will get bigger as the rupee depreciates. Thus, he integrates the external sector with the fiscal sector and in turn analyses its impact on GDP and other variables.

There are other models that have analysed the monetary sector in detail. Pani (1977) is by far the most elaborate treatment of India's money and credit markets. He has incorporated various institutional details and has a plausible endogenous explanation of a number of interest rates like call money rates, bank rate, deposit rate, a rate of return on variable dividend industrial securities, and the average rate of return on commercial bank loans and advances. The monetary sector is also thoroughly explored in Bhattacharya (1984). Behavioural functions are specified for currency in circulation, demand deposits, time deposits, bank credit, bank reserves, and various other monetary and financial variables. The supply of money depends on the interaction between demand and supply functions for monetary assets and liabilities. Rangarajan and Singh (1984) also deal with reserve money multiplier. Besides, Ahluwalia (1979) and Pandit (1973) have also attempted to model interlinkages of formal and informal money markets.

Many researchers have focused on the links between central government budget and its monetized deficit. Till recently, the presumption was that monetary policy was subservient to the government's fiscal policy. Bhattacharya and Guha (1992) analysed the interrelationships between public debt, growth, and inflation. This study analysed public debt at a disaggregated level. It was assumed that public debt consists of the government domestic debt, public enterprises domestic debt, and external debt. The government domestic debt has two components—monetized and non-monetized debt. The volume of monetized debt depends on the government's deficit financing which is endogenous to the model. Government's non-monetary borrowing is treated as an exogenous variable. It is also shown that external debt affects growth and inflation but domestic economic conditions do not determine external debt.

In another model on stabilization (Bhattacharya, Barman, and Nag 1994), extensive treatment was given to the linkages between the public sector revenue and expeditures on the one hand, and the real output, prices, and foreign exchange on the other. While focusing on the stabilization programme, the study explicitly included all relevant stabilization policy instruments in the fiscal and monetary sector and the linkages of these with the rest of the economy were analysed extensively. This is an issue-specific model that analyses stabilization policy option available to the Government of India. Reflecting this aspect, the model assumes that the government budget constraint determines the value of nominal public investment rather than the net RBI credit to government. Thus the value of gross nominal public investment is equal to current revenue plus gross fiscal deficit minus current expenditure and government net lending. Current revenue is divided into domestic tax receipts, import duty, and non-tax current revenue. Current expenditure is divided into interest on government debt and other current expenditure. Gross fiscal deficit has three components—net credit from RBI, net external borrowing, and net domestic non-monetized borrowing. One of the objectives of this model is to analyse the impact of various monetary policy instruments on money and bank credit. The money supply function therefore assumes that the money multiplier is not constant but depends on differential interest rates and cash reserve ratio. The model has two other price variables that are endogenously determined. The implicit GDP deflator is a simple function of the wholesale price index and a time trend while the implicit deflator for gross public investment is a function of wholesale price index alone. In the monetary sector, the demand for money and the demand for currency are a function of real gross national product, short-term interest rates, and expected prices. This determines the currency–money ratio. Changes in the money supply depend on changes in this currency–money ratio as well as the monetary base, reserves deposit ratio, and the time deposits to demand deposits ratio. As mentioned earlier, the demand for and supply of money determine aggregate price levels in the model. The overall model suggested that real output in India though essentially supply constrained is also sensitive to aggregate demand. A very tight monetary and fiscal squeeze therefore would affect not only the general price level but also real output. There is therefore a strong possibility of a trade-off between inflation and growth.

External Sector

Though foreign trade is an integral part of the national economy, the treatment given to this sector has been limited. The following reasons are responsible for this.

- In the protected regime characterized by fixed exchange rates, quota restrictions, heavy tariff barriers, and bulk of exports under rupee trade agreement, the scope of modelling the external sector was limited.
- Trade policies were not based on any long-term planning but rather on short-term crisis management. The development theories were pessimistic about export-led development due to inelastic price and income elasticities of demand for primary products and raw materials in the world markets.
- The share of exports was very small.

However, there are some models with focus on the external sector. For instance, Kannan (1985) provided an analysis of foreign trade; Pandit (1986) focused on the external trade and price formation; Marwah (1987) modelled the exchange rate; Ghose, Lahiri, and Wadhwa (1986) related quantitative restrictions and imports; Virmani (1991) analysed the role of supply and demand factors in influencing foreign trade. Besides, most general econometric models have estimated import and export functions. In most models, exports and imports are estimated separately for goods and services. In general, exports are determined by the world GDP, domestic prices relative to the world prices and exchange rates, while imports are influenced by the exchange rates, relative prices, and the GDP of the country. Different models have adopted different levels of aggregation while specifying export and import equations. While some models have one single equation for exports and imports each, others have more disaggregated specifications for exports and imports. For instance, Bhattacharya (1984) has analysed imports of capital goods and that of raw materials and other commodities separately while Pandit (1986) has a more detailed specification of exports and imports.

In the liberalized scenario, the external sector has assumed considerable importance. As a result recent contributions have seen the emergence of some detailed modelling on the external sector (Virmani 1991; Krishnamurty and Pandit 1995). Krishnamurty and Pandit (1995) employed a small open economy assumption to specify an infinitely elastic import supply function at fixed import price in international currency. Exchange rate then determines the price in local currency. The demand for imports is determined by the domestic level of economic activity (GDP and capital formation). For exports there is a downward sloping demand curve and an upward sloping supply curve. While demand depends on world GDP and relative prices, supply is affected by both relative prices in international currency and domestic level of output. Bhattacharya, Barman, and Nag (1994) also gave a detailed treatment to the foreign sector, with imports of goods being disaggregated into the import of food, capital goods, and the residual. Import of food is assumed to be exogenous while the import of capital goods is a function of the level of economic activity, price, and foreign aid. Residual imports, which are mostly intermediate materials, depend on manufacturing output, the unit value index of intermediate materials imports, and on non-food foreign and export earnings. The model also assumes exports trade in services is exogenously determined.

Foreign exchange availability in most models is assumed to be dependent on balance of trade, remittances, and foreign aid. Mammen (1999), however, endogenized the variable. It is explained in terms of the RBI holding of foreign assets along with inflows of private capital. However, private capital flows are taken to be exogenous. In most models foreign institutional investments are not considered at all. These investments started assuming significant proportion in recent years and have been included in the recent models. However, most models have assumed them to be exogenous along with external borrowings.

CONCLUDING REMARKS

A systematic review of the literature on the macroeconometric models of the Indian economy clearly highlights the fact that these models have traversed a long way over the years. The models that emerged in the 1980s and 1990s are more appropriate abstractions of the economy than those in the 1960s and the 1970s. Several complexities of the functioning of the economy have been effectively tackled. In the models of more recent vintages, intersectoral linkages have been captured more meaningfully, with a greater level of disaggregation permitting a more realistic treatment of policy issues. In several significant areas the emergence of some consensus can be clearly noticed, though there have been critical differences in other areas. All these aspects of the emerging macromodelling literature have been highlighted in this chapter. The quest for the most appropriate model for the Indian economy is, of course, far from over.

4

MODEL SPECIFICATION AND ESTIMATION

A systematic review of the literature clearly highlights that the modelling of the Indian economy has traversed a long way over the past forty odd years. However, till recently there had been no long-standing model of the Indian economy that could be used repeatedly for projections and policy analysis, with regular updating. Initiatives in this direction were taken in the 1990s when NCAER and IEG–DSE started institutionalized model building for the Indian economy. In 1997, the DPC of the IEG started work on the construction of another institutional macroeconometric model. The final version of this model is the result of several experiments carried out during the last few years of the model building process. Broadly, there are two versions of the model built in two stages of the model building process: a detailed and large model used to analyse macroeconomic structure and policy impact and a smaller version to simulate and forecast the alternative growth paths of the economy in the future. We shall present the first version of the model in this chapter while the second version will be presented in Chapter 7.

FRAMEWORK OF THE MODEL

Macroeconomic model builders are primarily faced with a choice between two alternative paradigms depending on the role that is assigned to output and price adjustments and on how markets function. These are the neoclassical and the Keynesian paradigms. A third alternative that came up specifically in the context of developing economies is known in the literature as structuralism. In practice, however, most macroeconomic models have put together different aspects of all these paradigms. This is known in the literature as the eclectic approach. The present model is no exception. Though it is Keynesian in outlook, it combines elements of neoclassical and structuralist views as well. For instance, the treatment given to agriculture is largely classical in the sense that given the level of technology, output is assumed to be determined by the supply side factors in the short term. Prices are also determined by the market clearing mechanism. The elements of unutilized capacity in the industrial and the service sectors, the investment function, price rigidities, and certain aspects of the fiscal and monetary sector in the model are based on the Keynesian approach while the capital stock-constrained output in the industrial sector and the cost-push approach to inflation are structuralist in nature. Keeping in view the liberalization process introduced in the economy in 1991, the model is designed to represent a market-oriented economy. It is broadly classified into four blocks. These relate to the production, fiscal, monetary, and external sectors.

The production block takes up the determination of quantity variables like output, consumption, investment, and price variables like GDP deflator, consumption deflator, investment deflator, and consumer and wholesale prices. Output is in real terms and disaggregated into four sectors—agriculture, industry, service, and public administration. Given sector-specific conditions, separate theoretical considerations guide the determination of output in each sector. Aggregate demand, on the other hand, is estimated in nominal terms as the sum of consumption, investment, and net exports. The private consumption function is specified on the basis of Modigliani's life cycle hypothesis and is a function of the rate of interest, net worth, and other factors. Private investment is disaggregated into those in agriculture, industry, and service sectors. Public investments are taken to be exogenously determined. Net exports are determined in the external sector. Thus, the monetary, fiscal, and external sectors are all interlinked to determine the aggregate demand. The aggregate price level is defined as the variable that equilibrates aggregate nominal demand and aggregate real output. Apart from the aggregate price, the model also estimates four sectoral prices, as well as the consumption and investment deflators. Sectoral prices are determined by the GDP deflator and by sector-specific factors. The GDP deflator is included as an explanatory variable in sectoral prices to capture the relationship between aggregate and sectoral prices. Fiscal and monetary sectors are specified in the spirit of the Keynesian framework. In the monetary sector, the rate of interest is determined by the equilibrium of the demand for and the supply of money. While dealing with the rate of interest, the focus has been on the prime lending rate, deposit rate, and the rate of return on government securities. The fiscal sector has a detailed and disaggregated representation of the revenue earned and the expenditure carried out by the government. This sector determines the deficit incurred by the government including the revenue and the fiscal deficit. The external block deals with trade and external transactions. There are separate behavioural equations for exports of goods, exports of services, imports of oil and non-oil groups, and imports of services. Separate equations are specified for net current transfers and capital transactions. The exchange rate is the equilibrating variable in this sector. All the equations in this sector are in dollar terms. The estimated values are converted into rupee terms using the $/Rs exchange rate while using them in other blocks. The structure of the four blocks is specified in Table 4.1.

Table 4.1 The Broad Framework of the Model.

	Quantity Variable	Price Variables
Production block, sectoral and aggregate price, agriculture, industry, service, and public administration	Sectoral and aggregate production, aggregate demand, private consumption, private investment	Service price index, consumption deflator, investment deflator, consumer and wholesale price index
Fiscal block	Current receipts, capital receipts and expenditures, and fiscal deficit	Rate of return on government securities, average interest rate on public debt
Monetary	Reserve money, money supply	Deposit rate, prime lending rate

(*Contd.*)

Table 4.1 (*Contd.*)

	Quantity Variable	Price Variables
External sector	Exports and imports of goods and services, remittances, FDI, external borrowings, foreign exchange reserves	Exchange rate

The size and the structure of each block are indicated in Table 4.2.

Table 4.2 Block-wise Number of Equations.

Blocks	Total number of technical equations	Total number of identities	Total number of behavioural equations	Total number of equations
Production block				
Agriculture	5	0	2	7
Industry	6	0	2	8
Services	4	0	2	6
Administration	1	0	1	2
Aggregate supply	2	3	0	5
Total Consumption and disposable income	10	5	2	17
Total investment	6	13	3	22
Aggregate demand	5	4	0	9
Capital stock	4	5	3	12
Prices	16	0	8	24
Fiscal sector				
Receipts	13	8	6	26
Payments	13	3	4	20
Deficit	3	3	0	6

(*Contd.*)

Table 4.2 (Contd.)

Blocks	Total number of technical equations	Total number of identities	Total number of behavioural equations	Total number of equations
Monetary sector				
Money supply	4	4	1	9
Interest rates	3	7	4	14
External sector				
Current Account	24	11	6	41
Capital Account	2	3	3	8
Exchange reserves	0	4	1	5
Exchange rate	2	2	1	5
Total	123	75	48	246

DATA AND ESTIMATION

The model is estimated using annual time series data for the period 1970–1 to 1998–9. The sources of data are summarized in Table 4.3.

Table 4.3 Sources of Data.

Source	Publishing agency	Data
White paper on national accounts statistics	Central Statistical Organization	CSO data for the new series from 1993–4 to 1998–9 from NAS 2000, for 1999–2000 from quick estimates and for 2000–1 from advanced estimates. Unpublished series from 1970–1 to 1992–3 based on the new base year for all variables
Report on currency and finance, *Handbook of statistics on Indian economy*, RBI monthly bulletins, and RBI Annual Report	Reserve Bank of India	Monetary and external sector data

(Contd.)

Table 4.3 (*Contd.*)

Source	Publishing agency	Data
Economic survey, Handbook-RBI, IPFS, budget paper, annexure-7	Department of Economic Affairs, Ministry of Finance, RBI	Fiscal sector data
International trade statistics	International Monetary Fund	World imports
International financial statistics	International Monetary Fund	LIBOR

It may be noted that the CSO data has been revised. The old data series has 1980–1 as the base year whereas in the new series the base year has been shifted to 1993–4. We have adjusted the old series in terms of both price correction and quantum correction.

Equations have been estimated using the OLS method. Most of the behavioural equations have been estimated in growth rates rather than in levels in order to avoid the problem of spurious regression that occurs in time series analysis. In 1991, major structural changes were introduced in the Indian economy. These changes are likely to have influenced the behavioural relationships and their strength between various variables. However, these are not likely to be reflected fully in the model estimation. This is because the results are based on a large part of the data that was generated in the pre-reform period when a number of markets were characterized by rationing equilibrium. As a result of this some of the specifications which should have been statistically significant do not yield satisfactory results. However, the model retains these specifications with the understanding that in future, with more data from the post-reform period, these specifications will be statistically significant. Besides, in order to take care of the regime changes, appropriate structural dummy variables have also been used. These structural dummies have names that start with the letter 'D' and are followed by numbers that indicate the years associated with the regime changes and QN. For example, D91QN is a dummy that takes care of the economic reforms that were initiated in 1991 and separates the pre-1991 period from the post-1991 period. In some cases, the year is preceded by D but not ended with QN, such variables take care of important events that might have influenced the relationship in a particular year only. Thus, D85 implies dummy for 1985.

Apart from taking care of regime changes as mentioned above, dummies have also been included in the regressions to account for outliers after all other ways of accounting for a particular large prediction error have been exhausted. In most cases outlier dummies have been named by using the prefix DUM before the name of the dependent variables in the corresponding regressions. For example, DUMEXP is the outlier dummy used in the exports (growth) equation.

EMPIRICAL PROPERTIES OF THE MODEL

A macroeconometric model is a monolithic structure made up of numerous individual equations and identities, each of which explains the structure or behaviour of a particular aspect of the economy. In this section, we shall present a detailed analysis of the individual equations of our model, together with their statistical properties and economic implications. We shall also discuss the important identities that ensure the closure of the model. For analytical convenience, we have classified the model into four sectors, that is the production sector, money supply and interest rates, the fiscal sector, and the external sector.

Production Sector

The production sector consists of three sub-sectors, that is, aggregate supply, aggregate demand, and prices.

Aggregate Supply

The production process is disaggregated into four sectors, that is agriculture, industry, service, and public administration and defence. Aggregate GDP (GDPCN) is the sum of the real output in the four sectors.

$$\text{GDPCN} = \text{YGACN} + \text{YGICN} + \text{YGSCN} + \text{YGDCN} \qquad (4.1)$$

where YGACN, YGICN, YGSCN, and YGDCN are the real output in the agriculture, industrial, service, and the public administration (and defence) sectors.

Agriculture Agriculture is defined to include gross value added in agriculture, forestry, and fishing. Agriculture includes agricultural crops and livestock products; forestry includes forestry, logging, and farmyard wood; and fishing includes commercial fishing, subsistence fishing, gathering of seaweeds, seashells, pearls, and fish curing.

In line with most existing models, this model also assumes agricultural output to be supply determined. In order to avoid multiplicity of equations and maintain simplicity in the model, one production function is specified for the entire agricultural sector. Production is postulated to be a function of capital stock while land and labour are excluded from this function. Labour is assumed to pose no constraint while any substantial change in total acreage in the short run is ruled out. Besides, as Agarwala (1970, p.79) explains 'extension of land in the Indian context is largely through capital expenditure in reclamation, land improvement etc. and these are taken into account in capital estimates'. Thus, the real agricultural output is a product of the agricultural capital stock and the productivity of agricultural capital. In the model this relationship is expressed by the following equation

$$\text{YGACN} = \text{KEACS}(-1)/\text{ACOR} \qquad (4.2)$$

where YGACN is the real agricultural output, KEACS is the agricultural capital stock, and ACOR is the agricultural capital–output ratio representing (the inverse of) the productivity of the agricultural capital stock. The productivity of the agricultural capital stock is not assumed to be a constant or exogenous variable, even in the short run. Given the technological level, there are year-to-year fluctuations in the value of this variable depending on variables like aggregate rainfall (RFAQI), fertilizer use (FERQI), and the ratio between agricultural price index and GDP deflator (RPAGR). This last variable represents the relative price of agricultural products and is a proxy for the price incentives experienced by the agricultural sector. The aggregate rainfall variable is somewhat erratic in explaining agricultural output because it does not take into account the geographical distribution of rainfall. This shortcoming is corrected by using a dummy variable (DUMACOR) that also takes care of other outliers. Taking all these into account the agricultural capital–output ratio is estimated as:

$$ACOR = 2.45 - 0.004*RFAQI - 0.011*FERQI$$
$$(25.28) \quad (-14.69) \qquad (-13.24)$$
$$- 0.005*RPAGR(-1) + 0.069*DUMACOR$$
$$(-5.14) \qquad (12.29)$$
$$R^2 = 0.98 \qquad DW = 1.80 \qquad (4.3)$$

The rainfall index RFAQI, (calculated by the Ministry of Agriculture on a year-to-year basis by assuming the long-term average to be 100) appears to be the single most significant variable with t-statistics of 14.69. The responsiveness of the capital–output ratio to the relative price variable is very small. A one per cent increase in this ratio decreases capital–output ratio by 0.005 per cent. Thus, the agricultural output in India is not highly responsive to price incentives. One of the options that was considered during the modelling process was the introduction of a suitable dummy variable that captures the effect of liberalization on the agricultural sector. Interestingly, the results showed that there were no significant effects of liberalization on this sector. This is perhaps due to the fact that there have been no significant reforms in this sector during the period of liberalization. In the final form of the model, we have dropped this dummy variable. Fertilizer use (FERQI), on the other hand, turns out to be highly significant with the t-statistics of 13.24. FERQI is calculated in the model by using the growth rate of fertilizer use (FERVP) and past values of fertilizer use (FERQI(– 1)). The growth rate of fertilizer use is estimated as a function of the growth rate in agricultural output (YGAVP) along with fertilizer price growth rate (PCFERPP) and agricultural price growth rate (PIAGRPP). Thus

$$FERQI = FERQI(-1)*(1+ 0.01*FERVP) \qquad (4.4)$$

where

$$FERVP = 4.826 + 0.315*YGAVP - 0.188*PCFERPP$$
$$(11.48) \quad (9.15) \qquad (-21.79)$$
$$+ 0.041*PIAGRPP + 12.095*DFERQI$$
$$(1.16) \qquad (34.96)$$
$$R^2 = 0.98 \qquad DW = 2.35 \qquad (4.5)$$

Equation 4.5 reveals that one percentage point growth in the fertilizer price affects fertilizer consumption growth by almost 0.2 percentage point. Apparently, the fertilizer demand is price inelastic.

This could perhaps be due to the effect of the Green Revolution, with the new variety of crops being significantly dependent on these fertilizers. In view of the price inelasticity, it is expected that any increase in fertilizer prices is likely to put a great burden on the farmers in terms of higher cost of production. The equation also shows that fertilizer consumption is significantly related to the agricultural growth rate. One percentage point increase in the growth of agricultural output increases fertilizer use by 0.3 percentage point implying that income elasticity of fertilizer-use is relatively higher. The agricultural price growth rate (PIAGRPP) turned out to be insignificant in influencing the fertilizer consumption. The equation thus indicates that fertilizer consumption is far more responsive to fertilizer price than to agricultural price. Clearly, the price responsiveness of Indian agriculture (both indirect through fertilizer consumption and direct) is still relatively weak.

Industry Industry includes gross value added at factor cost in mining, quarrying, registered and unregistered manufacturing, construction and electricity, gas and water supply. Unlike in the agricultural sector, production in the manufacturing sector is clearly not purely supply determined. On the supply side it is capital constrained with labour supply assumed to be infinitely large. The output levels are determined by the capital stock and the utilization of capacity. However, demand factors influence the capacity utilization rates and hence enter into the determination of output. These relationships are explained in the model through the following equations.

$$YGICN = KEICS(-1)/INDCOR \qquad (4.6)$$

where YGICN is the industrial output, KEICS is the capital stock, and INDCOR is the industrial capital–output ratio. INDCOR is estimated in the model as a function of the growth rate in agricultural output (YGAVP(– 1)), imports (M77CP), and government expenditures (RTEVP). While government expenditure is mainly a demand variable, imports are a supply-side variable, easing the input and capital goods constraints in this sector. The growth rate of agricultural output has a dual effect. Food items predominate in the consumption basket of the majority of the Indian population. As a result, a high agricultural growth rate increases demand for the industrial products by pushing down the agricultural prices on the one hand and pushing up the incomes on the other. This ensures larger spending on industrial products. On the supply side, the agricultural sector is a large supplier of raw materials to the industrial sector and is expected to have a positive impact on its output. The capital–output ratio function is therefore:

$$
\begin{aligned}
\text{INDCOR} = {} & 2.589 - 0.0075{*}\text{YGAVP}(-1) - 0.0029{*}\text{RTEVP} \\
& (157.09) \quad (-4.99) \qquad\qquad (-2.07) \\
& - 0.0015{*}\text{M77CP} + 0.5549{*}\text{D85QN} \\
& (-2.31) \qquad\qquad (23.78) \\
& + 0.5007{*}\text{DUMINDCOR} - 0.0358{*}\text{D91QN} \\
& (21.16) \qquad\qquad\qquad (-1.42) \\
R^2 = 0.983 & \qquad \text{DW} = 1.731 \qquad\qquad (4.7)
\end{aligned}
$$

The equation reveals that the growth in agricultural output and imports influences the industrial capacity utilization significantly. The impact of imports is however expected to weaken over time as capital goods and raw material imports (which formed the bulk of the import basket under the import substitution regime) are being substituted more and more by consumer goods imports. This implies that rather than ease the constraints in the industrial sector, the imports are going to bring down the demand for domestically produced industrial goods, thus creating a negative impact on this sector. It may be noted that an input like electricity affects industrial capacity utilization in a significant manner. We have not included electricity in the above equation, however, as it is already a part of industrial output and hence there are serious theoretical problems of estimating such an equation. Interestingly, the equation shows that the impact of government expenditure is positive and significant. The equation also includes a dummy variable D85QN for the post-1985 period. The results indicate that, contrary to expectations, capital–output ratio increased after 1985, the year of import rationalization, that is, capital's efficiancy fell in industry. Another dummy for the post-1991 period D91QN, on the other hand, shows that there was better capacity utilization in the post-liberalization period. However, the compound impact of both dummies indicates that capital intensity is still higher than earlier periods. This could possibly be due to the easier availability of more capital-intensive technology in recent years.

The INDCOR equation (Equation 4.7) has an important implication. It suggests that at any point of time, industrial production may be below the most efficient level. In other words, given the demand and supply side influences, potential industrial output may be higher than the actual industrial production creating the problem of less than full capacity utilization. In our model, therefore, we have separately estimated the potential output and the capacity utilization rate in industry. Potential output is based on the estimates of the most efficient capital–output ratio. Estimation of the potential output is fraught with conceptual and technical problems. In earlier versions of the model, an average capital–output ratio (for a given number of years) was taken to be the most efficient capital–output ratio. In order to have a better approximation, this model fits a non-linear time trend to the minimum capital–output ratios achieved over the years and assumes the values corresponding to the trend to be the most efficient capital–output ratios for that period. These most efficient capital–output ratios are thus the potential capital–output ratios, INDCORP. Thus,

$$\text{INDCORP} = \text{EXP}(0.758 + 0.012^*\text{TREND}) \quad (4.8)$$

Given the INDCORP, potential output is determined by the following equation.

$$\text{YCICN} = \text{KEICS}(-1)/\text{INDCORP} \quad (4.9)$$

The ratio of the potential and the actual output gives the capacity utilization rate,

$$\text{UTI} = (\text{YGICN}/\text{YCICN})^*100 \quad (4.10)$$

The capacity utilization rate influences the investment in the economy, which in turn affects the capital stock, industrial output, and prices. These links are discussed in later sections.

Services The service sector includes gross value addition in service-rendering enterprises like hotels and restaurants, wholesale and retail trade, railways and other transport, storage, communication, banking, insurance and business services, real estate and rental earnings from self-occupied dwellings and excludes public administration and defence which are treated separately. Following the standard practice, output in the service sector YGSCN is assumed to depend on the growth in the industrial and agricultural output. Besides, it was observed that there is a trend in the service sector. To take care of it and to examine if it is related with the industrial and the agricultural sectors, a trend variable is included in the model. Thus, the service sector output is determined by using the following two equations,

$$YGSCN = KESCS(-1)/SVSCOR \quad (4.11)$$

Here YGSCN is the output in the service sector, KESCS is the capital stock in this sector, and SVSCOR is the capital–output ratio in the service sector, which is determined by the following equation:

$$\begin{aligned} SVSCOR = \; & \underset{(360.13)}{4.790} - \underset{(-1.84)}{0.002}*RMATVP - \underset{(-2.24)}{0.003}*RMATVP(-1) \\ & - \underset{(-135.90)}{0.098}*TREND + \underset{(11.03)}{0.049}*DUMSVSCOR \end{aligned}$$

$R^2 = 0.998$ DW = 1.83 (4.12)

RMATVP and RMATVP(– 1) are the combined present and past growth rates in the real industrial and agricultural output. They are assumed to affect the output in the service sector by creating demand for services, thus having a positive impact on this sector. The results show that past (lagged) values of this variable are more significant than the present values. The trend variable is highly significant with t-statistics of 135.9 indicating a strong possibility of growth in services, which is independent of the agricultural and industrial sectors. It shows that the capital–output ratio in this sector is falling at the rate of approximately 0.1 per year. A possible reason for this could be that after higher investments in the initial years, this sector is now experiencing increasing returns to scale. A dummy for liberalization effects on the service sector was introduced in Equation 4.12 during the modelling process and showed insignificant results, implying that there has been no significant impact of liberalization on this sector. This dummy has been dropped in the final model.

Just as in the industrial sector, we define the potential output and the capacity utilization ratio in the services sector as well. SVSCORP is the potential capital–output ratio, which is estimated as

$$SVSCORP = EXP(1.480829 - 0.02605*TREND) \quad (4.13)$$

Given SVSCORP, potential output in the services sector(YCSCN) and the capacity utilization ratios in this sector (UTS) are worked out using the following equations:

$$YCSCN = KESCS(-1)/SVSCORP \quad (4.14)$$

$$UTS = (YGSCN/YCSCN)*100 \quad (4.15)$$

This ratio influences investments in the service sector and, in turn, the capital accumulation process.

Public Administration and Defence Real output in this sector (YGDCN) is calculated using its past level and the present growth rate (YGDVP) such that,

$$YGDCN = YGDCN(-1)*(1 + 0.01*YGDVP) \quad (4.16)$$

where, YGDVP is a function of the growth in the real expenditure on salary and wages by the government (RSWVPR).

$$\begin{aligned} YGDVP = \ & 2.231 + 0.584*RSWVPR + 3.041*DUMYGDVP \\ & (4.80) \quad (9.31) \qquad\qquad (11.24) \\ & - 0.353*D91QN \\ & (-0.70) \end{aligned}$$

$$R^2 = 0.91 \qquad DW = 1.701 \quad (4.17)$$

Equation (4.17) suggests that one percentage point growth in the salary and wages expenditure influences the growth in output in this sector by 0.58 percentage point, well below unity. A dummy for the liberalization period, D91QN, shows a negative coefficient but is not statistically significant. This implies that the government has been only marginally successful in bringing down the size of this sector. A plausible reason for this could be that while the central government has tried to decrease its size, the states have not done much in this regard.

Aggregate Demand

Aggregate demand reflects the expenditure side of the economy and is measured in nominal terms. It is the sum of the nominal values of private consumption (CPDWN), public consumption (which is itself the sum of salary expenditure (RSW) and non-salary expenditure (NSW)), private investment(IV7WN), public investment(IP7WN), and exports of goods and services (XGSWNR) net of imports (MGSWNR). Thus aggregate demand is expressed by the following equation:

$$\begin{aligned} GDPMP = \ & CPDWN + (RSW + NSW) + (IV7WN + IP7WN) \\ & + (XGSWNR - MGSWNR) + ERGDPMP \end{aligned} \quad (4.18)$$

It should be noted here that the values of exports and imports are estimated in dollar terms in the model (see the external sector). These estimated values are converted into rupee terms (in order to make them consistent and comparable with the rest of the model) by using a constant exchange rate (that is, the annual average) in terms of only one currency, that is the American dollar. This may lead to some measurement errors because the exchange rate varies on a day-to-day basis and hence does not remain constant. Besides, India trades with many other countries and hence it is not the American dollar alone that applies to valuations of exports and imports. The methodology adopted in the model, therefore, introduces a measurement error. This is taken care of by adding an additional error term (ERGDPMP) in the national income identity.

Private Consumption The consumption function has its genesis in the Keynesian absolute income hypothesis, which proposed that the levels of private consumption are determined by the current income levels. Later Duesenberry, in his relative income hypothesis, argued that consumption depends not only on the level of current income but also on past consumptions. The permanent income hypothesis of Friedman differentiated between permanent and transitory components of income and hypothesized consumption to be a function of permanent income, which is a weighted average of current and past incomes. Modigliani's life cycle hypothesis on the other hand introduced wealth into the consumption function. The neoclassical framework did not define a consumption function but postulated that savings is a positive function of the rate of interest. Since consumption is equivalent to income net of saving (in the absence of taxes), it is a negative function of the rate of interest in this framework. The present model is based on these theoretical considerations and includes changes in current disposable income (ZPDICN), changes in net worth (ZNWORTH), and real deposit rates (REALR13) as the determinants of change in real consumption (ZCPDCN). Thus the change in real consumption is estimated using the following function,

$$\begin{aligned}\text{ZCPDCN} = \underset{(4.62)}{5874.23} + \underset{(2.30)}{0.037}^{*}\ \text{ZNWORTH}(-1) + \underset{(12.53)}{0.380}^{*}\ \text{ZPDICN} \\ - \underset{(-2.99)}{507.567}^{*}\text{REALR13} + \underset{(15.506)}{14633.2}^{*}\text{DUMZCPDCN}\end{aligned}$$

$R^2 = 0.96$ DW = 2.10 (4.19)

Change in net worth (ZNWORTH) turns out to be significant (at 5 per cent level) in the consumption equation. Real deposit rate (REALR13) is also significant (at 5 per cent level), with a negative sign. However, it is the change in the disposable income (ZPDICN) that turns out to be the most significant variable affecting change in consumption. This upholds the Keynesian hypothesis and suggests that the current level of disposable income is the most important determinant of consumption in the Indian economy. Using the change in real consumption as well as past values of real consumption, we calculate the present values of real consumption in our model. The real consumption is then converted into nominal consumption by using the consumer deflator (which is estimated as a function of the industrial and agricultural prices and is presented in the section on prices) and it is the value of nominal consumption that goes into the calculation of the aggregate demand.

The value of net worth (NWORTH) used in the consumption function in Equation 4.19, is equal to the sum of real money supply (M37CS), the government's real borrowings from households, outstanding stocks (SCRHCN), and private capital stock (PVTCAP). While M37CS is determined in the monetary sector, SCRHCN is a fiscal sector variable. Thus consumption is linked with both the fiscal and the monetary sectors. PVTCAP is total private capital and this is determined from present and past values of private investments. The second variable in the consumption function is the real deposit rate (REALR13) and this is determined in the monetary sector. Finally, the value of real disposable income (PDICN) used in the equation, is derived from the value of nominal disposable income (PDIWN). PDIWN is defined as the sum of nominal net domestic product (NDPWN), interest payments (RIP), fiscal transfer payments (RTR), total transfer receipts (OTR), net factor incomes from abroad (NFIA), and an adjustment variable (ERPDIWN), net of income from entrepreneurship and property (GIEP), savings of non-departmental enterprises (SNDE), corporate tax (TCT), private corporate savings (PVTSAV), government miscellaneous revenue (GMR), and income tax (TIT). Private corporate savings is calculated from its growth rate (PVTSAVPP) and past values (PVTSAV(– 1)). The growth rate of private corporate savings is estimated in the model as a function of the industrial growth rate (YGIWNVP). Thus,

$$\text{PVTSAVPP} = -5.526 + \underset{(-0.33)}{}\;\underset{(2.18)}{2.346^{*}\text{YGIWNVP}} + \underset{(26.87)}{87.84178^{*}\text{DUMSAV}}$$

$R^2 = 0.96$ DW=1.88 (4.20)

The result shows that the industrial growth rate significantly explains the rate of growth of private corporate savings.

Public Consumption Together with private consumption, public consumption determines the total consumption and aggregate demand in the economy. In this model, public consumption (the sum of salary expenditure (RSW) and non-salary expenditure (NSW)) is determined in the fiscal block of the model.

Investments Investment plays a dual role in an economy. On the one hand it is a component of aggregate demand while on the other, it affects aggregate supply by adding to the capital stock. In this model, the nominal value of total investment forms a component of aggregate demand while the real fixed investment is used to determine the level of capital stock which in turn influences the supply side. Total real investment (I77CN) comprises private (IV7CN) and public investment (IP7CN).

I77CN = IV7CN + IP7CN (4.21)

Public investments are assumed to be exogenous in this model while private investments are estimated on the basis of theoretical considerations. The classical and Keynesian theories of investment both assume investment to be a function of interest rates and postulate an inverse relationship between them. The profit-based theories of investment, on the other hand, suggest that investments depend on aggregate profits and hence income levels (serving as proxies of profit) determine investment rates. Structuralist theories have also stressed on the complimentarity between public and private investments. In the present model, the investment equations are guided by all these theoretical considerations. However, together with these theoretical considerations, certain characteristics about the Indian economy are extremely important in understanding the investment behaviour during the period of study. Prior to 1991, private investment in India was strongly regulated by the government through licensing, credit control, and control over imported capital goods. This implies that while the theoretical considerations discussed above would determine some desired level of investments, the actual investment behaviour could be different from this desired level due to these controls. It further implies that as and when these controls were removed, the differences between the actual and the desired levels were expected to decrease. In order to capture all these factors, we have experimented with lagged dependent variables (that is, lagged values of investment) and two slope dummies in the investment function. The coefficient of the lagged dependent variable indicates the extent of the gap between the actual and desired levels of investments (with a higher value of the coefficient indicating a greater gap between the two). The first dummy shows whether the gap between the actual and desired levels of investments has narrowed in the post-1991 period following the initiation of the liberalization process. This dummy is named by prefixing the symbols D91 to the name of the (lagged) investment variable. The second dummy (D93LNDRN) shows whether investments have become more sensitive to lending rates in the post-1993 period following interest rate and credit decontrol. In order to bring out the sectoral specificities, separate investment functions have been estimated for agriculture, industry, and services sectors.

Real private investment in agriculture (IVACN) is determined by real agricultural income (YGACN) and interest rates (LNDRN), by real public investment in agriculture (IPACN) and relative price of agricultural products (RPAGR (– 1)). It may be noted that it is the growth rate of agricultural income that is considered rather than the GDP growth rate since incomes generated in other sectors are not allowed to be invested in agricultural activities. Also, we have taken nominal instead of real interest rates as the price effect already comes in through the relative price of agricultural products. A lagged dependent variable (IVACN (– 1)) and two slope dummies (D93LNDRN and D91IVACN (– 1)) are included to analyse the effects of liberalization.

$$\begin{aligned}
\text{IVACN} = {} & -11256.53 + 0.034^{*}\text{YGACN} - 118.443^{*}\text{LNDRN} \\
& \quad (-2.89) \qquad (8.103) \qquad\qquad (-2.45) \\
& -42.111^{*}\text{D93LNDRN} + 110.750^{*}\text{RPAGR}(-1) + \\
& \quad (-1.63) \qquad\qquad (3.22) \\
& 0.3959^{*}\text{IPACN}(-1) + 0.174^{*}\text{IVACN}(-1) + \\
& \quad (3.28) \qquad\qquad (2.23) \\
& 3301.152^{*}\text{DUMIVACN} + 0.182^{*}\text{D91IVACN}(-1) \\
& \quad (13.06) \qquad\qquad (3.84)
\end{aligned}$$

$R^2 = 0.97 \qquad \text{DW} = 2.34 \qquad\qquad (4.22)$

Equation (4.22) shows that real private investment in agriculture is determined significantly by the incomes generated within the sector though other variables including lending rate, relative price, and public investment all yield significant results. The 1993 dummy indicates that after 1993, investments have become even more sensitive to lending rates in this sector. The lagged dependent variable and the 1991 dummy indicate that there was about 17 per cent difference between desired and actual investments prior to 1991 but surprisingly, this gap seems to have doubled in the post-1991 period. This could be due to other socio-economic factors, including the uncertainty caused by WTO compulsions, leading to actual investments becoming tougher in this area.

In the industry sector, real private investment is assumed to be a function of real GDP (GDPCN) and real lending rates (RLNDRN). During the modelling process we also considered the lagged dependent variable (IVICN (– 1)) and two slope dummies (D93RLNDRN and D91IVICN (– 1)), included to analyse the effects of liberalization. In the final model, the 1991 dummy has been dropped as it indicated insignificant results.

$$
\begin{aligned}
IVICN = {} & \underset{(5.158)}{24591.24} + \underset{(6.304)}{0.061}*GDPCN - \underset{(-1.753)}{201.02}*RLNDRN \\
& - \underset{(-3.095)}{1098.68}*D93RLNDRN + \underset{(5.457)}{0.422}*IVICN(-1) \\
& + \underset{(12.591)}{33131.59}*DUMIVICN
\end{aligned}
$$

$R^2 = 0.990$ $\quad$ $DW = 2.109$ $\quad$ (4.23)

This equation again establishes that GDP is one of the most important variables affecting investment. The real private investment in industry is determined largely by GDP, as lending rates (prior to 1993) are not statistically significant. The 1993 dummy indicates that lending rates have, however, become very significant following decontrols in this sector. All these indicate that industry bore the brunt of the controls prior to 1993. This is further substantiated by the lagged dependent variable that indicates that the gap between actual and desired investment was at a high of 34 per cent before 1991. Interestingly, the 1991 dummy (that we have dropped from the final model) showed that there was almost no change in this gap in the post-liberalization period. This probably indicates that other forms of control remain in place and that deregulation has been largely notional in this sector.

The estimated equation (Equation 4.24) of real private investment in the service sector (IVSCN) includes real GDP (GDPCN), real lending rates (RLNDRN) along with the lagged dependent variable (IVSCN (– 1)) and two slope dummies (D93RLNDRN and D91IVSCN (– 1)), included to analyse the effects of liberalization.

$$\begin{aligned} IVSCN = &-3463.467 + 0.052{*}GDPCN - 192.388{*}RLNDRN \\ &(-1.313) \quad (4.938) \qquad\qquad (-1.826) \\ &-170.113{*}D93RLNDRN + 0.1990{*}IVSCN(-1) \\ &(-0.592) \qquad\qquad\qquad (1.181) \\ &-0.039{*}D91IVSCN(-1) + 8608.028{*}DUMIVSCN \\ &(-0.539) \qquad\qquad\qquad (5.618) \end{aligned}$$

$$R^2 = 0.953 \qquad DW = 2.176 \qquad (4.24)$$

Here, apart from GDP, the interest rates are also found to have a significant impact on investment (significant at 10 per cent level). However, credit decontrol in 1993 does not have a significant impact on investments in this sector. This could be due to the fact that the service sector gets its finances mostly from the unorganized sector and this sector has been largely untouched by the decontrol. The gap between actual and desired investment was about 20 per cent before 1991 and this has come down to about 16 per cent in recent times.

Using the three sectoral investment functions estimated above, we calculate the total private real investment (IV7CN) as the sum of these investment functions.

$$IV7CN = IVACN + IVICN + IVSCN \qquad (4.25)$$

Total private nominal investment (IV7WN) is calculated from private real investment using an investment deflator (IEDEF), which is determined in the section on prices. Again, total public investment in nominal terms (IP7WN) is calculated in the model as the sum of nominal government investment (GINV) and nominal investment of departmental public enterprises (PEINV). The sum of total private nominal investment (IV7WN) and total public nominal investment (IP7WN) is the total investment in nominal terms (I77WN) and this is an important constituent of the aggregate demand in the economy.

Apart from total investment, the model has also estimated equations for the stock investment. It is difficult to predict the behaviour of stock investments due to frivolous databases and high fluctuations in stocks. However, empirical exercises show that prices and levels of output influence the change in inventory. The use of these variables along with the real lending rate (as a proxy for interest cost of inventory holding) and the levels of accumulated inventories yielded satisfactory equations in all the three sectors. While in the service sector it is the output variable, in the industrial and agricultural sectors it is the stock of inventories that emerged as the most significant variable. The estimated equation for change in stocks in agriculture (N7ACN) is given by

$$\begin{aligned} N7ACN = {} & 972.966 - 0.038{*}AGRST(-1) - 25.427{*}PIAGRPP \\ & (1.92) \quad (-2.39) \qquad\qquad (-1.84) \\ & + 0.005{*}YGACN + 3027.392{*}DUMN7ACN \\ & (1.45) \qquad\qquad (10.62) \end{aligned}$$

$$R^2 = 0.86 \qquad DW = 1.80 \qquad (4.26)$$

The estimated equation for change in stocks in industry (N7ICN) is given by

$$\begin{aligned} N7ICN = {} & 8337.387 - 0.020{*}RLNDRN - 48.543{*}RLNDRN \\ & (8.33) \quad (-1.911) \qquad\qquad (-0.598) \\ & + 6682.591{*}DUMN7ICN \\ & (9.12) \end{aligned}$$

$$R^2 = 0.786 \qquad DW = 2.12 \qquad (4.27)$$

The estimated equation for change in stocks in services (N7SCN) is given by

$$\begin{aligned} N7SCN = {} & -1008.300 - 14.683{*}RLNDRN \\ & (-1.16) \quad (-0.29) \\ & + 4363.848{*}DUMN7SCN + 482.760{*}YGSVP \\ & (9.24) \qquad\qquad (3.06) \end{aligned}$$

$$R^2 = 0.784 \qquad DW = 2.23 \qquad (4.28)$$

Given the total investment and stock investment, fixed investment is calculated in each sector as the difference between the two. Cumulative fixed investment forms the capital stock, which enters the model on the supply side.

Net Exports Net exports are defined as the total exports of goods and services from the economy, net of imports. The estimated export and import functions are described in the external block of the model. However, as we have mentioned before, the estimated value of exports and imports (and hence, net exports) is in dollar terms. This value is converted into rupee terms using the exchange rate and then used in the determination of the aggregate demand for the economy.

Prices

General Price (GDP Deflator) The GDP deflator (PIGDP), representing the aggregate price levels in the economy, is determined by the interaction between the forces of aggregate demand and supply generated in the economy. It is calculated by dividing the nominal value of aggregate demand by the real value of aggregate production (supply) in the economy. Thus,

PIGDP = (GDPWN/GDPCN)*100 (4.29)

where GDPWN is the aggregate demand in nominal terms and GDPCN is the real value of aggregate supply.

Sectoral Prices Sectoral prices are estimated separately in order to take into account the sectoral specificities of the process of price determination. However, to ensure that there is no inconsistency between the aggregate price level and the sectoral prices, it is assumed that the aggregate price level has a significant influence on the sectoral prices. This is incorporated in the model by including the rate of growth of the GDP price deflator (PIGDPPP) in the determination of the sectoral price equations.

In the agricultural sector, prices are assumed to be determined by the interaction between the forces of demand and supply affecting this sector. In other words, a market clearing mechanism is assumed to operate to determine the agricultural prices. Therefore, both demand and supply factors are incorporated in the estimated equation for the rate of growth of agricultural prices (PIAGRPP) given below (Equation 4.30). The model uses nominal disposable income growth (DYPP) as a demand side variable, while on the supply side, present growth rate in agricultural output (YGAVP) and lagged growth rate in agricultural output (YGAVP(– 1)) are the variables included. It may be noted that in recent times, inspite of bumper agricultural crops, agricultural prices kept moving upwards due to continuous increase in minimum support prices. In order to take charge of this phenomenon, the model includes the growth rate of procurement price index (PROCPP) as a policy variable. Once the rate of growth of agricultural prices (PIAGRPP) is estimated, the agricultural prices (PIAGR) are calculated by using this estimated value and the past value of agricultural prices (PIAGR(– 1), as shown in Equation 4.31. Thus,

$$
\begin{aligned}
\text{PIAGRPP} = & -1.112 + 0.710{*}\text{DYPP} - 0.635{*}\text{YGAVP} \\
& \quad (-1.17) \quad (6.94) \qquad\quad (-9.39) \\
& -0.184{*}\text{YGAVP}(-1) + 0.201{*}\text{PIGDPPP} \\
& \quad (-4.79) \qquad\qquad\quad (1.45) \\
& +0.071{*}\text{PROCPP} + 4.786{*}\text{DUMPIAGRPP} \\
& \quad (1.72) \qquad\qquad\quad (8.06)
\end{aligned}
$$

$$R^2 = 0.96 \qquad \text{DW} = 2.10 \qquad (4.30)$$

and

$$\text{PIAGR} = \text{PIAGR}(-1){*}(1 + 0.01{*}\text{PIAGRPP}) \qquad (4.31)$$

Prices in the agricultural sector are found to be responsive to the disposable income and the current and past levels of agricultural output. With 1 per cent increase in growth of disposable income, growth of agricultural price goes up by about 0.7 per cent. This ratio is 1:0.6 for the current growth of agricultural output and 1:0.2 for lagged growth of agricultural output.

In the industrial sector, it is assumed that prices are based on mark-up cover cost and hence considerable emphasis has been placed on the cost side factors. Thus the rate of growth of industrial prices (PIINDPP) is estimated as a function of the lending rate (LNDRN) representing interest cost, the growth rate of adjusted import prices (MGOPPEXR) and the growth rate of agricultural prices (PIAGRPP), both representing the cost of raw materials. We assume that an increase in capacity utilization puts pressure on prices and this effect is captured by including the capacity utilization ratio (UTI). We also include the rate of growth of aggregate prices (PIGDPPP) to capture the aggregate price effect and a dummy (D91QN) for the post-1991 period to capture the liberalization effect. Once the growth rate of industrial prices is estimated, the industrial price level is determined by using this growth rate and past values of industrial prices (Equation 4.33).

Thus,

$$
\begin{aligned}
\text{PIINDPP} = & -2.389 + 0.221^{*}\text{LNDRN} + 0.458^{*}\text{PIGDPPP} \\
& (-0.77) \quad (2.10) \qquad\qquad (7.88) \\
& + 0.069^{*}\text{PIAGRPP}(-1) + 0.046^{*}\text{MGOPPEXR} \\
& \quad (2.28) \qquad\qquad\qquad (4.54) \\
& + 0.0235^{*}\text{UTI}(-1) + 3.727^{*}\text{DUMPIND} \\
& \quad (0.87) \qquad\qquad (9.66) \\
& - 0.967^{*}\text{D91QN} \\
& \quad (2.48)
\end{aligned}
$$

$R^2 = 0.97$ $\quad$ DW = 1.92 $\quad$ (4.32)

and,

PIIND = PIIND(– 1)*(1 + 0.01*PIINDPP) (4.33)

In the equation (Equation 4.32), the above adjusted import price (MGOPPEXR) is from the external sector. There the import price is adjusted for the average tariff rate and the exchange rate. Real lending rates are determined in the monetary sector. The results show that all the cost variables are positively related to industrial prices and they are all statistically significant. Capacity utilization is also positively related but it is not significant. Moreover, the aggregate price effect as well as the liberalization effect are both significant. The liberalization effect is significant due to two reasons. First, import liberalization has led to downward pressure on prices from cheaper imports. Second, foreign investment in domestic firms has also led to more competition in the domestic market.

Prices in the service sector are based mostly on labour costs. In this model, the rate of growth of prices in the service sector (PISVSPP) is a function of the consumer price index (CPIPP), which is used as a proxy for labour costs. We also include the rate of growth of aggregate price (PIGDPPP) and a dummy for the post-1991 period (D91QN). Next, the services price (PISVS) is calculated in Equation 4.35 using the estimated growth rate and past values of prices in this sector. Thus,

$$
\begin{aligned}
\text{PISVSPP} = & \ 3.508 + 0.262^{*}\text{PIGDPPP} + 0.286^{*}\text{CPIPP} \\
& (3.34) \quad (1.49) \qquad\qquad (2.36) \\
& + 8.104^{*}\text{DUMPISVS} - 0.377^{*}\text{D91QN} \\
& \quad (10.85) \qquad\qquad (-0.42)
\end{aligned}
$$

$R^2 = 0.87$ $\quad$ DW=2.12 $\quad$ (4.34)

and,

PISVS = PISVS(– 1)*(1 + 0.01*PISVSPP) (4.35)

The results show that the 1991 dummy has the right sign but is not statistically significant, implying only a slight effect of liberalization. This is possibly due to the fact that only some specific parts of this sector (telecommunication, etc.), have experienced more competition in the post-liberalization era.

The rate of growth of price in the public administration sector (PIGOVPP) is also largely dependent on labour costs and is determined in the model by the CPI. Once the growth rate of prices in the public administration sector is estimated, the price level is determined by using this growth rate and past values of prices (Equation 4.37). Thus,

PIGOVPP = 2.500 + 0.725*CPIPP + 7.649*DUMPIGOV

(4.30) (12.69) (8.88)

$R^2 = 0.87$ DW = 1.58 (4.36)

and,

PIGOV = PIGOV(– 1)*(1 + 0.01*PIGOVPP) (4.37)

The results support the hypothesis that prices in the public administration sector are largely influenced by labour costs though the coefficient is 0.7, indicating that there are other factors that are also important.

The consumption and investment deflators (used in the section on aggregate demand to determine the nominal values of consumption and investment, respectively) are separately estimated in the model. The rate of growth of the consumption deflator (CPDDEFPP) is a function of the rate of growth of the consumer price index (CPIPP). Thus,

CPDDEFPP = 2.229 + 0.717*CPIPP + 2.047*DCPDDEF

(4.519) (15.302) (3.166)

$R^2 = 0.903$ DW = 1.990 (4.38)

The consumption deflator should be having a one-to-one relation with the CPI but the results show that the coefficient is 0.71 only. This is due to the fact that the deflator uses 1993–4 as the base year while the CPI uses 1981–2 as its base year and there is a difference in the basket of commodities associated with these two different base years.

The investment deflator is largely determined by domestic industrial prices and import prices. The rate of growth of the investment deflator

(IEDEFPP) is, therefore, a function of the rate of growth of industrial prices (PIINDPP) and the rate of growth of import price (MGOPPEXR) adjusted for tariffs and the exchange rate. Thus,

$$\begin{aligned} \text{IEDEFPP} = {} & \underset{(2.804)}{2.840} + \underset{(6.00)}{0.679}*\text{PIINDPP} + \underset{(4.570)}{5.165}*\text{DUMIEDEF} \\ & + \underset{(2.88)}{0.060}*\text{MGOPPEXR} \end{aligned}$$

$R^2 = 0.833$ DW = 2.358 (4.39)

The CPI and the WPI are also determined in the model. Their growth rates (CPIPP and WPIPP) are estimated as functions of the growth rate of agricultural and industrial prices (PIAGRPP and PIINDPP respectively). The estimated equations (Equations 4.40 and 4.41) for these growth rates are as follows:

$$\begin{aligned} \text{CPIPP} = {} & \underset{(0.092)}{0.097} + \underset{(3.922)}{0.290}*\text{PIAGRPP} + \underset{(5.413)}{0.703}*\text{PIINDPP} \\ & + \underset{(6.446)}{7.315}*\text{DUMCPI} \end{aligned}$$

$R^2 = 0.887$ DW= 2.049 (4.40)

$$\begin{aligned} \text{WPIPP} = {} & \underset{(3.20)}{0.163} + \underset{(68.93)}{0.244}*\text{PIAGRPP} + \underset{(116.77)}{0.735}*\text{PIINDPP} \\ & + \underset{(152.27)}{1.041}*\text{DUMWPI} \end{aligned}$$

$R^2 = 0.999$ DW = 2.050 (4.41)

The industrial price growth rate appears to have a greater impact on the growth of CPI and WPI. The ratio is almost 30:70 in the case of the WPI while it is almost 25: 75 in the case of CPI. This reflects the weightage system in the price index. In the present system, greater weightage is given to the industrial prices.

Money Supply and Interest Rates

Money Supply

Money supply (broad definition) consists of currency and total deposits held by the non-bank public. The analysis of the total supply of money in an economy is based on the theory of the money multiplier. This theory suggests that total money supply (M) is a multiple of high powered or reserve money (H) also known as the monetary base. Thus,

$$M = mH \tag{4.42}$$

Here the multiple m is the money multiplier. In the model, the monetary base (M07WS) consists of the central bank credit to the government (SCRBI), the foreign exchange reserves (FERWNR), and net non-monetary liabilities (NNML). Thus,

$$M07WS = SCRBI + FERWNR - NNML \tag{4.43}$$

While SCRBI is determined in the fiscal sector, FERWNR is an external sector variable. Thus, it is an important identity that establishes interlinkages between the monetary, fiscal, and external sectors. NNML is an exogenous variable.

The money multiplier is not a constant term. Several factors including the bank rate, commercial bank advance rates, the desired currency–money supply ratio, commercial bank reserve–deposit ratio, and the liquidity position of banks may have a significant impact on the value of money multiplier. In this model, the commercial bank's CRR, the bank rate (BNKRN), and the lending rate (LNDRN) are assumed to be the determinants of the money multiplier. Thus the estimated equation for the growth rate of money supply (M37VP) is in terms of the growth rate of reserve money (MO7VP), change in the cash reserve ratio (ZCRR), change in the bank rate (ZBNKRN), and change in the lending rate (ZLNDRN). A dummy is added (D93ZLNDRN) to analyse the effect of credit decontrol.

Thus,

$$\begin{aligned} M37VP = {} & \underset{(19.57)}{11.876} + \underset{(8.36)}{0.326}{*}M07VP - \underset{(-0.92)}{0.179}{*}ZCRR \\ & - \underset{(-5.46)}{1.001}{*}ZBNKRN + \underset{(0.02)}{0.003}{*}ZLNDRN \\ & + \underset{(2.73)}{0.759}{*}D93ZLNDRN + \underset{(10.00)}{5.314}{*}DUMM37VP \end{aligned}$$

$$R^2 = 0.944 \qquad DW = 2.375 \tag{4.44}$$

Equation 4.44 shows a strong positive relationship between high-powered money and money supply with t-statistic of 8.36. One per cent growth in the reserve money leads to 0.32 per cent change in money supply growth. The CRR, which is the most widely used instrument of monetary policy in India and has a direct impact on the money supply growth rate, shows significantly less responsiveness. The equation reveals a 0.18 per cent decline in money supply growth with 1 per cent increase in CRR. The bank rate affects money supply indirectly by influencing the cost of credit and the rate of interest in the economy. Here the results show that a change in the bank rate is a significant determinant with a negative sign. The lending rate has a positive effect on the money supply through the money multiplier. The results show that for the pre-reform period, the lending rate had a positive effect though it is not statistically significant. This is probably due to the fact that credit creation was tightly controlled in this period. The 1993 dummy shows that after decontrol of credit markets, the lending rate has become highly significant in the determination of money supply. The role of the lending rate in changing money supply seems to have become significant in the post-liberalization period implying that the money supply is becoming more and more endogenous in this period.

Once the growth rate of money supply is estimated, the level of (nominal) money supply (M37WS) is derived by adding this growth to the past period's money supply (Equation 4.44). Real money supply (M37CS) is then calculated by using the consumer price deflator (CPDDEF). Thus,

$$M37WS = M37WS(-1)*(1 + 0.01*M37VP) \quad (4.45)$$

and,

$$M37CS = (M37WS/CPDDEF)*100 \quad (4.46)$$

Interest Rates

It has been explained in the section on prices that the aggregate price level in this model is determined by the aggregate demand and supply in the economy. Thus prices are not an exclusively monetary phenomena, even though money affects prices through its effects on aggregate demand and supply. In fact, in keeping with this Keynesian spirit, this model assumes that it is the interest rates that are affected by the disequilibrium in the money market, although other factors like the fiscal deficit and the bank rate are also important in the determination of the interest rate. There are four market-determined interest rates that are considered here namely, the deposit rate, the lending rate, the interest rate on government securities, and the average interest rate on public debt.

The deposit rate (R13RN) is assumed to be an equilibrating variable in the money market determined by the interaction between money demand and supply. Therefore, the higher the excess money supply (MYVP) in the economy, the lower must be the deposit rate, in order to maintain equilibrium between the demand for and the supply of money. We also assume that banks take into account the lending rate to the corporate sector (LNDRN) and to the government (RORGS) while determining the deposit rate. A lagged dependent variable (R13RN(– 1)) is added to estimate the gap between actual and desired lending rates and a slope dummy (D93R13RN(– 1)) for the post-1993 period is included to see how far this gap has been closed following interest rate decontrol. Thus,

$$\begin{aligned} R13RN = \; & 1.514 - 0.020{*}MYVP + 0.559{*}R13RN(-1) \\ & (5.699) \quad (-2.976) \qquad (12.712) \\ & + 0.129{*}D93R13RN(-1) + 0.149{*}LNDRN \\ & (12.078) \qquad\qquad (10.599) \\ & + 0.035{*}RORGS + 2.092{*}DUMR13RN \\ & (2.511) \qquad\qquad (23.357) \end{aligned}$$

$R^2 = 0.994$ DW=1.768 (4.47)

Here the excess supply of money (MYVP) is equal to the difference between the growth in nominal money supply (M37VP) and the growth of real output (GDPVP) such that,

$$MYVP = M37VP - GDPVP \qquad (4.48)$$

The results show that the lending rate to the corporate sector is the most significant determinant of the deposit rate although the lending rate to the government and the excess money supply are significant as well. The gap between the actual and desired rates is almost 56 per cent in the pre-reform era. Furthermore, the gap increases after the decontrol of 1993, showing that the decontrol has not been successful in bringing down the rigidities in this market.

The lending rate (LNDRN) is estimated in Equation 4.49 as a function of the bank rate (BNKRN), the cash reserve ratio (CRR), and rate of return on government securities (RORGS). All these variables are assumed to have a positive impact on the lending rate. A lagged dependent variable (LNDRN(– 1)) is added to estimate the gap between actual and desired lending rates and a slope dummy (D93LNDRN(– 1)) for the post-1993 period is included to see how far this gap has been closed following interest rate decontrol.

$$\begin{aligned} LNDRN = {} & 0.698 + 0.337{*}BNKRN + 0.045{*}CRR \\ & (0.87) \quad (2.52) \qquad\qquad (0.67) \\ & + 0.018{*}RORGS - 0.099{*}D93LNDRN(-1) \\ & \quad (0.46) \qquad\qquad (-5.63) \\ & + 0.702{*}LNDRN(-1) + 3.588{*}DUMLNDRN \\ & \quad (7.88) \qquad\qquad (7.59) \end{aligned}$$

$R^2 = 0.96 \qquad DW = 2.07 \qquad (4.49)$

The results show that the bank rate is the most significant determinant of the lending rate. The gap between the actual and desired rates is very large, almost 70 per cent in the pre-reform era. The gap does diminish somewhat after the decontrol of 1993 but it is still about 60 per cent, showing that the decontrol has had only partial effects.

The rate of return on government securities (RORGS) is endogenously determined as a function of the fiscal deficit to GDP ratio (FDGGDP). An increase in the fiscal deficit is expected to raise the rate of return on government securities. A lagged dependent variable (RORGS(– 1)) is added to estimate the gap between the actual and desired rates and a slope dummy (D93RORGS(– 1)) for the post-1993 period is included to see how far this gap has been closed following interest rate decontrol.

$$\begin{aligned} RORGS = {} & 0.465 + 0.311{*}FDGGDP + 3.463{*}DUMRORGS \\ & (0.52) \quad (2.03) \qquad\qquad (2.77) \\ & + 0.715{*}RORGS(-1) - 0.078{*}D93RORGS(-1) \\ & \quad (6.02) \qquad\qquad (-1.29) \end{aligned}$$

$R^2 = 0.90 \qquad DW = 2.24 \qquad (4.50)$

The results reveal a significant relationship between the rate of return on government securities (RORGS) and the fiscal deficit to GDP ratio (FDGGDP). The gap between the actual and desired rates is again very large as in the case of the lending rates. It is almost 71 per cent in the pre-reform era. The gap diminishes somewhat after the decontrol of 1993 coming down to about 63 per cent. This again shows that the decontrol has had only partial effects.

The fourth interest rate in the model is the average interest rate on public debt (AVR). It is the ex-post rate of interest that the government pays for accumulating debt. Clearly, this rate is affected by present as well as past interest rates corresponding to the different vintages of the stock of debt. Here, it is estimated as a function of the rate of return on government securities (RORGS), the deposit rate (R13RN), as well as a lagged dependent variable (AVR(– 1)) that estimates the effect of the past interest rates.

$$\begin{aligned} AVR = {} & \underset{(0.0007)}{0.0001} + \underset{(2.026)}{0.035}*RORGS + \underset{(0.638)}{0.0335}*R13RN \\ & + \underset{(24.709)}{0.943}*AVR(-1) + \underset{(7.767)}{1.201}*DUMAVR \end{aligned}$$

$R^2 = 0.99$ DW = 2.27 (4.51)

The results indicate that the effect of past interest rates is the most significant determinant of the average interest rate although the rate of return on government securities is important as well.

Fiscal Sector

The fiscal block incorporates different components of the receipts and expenditures of the government. It involves the combined budgetary transactions of the centre, state, and the union territories.

Expenditure

The total expenditure of the government (TE) is equal to the sum of the capital expenditure (CE) and the revenue expenditure (RE). The capital expenditure is composed of two parts, government investments (GINV) and other capital expenditures (OCE), both of which are treated as policy variables in the model. The revenue expenditure consists of salaries and wages (RSW), non salaries and wages (NSW), interest payments (RIP), subsidies (RSUB), fiscal transfer payments (RTR), and other revenue expenditures (REO). Of these components, fiscal transfer payment (RTR) is assumed to be a policy variable. Interest payment (RIP) is calculated as the product of the average interest rates on public debt and the stock of public debt. The rest, that is, salaries and wages, non salaries and wages, subsidies and other revenue expenditures are estimated in the model.

The salaries and wages variable (RSW) includes all compensation paid to government employees like salaries, wages, pension, provident fund, etc. Its growth rate (RSWVP) is expected to depend on employment growth in public administration (EMPGOVPP) and growth in consumer prices (CPIPP). Two dummy variables (D87 and D97) capture the effect of pay hikes due to the fourth pay commission (1987) and the fifth pay commission (1997).

$$
\begin{aligned}
RSWVP = \; & 9.936 + 1.267{*}EMPGOVPP + 0.265{*}CPIPP \\
& (7.69) \quad (2.36) \qquad\qquad\qquad\quad (3.40) \\
& + 6.432{*}D87 + 11.861{*}D97 + 6.598{*}DUMRSW \\
& \quad (2.76) \qquad\quad (6.25) \qquad\quad (4.53)
\end{aligned}
$$

$R^2 = 0.81$ DW = 1.79 (4.52)

From the estimated Equation 4.52, it is clear that the variable salaries and wages (RSW) grows at a faster rate than does employment in public administration. This may be due to the fact that in recent times there has been an increase in casualization of the public sector workforce. The variable EMPGOV does not include this workforce and this has resulted in the total salaries and wages expenditure going up at a faster rate than EMPGOV. The proxy for inflation CPIPP is a significant determinant although the coefficient is only 0.26. However, considering that salaries and wages are in real terms, this implies that the elasticity of prices with respect to nominal values of salaries and wages is 1.26. The effect of the fourth and the fifth pay commissions is highly significant.

Non salaries and wages (NSW) represent the government's consumption expenditure other than salaries and wages, including all office expenditures. The growth rate of non salaries and wages (NSWVP) is determined by the growth rate of salaries and wages (RSWVP). A dummy variable (D91QN) represents the post-1991 period when the government policy was oriented towards bringing down such consumption expenditures.

$$
\begin{aligned}
NSWVP = \; & 10.032 + 0.336{*}RSWVP - 2.800{*}D91QN \\
& (4.14) \qquad (2.20) \qquad\qquad (-1.75) \\
& + 12.644{*}DUMNSW \\
& \quad (12.25)
\end{aligned}
$$

$R^2 = 0.86$ DW = 1.72 (4.53)

The results suggest that salaries and wages are a significant determinant of the non salaries and wages expenditure with an elasticity of 0.3. The dummy for the post-1991 period has the right sign though it is significant only at 10 per cent level. This suggests that it is proving difficult for the government to bring down these consumption expenditures.

Subsidy growth rate (RSUBVP) is a function of the growth rate of fertilizer prices (PCFERPP) and the growth rate of procurement prices (PROCPP). One of the important aspects of the reforms that were initiated in 1991 was the government's attempt to bring down expenditure on subsidies. D91QN is a dummy variable that captures this aspect.

$$\begin{aligned} RSUBVP = {} & \underset{(9.06)}{18.979} - \underset{(-4.02)}{0.221}*PCFERPP + \underset{(1.74)}{0.428}*PROCPP \\ & - \underset{(-7.65)}{18.808}*D91QN + \underset{(9.90)}{20.941}*DUMRSUB \end{aligned}$$

$R^2 = 0.88$ DW = 2.37 (4.54)

The results indicate that expenditure on subsidies is influenced by procurement prices (significant at the 10 per cent level) as well as the price of fertilizers. The results also bring out the fact that subsidy growth rate declined significantly after 1991.

Other revenue expenditures (REO) are incurred in the process of providing public goods and services. In fact, these are the overhead expenditures associated with revenue expenditures. Thus an increase in any of the revenue expenditures leads to a proportionate increase in REO. This is captured in the model by assuming that the growth rate of other revenue expenditure (REOVP) is a function of the growth rate of total revenue expenditure (REVP).

$$REOVP = \underset{(-0.68)}{-3.570} + \underset{(3.23)}{1.027}*REVP + \underset{(21.97)}{76.054}*DUMREOVP$$

$R^2 = 0.962$ DW = 1.98 (4.55)

The results point to the one-to-one correspondence between total revenue expenditures and other revenue expenditures, thus vindicating the underlying assumptions.

Receipts

The receipts side of the government budget consists of revenue receipts (RR) and capital receipts (CR). The revenue receipts has two components, tax receipts (TAX), and non-tax receipts (NTAX).

$$RR = TAX + NTAX \tag{4.56}$$

The tax receipts can be sub-divided into two parts, direct taxes (DT) and indirect taxes (IDT).

$$TAX = DT + IDT \tag{4.57}$$

Direct taxes consist of income tax (TIT), corporate tax (TCT), and other direct taxes (ODT).

$$DT = TIT + TCT + ODT \tag{4.58}$$

The levels of income tax receipts (TIT) and corporate tax receipts (TCT) are calculated from their past values and their estimated growth rates. Other direct taxes (ODT) consist mainly of agricultural income tax, land revenue tax, and other direct taxes imposed from time to time such as interest tax and profession tax. Here they are assumed to be an exogenous variable.

Income tax growth rates (TITVP) are determined by the growth rate of nominal non-agricultural output (YGNWNVP). A slope dummy (D91YGNWNVP) is introduced to capture the government's efforts towards better fiscal performance from 1991 onwards. Another dummy (DUMITRD) is used to take care of tax reforms after 1993.

$$\begin{aligned} TITVP = & -3.385 + 0.990{*}YGNWNVP + 1.014{*}D91YGNWNVP \\ & (-0.726) \quad (3.219) \qquad\qquad\qquad (3.002) \\ & -8.153{*}DUMITRD + 15.887{*}DUMTIT \\ & (-1.42) \qquad\qquad\qquad (10.33) \end{aligned}$$

$$R^2 = 0.84 \qquad DW = 2.39 \tag{4.59}$$

In an economy with progressive rates of taxation, revenue from income tax should grow faster than the nominal non-agricultural output but the estimated equation (Equation 4.59) shows that there is a one-to-one relationship between the two. This indicates the prevalence of large-scale tax evasion. However, the slope dummy term (D91YGNWNVP) indicates that after 1991, the collections increased significantly. This could be partly due to more stringent measures and partly due to the fact that after 1991, the government came up with certain voluntary disclosure schemes like VDIS that mobilized past tax evasions. The dummy for the post-1993 period, however, shows negative results implying that tax reforms including the reduction of tax rates have, in fact, adversely affected the government's capacity to raise tax revenue.

Corporate tax growth rates (TCTVP) also depend largely on growth rate of nominal non-agricultural output (YGNWNVP). As in the case of income taxes, a slope dummy (D91YGNWNVP) is introduced to capture the government's efforts towards better fiscal performance from 1991 onwards and another dummy (DUMITRD) to take care of tax reforms since 1993.

$$\begin{aligned} TCTVP = {} & \underset{(0.28)}{1.226} + \underset{(2.486)}{0.696}*YGNWNVP + \underset{(1.025)}{0.350}*D91YGNWNVP \\ & + \underset{(10.63)}{15.808}*DUMTCT - \underset{(-0.434)}{2.487}*DUMITRD \end{aligned}$$

$R^2 = 0.89$ DW = 2.27 (4.60)

The elasticity of the corporate tax growth rate with respect to non-agricultural output growth is even smaller than that of the income tax growth rate with respect to the latter. Thus tax evasion seems to be even larger in the corporate sector. This may be facilitated by various tax incentives given on investment by the government. As in the case of income taxes, the dummy variables indicate that after 1991, the collections increased, although the post-1993 period shows negative results implying that tax reforms (including the reduction of tax rates) have adversely affected the government's capacity to raise tax revenue. However, these results are much less significant statistically, compared to the results in the case of income tax.

Total indirect taxes (IDT) have four components. These are excise tax (TEX), sales tax (TST), customs tax (TCM), and other indirect taxes (OIDT).

$$IDT = TEX + TST + TCM + OIDT \quad (4.61)$$

The levels of these components are calculated from their past values and their growth rates. The growth rates of the first three are estimated in the model while the growth rate of other indirect taxes (OIDTVP) is treated as an exogenous variable.

The excise tax growth rate (TEXVP) depends mainly on the growth rate of industrial output (YGIVP) and the growth rate of industrial prices (PIINDPP). The estimated equation (Equation 4.62) includes a dummy (D91QN) to take care of structural changes that resulted after the reforms in 1991 and another dummy (DUMITRD) to take care of tax reforms from 1993 onward.

$$\begin{aligned} TEXVP = & -0.0865 + 0.515{*}YGIVP + 0.953{*}PIINDPP \\ & (-0.03) \quad (2.40) \qquad\qquad (5.33) \\ & + 4.877{*}D91QN + 16.353{*}DUMTEX \\ & (1.49) \qquad\qquad (8.79) \\ & - 7.509{*}DUMITRD \\ & (-2.20) \end{aligned}$$

$R^2 = 0.81$ DW = 2.27 (4.62)

The elasticity of excise taxes with respect to industrial output is 0.5 indicating once again that there is massive tax evasion. Interestingly, the elasticity is much higher (almost one) with respect to industrial prices showing that it is far easier to monitor industrial prices than industrial output and hence, evasion is easier with output growth. The dummy variables indicate that after 1991, the collections increased, although this result is not statistically significant. The dummy for the post-1993 period shows negative results implying that tax reforms have adversely affected the government's capacity to raise tax revenue from excise taxes as well.

The sales tax growth rate (TSTVP) depends on the growth rate of aggregate real output (GDPVP) and the growth rate of aggregate prices (PIGDPPP). The estimated equation also includes a dummy (D91QN) to take care of structural changes that resulted after the reforms in 1991.

$$\begin{aligned} TSTVP = & \ 9.409 + 0.459{*}GDPVP + 0.645{*}PIGDPPP \\ & (4.79) \quad (2.41) \qquad\qquad (4.21) \\ & + 6.503{*}DUMTST - 1.363{*}D91QN \\ & (10.51) \qquad\qquad (-1.09) \end{aligned}$$

$R^2 = 0.86$ DW = 2.12 (4.63)

The results of Equation 4.63 indicate that the elasticity of sales tax with respect to both output and prices are far below unity, further strengthening the hypothesis of widespread tax evasion. Surprisingly, while other direct and indirect taxes have shown a higher growth rate after 1991, sales tax growth rates seem to have fallen in this period, indicating that the efficiency of sales tax collection has gone down.

The customs tax growth rate (TCMVP) depends on growth rate of imports (M77VPR) and the growth rate of average tariff (AVGTARVP).

$$TCMVP = \underset{(1.03)}{1.318} + \underset{(14.21)}{0.833}*M77VPR + \underset{(18.48)}{1.088}*AVGTARVP - \underset{(-4.34)}{12.348}*DUMTCM$$

$R^2 = 0.93$ DW = 2.25 (4.64)

The customs taxes show an almost one-to-one correspondence with average tariff rates and a slightly lower elasticity with respect to imports. This indicates that evasion of customs duties is far more difficult than the evasion of other kinds of taxes.

Two important conclusions may be drawn from all these indirect tax equations. One, indirect taxes are less income elastic than the direct taxes. In all the equations, from Equation 4.62 through 4.64, the coefficient is much smaller than one. Two, liberalization does not seem to have influenced the indirect tax receipts significantly. Furthermore, income tax receipts are the most income elastic while sales tax is the least income elastic. These results have important policy implications and require further explorations.

The other component of revenue receipts is non-tax receipts (NTAX). These receipts can be subdivided into four parts, that is, income from entrepreneurship and property (GIEP), government's miscellaneous revenue (GMR), official transfer receipts in rupees (OTRECR), and other non-tax receipts (ONTX).

NTAX = GIEP + GMR + OTRECR + ONTX (4.65)

Here GIEP, GMR, and OTRECR are assumed to be exogenous variables, while ONTX is endogenously determined. Other non-tax receipts (ONTX) include receipts like judicial fees, stamp paper, etc., and its growth rate (ONTXVP) is primarily determined by the growth rate of nominal non-agricultural output (YGNWNVP). The estimated equation includes a dummy (D91QN) to take care of structural changes that resulted after the reforms in 1991.

$$ONTXVP = -\underset{(-1.23)}{12.720} + \underset{(2.32)}{1.618}*YGNWNVP - \underset{(-0.95)}{3.578}*D91QN + \underset{(20.23)}{135.728}*DUMONTX$$

$R^2 = 0.95$ DW = 2.27 (4.66)

The results indicate that the elasticity of non-tax receipts with respect to output in non-agricultural sector is higher than unity.

In order to balance the government budget, capital receipts (CR) must be equal to the difference between the total expenditure (TE) and the revenue receipts (RR).

$$CR = TE - RR \tag{4.67}$$

The difference between the capital receipts (CR) and the other capital receipts (OCR) gives us the fiscal deficit (FDGWN). OCR consists mainly of divestment of shares of public enterprises and is assumed to be exogenous to the model.

$$FDGWN = CR - OCR \tag{4.68}$$

The fiscal deficit is financed by four different sources. These are: net RBI credit to the government (CRBI), government's external borrowing (CRE), government's borrowing from the household (CRH), and the governments market borrowings (CRM). Net RBI credit to the government is assumed to be an exogenous policy variable determined by the monetary authorities. This assumption implies that the RBI exercises significant autonomy vis-à-vis the government. As a result there is no automatic monetization, that is, deficits do not result in increased reserve money automatically. The government's external borrowing is also an exogenous variable since it is determined by foreign governments and international financial institutions.

The government's borrowing from the household (CRH) is that component of the household's savings like postal savings, household's contribution to the provident fund, etc., which is invested with the government. It is a function of the nominal disposable income (PDIWN) and the deposit rate (R13RN).

$$\begin{aligned} CRH = &-5340.324 + 0.014{*}PDIWN + 728.733{*}R13RN \\ &(-3.93) \qquad (20.30) \qquad\qquad (4.19) \\ &+ 7858.352{*}DUMCRH \\ &\quad (11.33) \end{aligned}$$

$$R^2 = 0.98 \qquad\qquad DW = 1.82 \tag{4.69}$$

The results of Equation 4.69 indicate that both the nominal disposable income and the deposit rate are significant determinants of the government borrowings from the household.

The government's market borrowing (CRM) are loans taken by the government from banks and other financial institutions. Once the net RBI credit to the government (CRBI), government's external borrowing (CRE), and the government's borrowing from the household (CRH) are determined, the government's market borrowing finances the rest of the fiscal deficit. This assumption rules out the possibility of automatic monetization of fiscal deficits through an increase in money reserves.

The difference between the fiscal deficit (FDGWN) and the non-debt fiscal deficit (CRO) gives the change in the stock of public debt. Adding this change in the stock of public debt to the past stock of public debt (PD (-1)), gives the present stock of public debt (PD). Thus,

$$PD = PD(-1) + FDGWN - CRO \quad (4.70)$$

External Sector

The balance of payments account is made up of the current and capital account balance. All the equations for the current and capital account balance are estimated in dollar terms. Since the rest of the model is in rupee terms, for a number of variables in this sector, the rupee values have also been calculated. While converting the dollar values to rupee, a constant exchange rate (that is, the annual average) in terms of only one currency, that is, the American dollar is used. Clearly this may lead to some measurement errors, firstly because the exchange rate varies on a day-to-day basis and hence does not remain constant and secondly, India trades with many other countries and hence it is not the American dollar alone that applies to valuations of exports and imports. This is taken care of in the model by accommodating an error term in the appropriate equations.

The Current Account Balance

The current account balance (CABWN) is equal to exports related to free-on-board values (EXPFOB) minus imports related to cost-insurance-freight values (IMPCIF) plus the net invisibles (NETINVS).

$$CABWN = EXPFOB - IMPCIF + NETINVS \quad (4.71)$$

Here, the variable export-f.o.b. (EXPFOB) is the merchandise exports taken from the RBI's balance of payments accounts. However, the export (X77WN) function estimated below uses data from the

Directorate General of Commercial Intelligence and Statistics (DGCIS). These data are not adjusted for 'free-on-board' valuation and hence are different from the data for exports-f.o.b. Hence, we need an adjustment variable (EXPERR) to describe the relation between export-f.o.b. (EXPFOB) and export (X77WN). Clearly, the value of this variable is nothing but the difference between the values of exports from the two different sources. Using this adjustment variable we can write:

$$\text{EXPFOB} = \text{X77WN} - \text{EXPERR} \tag{4.72}$$

Similarly, we need an adjustment variable (IMPERR) to describe the relationship between imports related to cost-insurance-freight (IMPCIF), which is the merchandise imports taken from the RBI's balance of payments accounts, and the import (M77WN) function estimated below using data from DGCIS. Again, this adjustment variable is defined as the difference between the values of imports from the two sources. This implies,

$$\text{IMPCIF} = \text{M77WN} - \text{IMPERR} \tag{4.73}$$

Exports Exports (X77WN) are the demand for domestic products in foreign markets. They are determined by domestic prices, (nominal) foreign exchange rates, and volume of world trade. Thus the estimated equation for growth in exports (X77VP) is a function of the growth rate of wholesale prices (WPIPP), the growth in exchange rate (EXRPLVP) and the world import growth rate (MWTVP)—a proxy for world trade. Under the erstwhile policy regime, particularly till 1993, exchange rate variations were tightly regulated by the RBI. After 1993, exchange rates were liberalized and began to fluctuate more freely. In order to take into account this change in policy regime, a dummy variable (D93EXPRLVP) is also included in Equation 4.74.

$$\begin{aligned}
\text{X77VP} = {} & \underset{(2.58)}{2.413} + \underset{(3.540)}{0.239}{*}\text{EXRPLVP} + \underset{(3.04)}{0.406}{*}\ \text{D93EXRPLVP} \\
& + \underset{(12.308)}{0.713}{*}\ \text{MWTVP} - \underset{(-1.87)}{0.190}{*}\text{WPIPP} + \underset{(12.60)}{8.333}{*}\text{DUMEXP}
\end{aligned}$$

$$R^2 = 0.959 \qquad \text{DW} = 1.908 \tag{4.74}$$

The results show that Indian exports are definitely sensitive to world imports although the elasticity is significantly less than one. This implies that a rise in world trade will result in India losing its share in the international market. On the other hand, this also partially insulates the domestic economy against a fall in world trade. The responsiveness of exports to exchange rate variations is significant. Moreover, this responsiveness increased substantially after 1993. The impact of domestic prices is along expected lines.

Imports Imports are generally influenced by levels of economic activity (that is, GDP), exchange rate, average tariff rate, and certain important price variables. Unlike exports, we disaggregate imports into two groups namely, imports of oil and imports of non-oil commodities. These are given separate treatment because the same variables have remarkably different effects in each of these categories, both in terms of direction as well as magnitudes.

The growth rate of oil imports (IMPOILPP) is a function of the rate of growth of GDP (GDPVP(-1)), the rate of growth of the exchange rate (EXRPLVP), the rate of growth of average tariff rate (AVGTARVP) as well as the growth in the price of oil (PCOILPP). A dummy variably (D93EXRPLVP) captures the effects of the regime change after 1993.

$$\begin{aligned} \text{IMPOILPP} = & -3.713 + 1.583^{*}\text{GDPVP}(-1) + 0.866^{*}\text{PCOILPP} \\ & (-0.89) \quad (2.31) \qquad\qquad\qquad (18.1) \\ & -0.627^{*}\text{EXRPLVP} + 33.987^{*}\text{DUMIMPOIL} \\ & (-2.56) \qquad\qquad (9.38) \\ & -0.281^{*}\text{AVGTARVP} - 0.239^{*}\text{D93EXRPLVP} \\ & (-1.43) \qquad\qquad (-0.40) \end{aligned}$$

$R^2 = 0.969$ DW = 1.743 (4.75)

The oil import equation (Equation 4.74) is highly responsive to the oil price. With a one per cent change in oil price, there is almost 0.9 per cent change in the imports, which implies almost a one-to-one correspondence. This could be due to the highly inelastic nature of oil imports. The level of economic activity as well as the exchange rate are both significant, with the former having an elasticity higher than unity. The average tariff rate and the 1993 dummy are statistically insignificant. During the process of modelling this import function, a lagged dependent variable was tried in order to check whether there was any discrepancy between actual and desired import of oil. The coefficient of this lagged dependent variable (which has not been included in the final result) indicates that there was not much discrepancy between the two. This indicates that the authorities had always given priority to oil imports and never compromised on this point.

The nature of non-oil imports has changed significantly over the past decades. Before 1991, these imports consisted mostly of essentials and investment goods. During the last decade however, the stress has shifted to consumer imports. The growth rate of non-oil imports (IMPNONOILPP) is a function of the rate of growth of GDP (GDPVP), the rate of growth of the exchange rate (EXRPLVP), the rate of growth of average tariff rate (AVGTARVP) as well as the growth in the price of non-oil commodities (PCNONOILPP), and the growth in the price of industrial commodities (PIINDPP). A dummy variable (D93EXRPLVP) captures the effects of the regime change after 1993. As opposed to oil imports, non-oil imports slow down considerably with a hike in import prices. Besides, the import growth rate of non-oil commodities is much more responsive to GDP growth rate and the exchange rate growth than the oil import growth rate. The equation also suggests that high domestic industrial prices may shift the consumer preference for imported products. With trade liberalization, therefore, domestic industry has to produce at competitive prices to compete with the importers. Improvements in efficiency and competitiveness have therefore become important issues for them to survive. Average tariff rates also seem to exert substantial impact on import growth rate of the non-oil products. The 1993 dummy is statistically insignificant.

$$
\begin{aligned}
\text{IMPNONOILVP} = & -1.721 + 1.771^{*}\text{GDPVP} \\
& (-0.75) \quad (9.47) \\
& -0.078^{*}\text{PCNONOILPP} + 0.870^{*}\text{PIINDPP} \\
& (-2.69) \qquad\qquad (4.71) \\
& -0.802^{*}\text{EXRPLVP} + 0.269^{*}\text{D93EXRPLVP} \\
& (-10.77) \qquad\qquad (1.66) \\
& -0.204^{*}\text{AVGTARVP} + 12.188^{*}\text{DUMIMPNOIL} \\
& (-4.24) \qquad\qquad (11.99)
\end{aligned}
$$

$R^2 = 0.98$ $\qquad$ $DW = 2.36$ $\qquad$ (4.76)

Net Invisibles Net invisibles (NETINVS), the other component of the current account balance, consists of net receipts of non-factor services (that is, receipts of non-factor services (NFSRE) minus payments of non-factor services (NFSPT)), private transfer receipts (PTREC), official transfer receipts (OTREC), and net investment income (NINV). While the first three components are estimated in the model in terms of their growth rates, the last two are exogenous variables.

Non-factor Services Growth Rate: The growth in the receipts of non-factor services (NFSREVP) is a function of total trade growth rate (TTRADEVP) and growth in the exchange rate (EXRPLVP). A dummy variable (D93QN) is introduced to capture the effects of the regime changes after 1993.

$$\begin{aligned} NFSREVP = & -1.615 + 1.067*TTRADEVP + 22.342*DUMNFSRE \\ & (-0.71) \quad (9.88) \qquad\qquad (12.89) \\ & + 0.081*EXRPLVP + 0.875*D93QN \\ & \quad (0.55) \qquad\qquad (0.40) \end{aligned}$$

$R^2 = 0.912$ DW = 1.64 (4.77)

The results show that receipts of non-factor services are significantly explained by total trade with an almost one-to-one correspondence. The exchange rate effects are insignificant while the regime changes following liberalization show only mild effects.

The growth in non-factor services payments (NFSPTVP) is influenced by the total trade growth (TTRADEVP) and the exchange rate growth (EXRPLVP). A dummy variable (D93QN) is introduced to capture the effects of the regime changes after 1993.

$$\begin{aligned} NFSPTVP = & \ 4.528 + 0.262*TTRADEVP + 27.812*DUMNFSPT \\ & (2.08) \quad (2.52) \qquad\qquad (15.45) \\ & + 2.091*D93QN + 0.114*EXRPLVP \\ & \quad (0.98) \qquad\qquad (0.79) \end{aligned}$$

$R^2 = 0.91$ DW = 1.58 (4.78)

The exchange rate variations are not found to influence the non-factor services payments substantially. Like the non-factor services receipts, non-factor services payments are also influenced substantially by the total trade growth. Here again, regime changes following liberalization show only mild effects.

Private Transfers Receipts Growth Rate: Apart from the trade in goods and services, private transfers are also an important component of current account balance. Non-resident Indian (NRI) remittances contribute a sizeable amount of foreign reserves in this category. These remittances come mainly from the Middle East. The rise in oil prices benefits the Middle East economy, which in turn affects the remittances as well. Therefore, these are expected to be a positive function of the oil prices. It may however be noted that if oil price rise is due to war-like conditions as in 1991, then the remittances may decline even in the face of increasing oil prices. Apart from the oil price, exchange rate variations may also influence the remittances from abroad. A depreciation of rupee may slow down the flow partly due to greater conversion rate of rupee in terms of dollar and partly due to less willingness of NRIs to convert dollars into rupees. The private transfers receipts growth rate (PTRECVP) is a function of growth of oil prices (PCOILPP) and growth of exchange rate (EXRPLVP). Two dummy variables (D91 and D93) capture the effects of the deregulation that brought these flows to the official channel.

$$\begin{aligned} PTRECVP = {} & \underset{(6.85)}{21.940} - \underset{(-6.67)}{2.540}{*}EXRPLVP + \underset{(3.602)}{0.145}{*}PCOILPP \\ & + \underset{(9.744)}{153.065}{*}D91 + \underset{(5.434)}{62.575}{*}D93 \\ & + \underset{(10.391)}{83.277}{*}DUMPTREC \end{aligned}$$

$$R^2 = 0.911 \qquad DW = 2.14 \qquad (4.79)$$

The estimated equation shows a small though positive responsiveness of the private receipts growth rates to the oil price. However, it is significantly affected by the exchange rate variation. One per cent change in the exchange rate leads to almost two and a half per cent change in the net receipts. Thus the positive impact of depreciation of rupee on trade may be offset by decline in the growth of remittances. The dummies for 1991 and 1993 show positive and significant results.

Capital Account

Capital account balance (KABWN) consists of net foreign direct investment flows (FDI), foreign portfolio investment (FPI), other commercial borrowing (OCB), external commercial borrowing (EXTB), NRI deposits (NRI), rupee debt service (RPDEBT), and net residual capital flows (RESCAP).

$$\text{KABWN} = \text{FDI} + \text{FPI} + \text{OCB} + \text{EXTB} + \text{NRI} + \text{RPDEBT} + \text{RESCAP} \quad (4.80)$$

While FDI, OCB, EXTB, and NRI are endogenously determined, FPI, RPDEBT, and RESCAP are treated as exogenous variables. Unlike the current account equations, which are in growth terms, capital account equations are in terms of the absolute levels. This is due to the nature of data. The values are large and they tend to oscillate so much that the growth rates have large errors.

FDI Theoretically and empirically there is ample evidence to suggest that FDI is related directly to the growth rate of the host countries and that the causality runs from growth rate to FDI. Beside GDP growth, exchange rate variations are also incorporated in the model. The hypothesis is that as the domestic currency depreciates, dollar equivalent of rupee profits declines. Since foreign investors are more interested in return in dollar terms and not in rupee terms, rupee depreciation may discourage them from investing in India. In the model, FDI is estimated as a function of GDP growth (GDPVP (– 1)) and growth of exchange rates (EXRPLVP). A dummy (D91QN) is included to capture the liberalization effect.

$$\underset{}{\text{FDI}} = \underset{(-0.04)}{-3.262} + \underset{(2.90)}{39.667}\text{*GDPVP}(-1) + \underset{(18.64)}{1761.209}\text{*D91QN}$$

$$\underset{(-4.30)}{-24.667}\text{*EXRPLVP} + \underset{(12.25)}{847.332}\text{*DUMFDI}$$

$R^2 = 0.96$ DW = 1.92 (4.81)

GDP and exchange rates emerge as significant variables with stipulated signs. The results also show that FDI increased substantially in the post-1991 period.

NRI Deposits The NRI deposits are determined by the return on these deposits relative to international levels and this is approximated by the difference between the domestic deposit rates and London Interbank Offered Rate (LIBOR). Beside returns, the performance of the economy in terms of the GDP growth rates and the exchange rate growth also influence the NRI deposits by affecting their confidence in the economy. While GDP growth rate and rate of interest affect these deposits positively, growth of exchange rate influences it adversely. The estimated equation, Equation 4.82 for NRI deposits (NRI) is a function of GDP growth rate (GDPVP), growth of exchange rate (EXRPLVP), and deposit rates relative to LIBOR (R13RN1). A dummy variable (D93QN) is included to capture the deregulations.

$$\begin{aligned} NRI = {} & \underset{(5.81)}{889.434} + \underset{(2.09)}{49.496}{*}GDPVP - \underset{(-0.41)}{3.755}{*}EXRPLVP \\ & + \underset{(4.89)}{122.660}{*}R13RN1 + \underset{(8.89)}{1092.356}{*}DUMNRI \\ & - \underset{(-1.31)}{297.814}{*}D93QN \end{aligned}$$

$$R^2 = 0.86 \qquad DW = 1.78 \qquad (4.82)$$

While GDP and interest rates emerge as significant variables with positive signs, exchange rate is insignificant. Thus exchange rates variations that affect remittances significantly do not appear to affect deposits. The dummy for 1993 has a negative coefficient indicating a fall in NRI deposits after 1993, probably due to a definite policy to discourage these deposits by bringing down interest rates.

Other Commercial Borrowings Other commercial borrowings (OCB) are the private external borrowings and are determined by the performance of the economy as well as the relative cost of domestic versus foreign borrowings. Thus, the rate of growth of GDP (GDPVP), exchange rate growth (EXRPLVP), domestic lending rates (LNDRN), and international rate of interest (LIBOR) reflecting the cost of borrowing internationally, are expected to be the determinants of OCB. A dummy variable (D91QN) is included to capture the effects of reforms.

The estimated equation exhibits a positive relationship between OCB and the lending rate and a negative relationship with LIBOR. The GDP growth rate is moderately significant (at almost ten per cent level of significance) while exchange rate effects are insignificant. The results also show that these borrowings seem to have declined significantly in the post-reforms period.

$$\text{OCB} = -693.959 + 113.898^{*}\text{LNDRN} - 63.418^{*}\text{LIBOR}$$
$$(-1.00) \quad (2.38) \quad (-1.25)$$

$$-\,8.903^{*}\text{EXRPLVP} - 207.056^{*}\text{D91QN} + 60.769^{*}\text{GDPVP}$$
$$(-0.53) \quad (-0.57) \quad (1.70)$$

$$+\,1673.148^{*}\text{DUMOCB}$$
$$(8.02)$$

$R^2 = 0.80$ DW = 2.29 (4.83)

The government commercial borrowings (EXTB) are calculated by adding government external borrowings in dollars (CRED) and adjusted government borrowings (EXTBAD). The last two variables are treated as exogenous to the model.

EXTB = CRED + EXTBAD (4.84)

Foreign Exchange Reserves

The foreign exchange reserves of the economy (FERWN) is the sum of past foreign exchange reserves (FERWN(– 1)) and the change in foreign exchange reserves (ZFERWN). Here, the change in foreign exchange reserves is the sum of the current account balance (CABWN), the capital account balance (KABWN), and an adjustment variable (RESFERWN) that takes care of errors and omissions in the balance of payments accounts. Thus,

FERWN = FERWN (– 1) + ZFERWN (4.85)

where,

ZFERWN = CABWN + KABWN + RESFERWN (4.86)

Exchange Rate

The (nominal) foreign exchange rate of the economy (EXRPL) is the sum of the past foreign exchange rate (EXRPL (-1)) and the change in foreign exchange rate (ZEXRPL).

EXRPL = EXRPL (– 1) + ZEXRPL (4.87)

The change in the foreign exchange rate (ZEXRPL) is determined in the foreign exchange market as a result of the interaction between the foreign exchange receipts and foreign exchange payments. It is estimated in the model as a function of foreign exchange receipts

(FERRE), foreign exchange payments (FERPT), and rate of inflation in terms of the wholesale price index (WPIPP (– 1)). According to the theoretical literature, the relative inflation in a country, based on the domestic and international inflation rates, plays an important role in this exchange rate determination process. In India, however, the exchange rate had been highly regulated till 1993. Even after deregulation, the exchange rates have shown less sensitivity to world prices than to the domestic market forces. In view of this, the model includes only domestic inflation and not world inflation in the exchange rate determination. Two dummy variables (D91 and D93) were added to take care of the exchange rate devaluation in 1991 and the shift to market-led exchange rates in 1993.

$$\begin{aligned} ZEXRPL = & -0.539 - 5.144{*}FERRE + 0.0001{*}FERPT + 5.396{*}D91 \\ & (-2.42) \quad (-1.81) \qquad\qquad (3.36) \qquad\qquad (11.54) \\ & + 3.805{*}D93 + 0.028{*}WPIPP(-1) + 1.384{*}DUMZEXR \\ & \quad (7.76) \qquad\quad (1.79) \qquad\qquad\qquad (7.16) \end{aligned}$$

$$R^2 = 0.94 \qquad DW = 1.99 \qquad (4.88)$$

From the results it appears that foreign exchange rate changes are greater in response to payments than receipts. This reflects rigidities in the foreign exchange markets. It depreciates faster with increase in payments but does not appreciate at the same rate when receipts improve. Domestic inflation has a moderate effect on the change in exchange rates while both the dummies are highly significant. It may be noted that the implicit real exchange rate behaviour can be derived as a reduced form of exchange rate and domestic price functions. However, we focus more on the impact of nominal exchange rate on trade and balance of payments.

5

INFERENCES AND VALIDATION OF THE MODEL

A macroeconometric model is a monolithic structure made up of individual equations and identities, each of which explains the structure or behaviour of a particular aspect of the economy. The last chapter described a macroeconometric model of the Indian economy, with a detailed explanation of the behavioural equations and important identities of the model. However, an understanding of these equations and identities does not, by itself, give us sufficient insight into the working of the model. For this it is important to look at two more aspects of the model. The first aspect is the mechanics of the model, that is, the different ways in which these equations and identities interact with each other giving rise to an interlinked system that hangs together. The second aspect is the validation of the model, that is, a test of how well the model performs in terms of explaining the real world. In this chapter, we shall present these two aspects of the model.

THE MECHANICS OF THE MODEL

One way to understand the interlinked system is to look at how output, prices, and other major macro variables are determined in the model and what are the different channels and transmission mechanisms through which different sectors of the economy affect these variables. In this chapter we shall try to do this by discussing how the important macro variables in our structural model are determined. Another very important objectives of a macromodel is to analyse alternative policies that can be persued by the State. Towards this end, the macromodel must involve those sectors of the economy where these policies are implemented. This would automatically include the fiscal and the monetary sectors. Another sector that is becoming increasingly important due to the present trends towards liberalization and globalization is the external sector. Our model deals with these three sectors in some detail, incorporating their effect on output and prices.

Output and Prices

The determination of the level of output (or in some cases its growth rate) is of course at the heart of most macromodels. The history of macroeconometric modelling indicates that initial efforts in this field were motivated by the business cycle literature and as a result most of them tried to provide a cogent framework that explains the short run (cyclical) behaviour of output. Similarly, most of the macroeconometric models constructed for the Indian economy are primarily concerned with the determination of aggregate output, although there are distinct differences within them in terms of their framework as well as their level of disaggregation. In our model, we have disaggregated total output into four parts. These are agricultural output, industrial output, output from the service sector, and the output from public administration. In the first three sectors, the sectoral output is the product of the existing stock of capital and the output to capital ratios. In the fourth sector, that is public administration, the salaries and wages paid by the government determine the sectoral output. This implies that the first three sectors of our model are capital constrained, and so, investment decisions in these sectors become extremely crucial in determining the levels and growth rates of output. Towards this end, we have estimated investment functions for the three sectors separately. These are assumed to be functions of the income levels and interest rates, apart from some sector specific variables like the agricultural terms of trade for investment in the agricultural sector. The investment functions in the industrial and services sectors are also affected by the capacity utilization rates in these sectors. The rate of capacity utilization measures how intensively the capital is being used in comparison to the maximum intensity with which the same capital can be used. It is assumed that the highest value of the output–capital ratio in the given period represents the maximum possible intensity. Thus, any value that is lower than this maximum implies that capacity is not being fully utilized in the sector and this affects the investment function in the sector adversely.

Investment, of course, adds to the existing capital stock and hence increases the productive capacity. However, output is determined not only by the productive capacity but also by the intensity of its use, which is given by the output–capital ratios. In our model, the output–capital ratios of the three capital-constrained sectors are estimated separately. In the agricultural sector, the output–capital ratios are determined by rainfall, fertilizer use, and the agricultural terms of trade vis-à-vis the aggregate price level. It may be noted that all these are supply side factors. In the industrial sector, on the other hand, both demand and supply factors affect the output–capital ratios. On the demand side we have government expenditures that are assumed to affect the output–capital ratios while on the supply side it is the import growth rate. The agricultural growth rate is another factor that affects industrial output–capital ratio both from the demand as well as the supply side. Finally, in the service sector, it is assumed that the output–capital ratio is determined by the growth rate of the other sectors.

The determination of the price level is another very important objective of most macromodels. Sometimes instead of price levels, the models try to analyse and forecast the rate of inflation, that is, the rate of change of prices in the economy. In our model the level and growth rate of aggregate prices are both determined endogenously (that is, within the model). Apart from the aggregate price, the model also estimates four sectoral prices as well as the consumption and investment deflators. The WPI and the CPI—the two composite price indices used widely to measure the inflationary tendencies in the economy—are also estimated in the model.

The mechanics of price formation has been one of the basic issues in the macroeconomic literature over which there is no consensus even today. In the classical framework, there is a dichotomy between the real and the nominal sectors of the economy. This implies that, while real factors (like the size of the labour force or its productivity) determine the level of output, the supply of money and the velocity of its circulation determine the nominal demand for the output and hence the price level. This is the classical concept of the 'neutrality of money' implying that money determines price and has no role to play in the determination of output. The Keynesian revolution, of course, countered the concept of neutrality of money by explaining the linkages between the real and the monetary sectors, especially through the interest rate mechanism. Subsequent work in the Keynesian tradition assumed that price levels were determined by maintaining a mark-up over and above the cost of production. It should be remembered, however, that both the classical as well as the Keynesian approaches were in the context of developed economies. In the case of less developed economies and particularly India, early studies supported some form or the other of the Quantity Theory of Money. This view was later moderated as it was realized that money did have an effect on prices but there were other factors, including the price of imports, government's procurement policies, etc., that also had significant impact on prices. As a result, most macroeconometric models of the Indian economy at present explain prices in terms of the liquidity situation in the economy as well as a host of other factors.

In our model, different prices are determined by different mechanisms. The aggregate price level is determined by the aggregate nominal demand and the aggregate output produced in the economy. The aggregate nominal demand is the sum of the nominal values of consumption, investment, and net exports. The total output is the sum of the output from each of the four sectors—agriculture, industry, services, and public administration. Given the total output from these sectors, the equilibrium aggregate price is that which equates the nominal values of this output to the value of nominal demand. It will be noticed immediately that money does not determine prices directly in this model. Of course, the supply of money affects aggregate demand through its effects on consumption and investment, and hence has an effect on prices indirectly. The four sectoral prices are estimated separately. The agricultural price is assumed to be completely market determined and hence, it is a function of demand and supply factors in the agricultural sector. The prices in the other three sectors are determined by mark-up pricing. One point that needs to be discussed at this point is the relationship between the aggregate price level and the sectoral prices. Clearly, the aggregate price level of an economy and the set of sectoral prices cannot be totally independent of each other. There are two ways in which this issue can be dealt. The first is to assume that the aggregate price level is some combination of the individual sectoral prices. In such a case, of course, the economy-wide aggregates (that is, aggregate demand and supply) play no role in the determination of the aggregate price level. Alternatively, we may assume that the aggregate demand and supply determines aggregate prices and there is some adjustment mechanism that ensures that the sectoral prices are consistent with this aggregate price level. Our model adopts this second approach. In order to ensure that the sectoral prices are consistent with the aggregate price level, it is assumed that the latter influences all sectoral prices. Apart from the aggregate and sectoral prices, the model also determines the consumption and investment deflators as well as the wholesale and consumer price indices.

The Monetary Sector

Money is perhaps the biggest source of controversy in macroeconomics. Theoretical debates on the nature of money as a commodity and why it exists in an economy are yet to be settled. For a macroeconometric model however, the more important issues are identifying the factors that determine the stock of money in an economy and the effect that money has on the output and prices in the economy. The theories of money supply provide a framework for analysing the determinants of the stock of money. The traditional approach in this area has been to assume that the supply of money is determined exogenously by a policy-determined money reserve (or monetary base) and a stable money multiplier. This was challenged by the post-Keynesian theories, which claimed that the stock of money is determined endogenously, and it is the rates of interest that are determined exogenously by the monetary authorities. In our model, the monetary base broadly consists of the outstanding RBI credit to the government and the foreign exchange reserves. Since the stocks of foreign exchange reserves are determined endogenously, the monetary base automatically becomes endogenous as well. However, the monetary authorities do have some control over the stock of money through the bank rate and the CRR as these two variables determine the value of the money multiplier. It may be noted here that our model assumes that the RBI exercises significant autonomy vis-à-vis the government. This is reflected in our model by the lack of any automatic monetization of the fiscal deficit. In fact, it is assumed that the net RBI credit to the government is exogenous since it is fixed by the RBI, and it is the government market borrowing from commercial banks and financial institutions that becomes the adjusting variable in balancing the government's budget. It is, of course, true that for a large part of the period which is considered in our study, the RBI was not autonomous in the sense described above. However, our model has been constructed to describe a liberalized market economy (in line with the characteristics of the Indian economy after, say, 1993) and it is in this context that the assumption of the RBI autonomy must be understood.

Interest rates have for long been the primary tools of monetary policy. However, with financial liberalization, these rates are no longer fixed exogenously by the monetary authorities, but are determined endogenously by the markets. In our macromodel, we have four different interest rates that are determined in this manner. These are the deposit rate, the lending rate, the rate of return on government securities, and the average rate of interest on public debt. These four interest rates interact with each other to give the interest rate structure. There are two important determinants of this interest rate structure in our model. The first is the money market equilibrium (driven by the demand and supply of money) that determines the deposit rates and hence affects the structure of interest rates. The second determinant is the fiscal deficit of the government that affects the rate of return on government bonds and hence the interest rate structure.

As we have mentioned earlier, the effects of money and monetary policy on output and prices have remained one of the most contentious issues in macroeconomics. In our model, the bank rate and the CRR are the two policy variables that are used by the monetary authorities to fulfil their policy objectives. The stock of money affects the economy through various channels. The equilibrium in the money market determines the interest rate structure and hence investments. Thus money has an effect on the productive capacity and output. On the other hand, money affects aggregate demand through its effects on consumption and investment. Since aggregate demand and output determine the aggregate price levels, it is easy to see that money affects both prices and output in our model. Some of these interlinkages are represented in Figure 5.1.

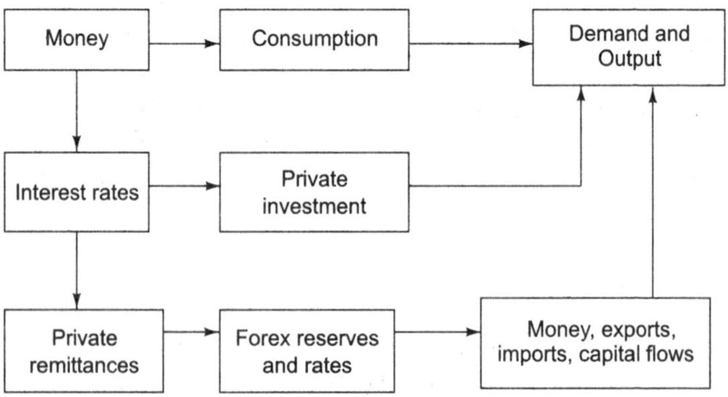

Figure 5.1 Effect of Monetary Variables on Demand and Output.

The Fiscal Sector

The fiscal sector has a significant impact on various components of the economy through policy choices that are implemented in different parts of this sector. For analytical convenience, it is useful to think that this sector comprises of three parts, namely the expenditure of the government, the revenue earned by the government, and the deficit incurred by the government. The expenditure of the government includes public investments in different sectors, which in turn increase the capital stock and output in these sectors. Moreover, public investment in the service sector gives rise to private investment in that sector and hence affects output even more. This 'crowding in' effect is however not found to be significant in the other sectors. Another component of government expenditure is the salary and wage bill. This determines the GDP from public administration and hence total supply. The total expenditure of the government also stimulates industrial demand and output. Figure 5.2 depicts these effects.

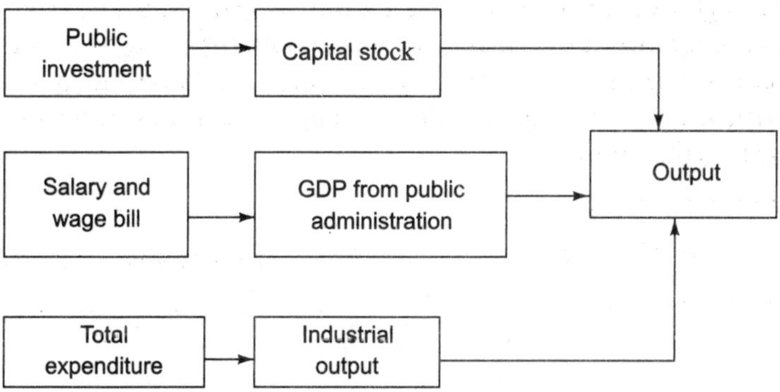

Figure 5.2 Effect of Government Expenditure on Output.

On the revenue side, a number of taxes have significant effects on different parts of the economy. The direct taxes bring down disposable income and hence consumption expenditure and aggregate demand. Customs taxes influence imports and hence affect the industrial output. The average tariff rate is a fiscal policy variable that is becoming particularly important in the context of the World Trade Organization (WTO) agreements. In our model, it affects the economy through its effects on imports, which in turn has effects on both aggregate demand and industrial output (see Figure 5.3).

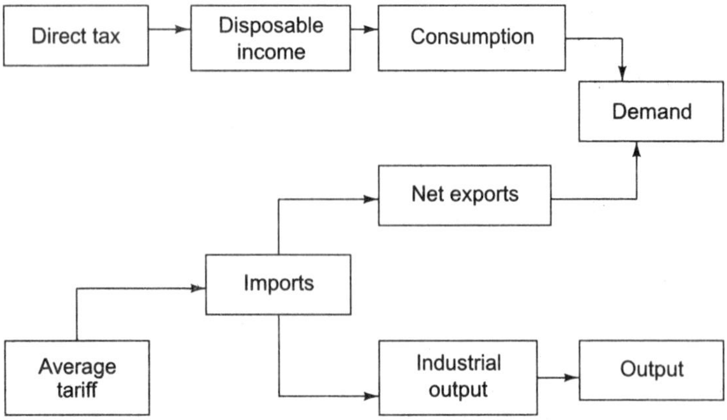

Figure 5.3 Effect of Taxes on Demand and Output.

The third component of the fiscal sector is the deficit incurred by the government, and this also has a significant impact on the economy through its pressure on the rate of return on government bonds. In our model, the fiscal deficit as a ratio to GDP determines the interest on government bonds, which in turn affects the whole interest rate structure and the resultant effects on output and prices. Figure 5.4 depicts this effect.

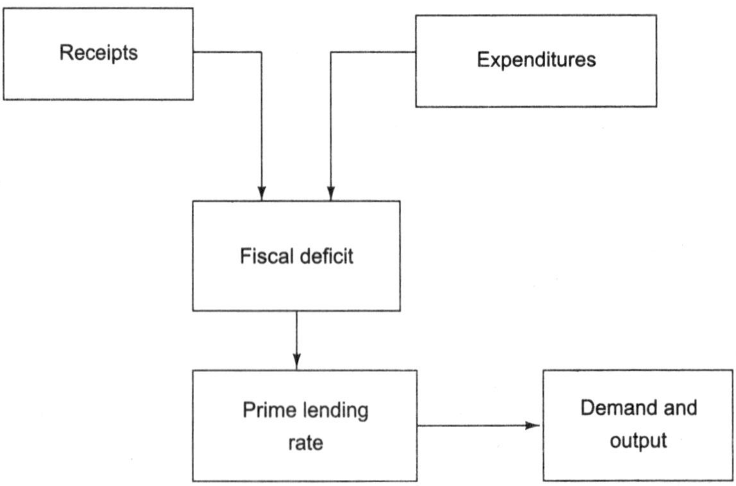

Figure 5.4 Effect of Fiscal Deficit on Demand and Output.

Thus, on the one hand, an expansionary fiscal policy can stimulate industrial output or public investment while on the other, it can increase interest rates and thereby decrease private investment. It may be pointed out here that the expansionary effect of a fiscal stimulus on industrial output can only act upto the point where capacity is fully utilized. Any further expansion of government expenditure after that would be inflationary in nature.

THE EXTERNAL SECTOR

The Indian policy makers during the first three or four decades after independence were greatly influenced by the theories of import substitution and export pessimism. As a reflection of this mindset, the early macromodels of the Indian economy also neglected the external sector. This has, of course, changed drastically in the last decade or so and the Indian economy is more open today then ever before. In the context of the WTO agreements, it is conceivable that in the future, the external sector will play a very significant role in the working of the domestic economy. Our macromodel tries to incorporate the mechanisms through which the external sector affects different components of the domestic sector. These involve various components of the current and the capital accounts as well as the foreign exchange reserves that accumulate from the transactions in the external sector. From the current account, the volume of imports determines the industrial output and total GDP. Import prices, similarly, affect industrial prices and the WPI. The net exports also affect aggregate demand and price through the open economy multiplier. The current and capital account transactions determine the demand and supply of foreign exchange, which in turn determines the exchange rate. Conversely, the exchange rate itself affects a number of variables in the external sector and, through the transmission mechanism described above, the overall economy. One of the most important of such mechanisms is the monetary effect of the foreign exchange reserves. In our model, the foreign exchange reserves created by the balance of payments in the external sector adds to the monetary base of the economy. Thus all transactions in this sector have an impact on the supply of money in the economy and the resultant effect on aggregate output and prices. Figure 5.5 depicts these effects.

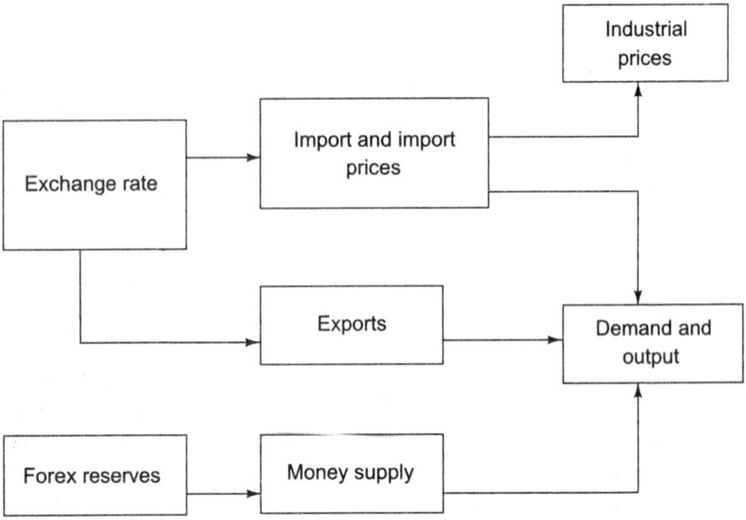

Figure 5.5 Effect of the External Sector on Demand and Output.

TRADE-OFFS

The usefulness of a large macroeconometric model like the present one lies in its capacity to incorporate various interlinkages between different components of the economy. This gives rise to the possibility that a policy stimulus in one part of the model may get translated to the other parts through a number of channels. Of course, in some cases the same stimulus may give rise to very different kinds of effects through different channels. For example, a change in a particular policy variable may lead to an increase in output in a particular sector but the same could lead to a decrease in output in another sector. In such a case there is a trade-off between these effects that must be considered for any policy planning. There are a number of trade-offs that have been incorporated in our model and we shall now consider a few of them.

Effects of a Change in Average Tariff Rate

An increase in average tariff rate can lead to lower fiscal deficit and prime lending rate and hence higher output. On the other hand, it may lead to lower output due to lower imports and industrial output. Figure 5.6 depicts this trade-off.

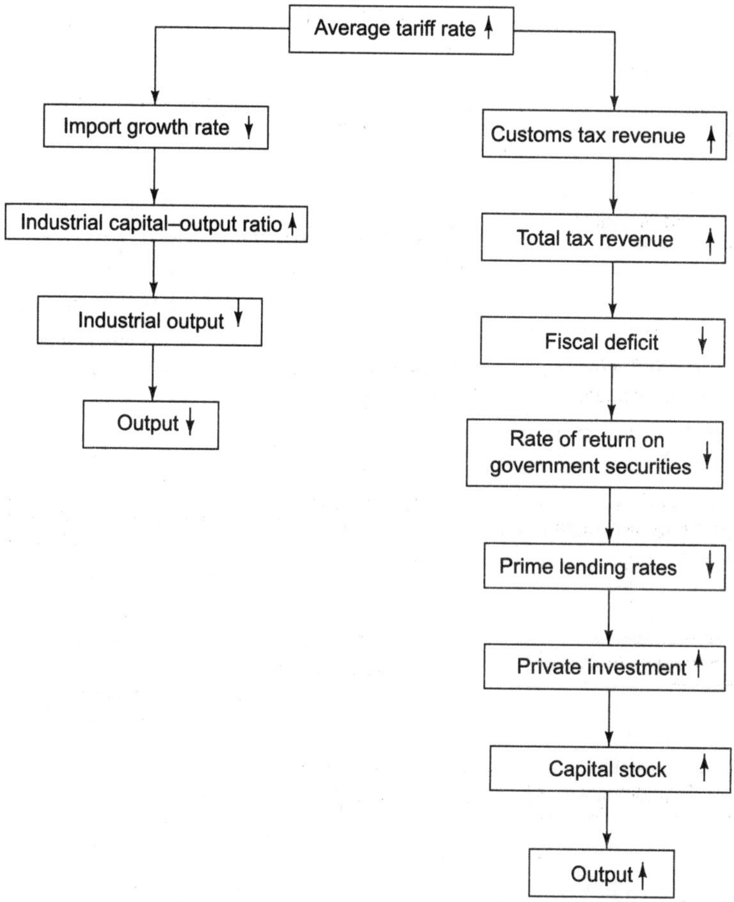

Figure 5.6 Effect of Changes in Average Tariff Rate on Output.

Effects of a Change In Fertilizer Price

An increase in fertilizer prices may lead to a fall in output due to a fall in fertilizer consumption and agricultural GDP. Output may also fall as a result of a fall in subsidies and hence a fall in total government expenditure, resulting in a fall in industrial GDP. Conversely, an increase in fertilizer price may lead to an increase in output, through a fall in subsidy, fiscal deficits, and hence prime lending rates. Figure 5.7 represents these linkages.

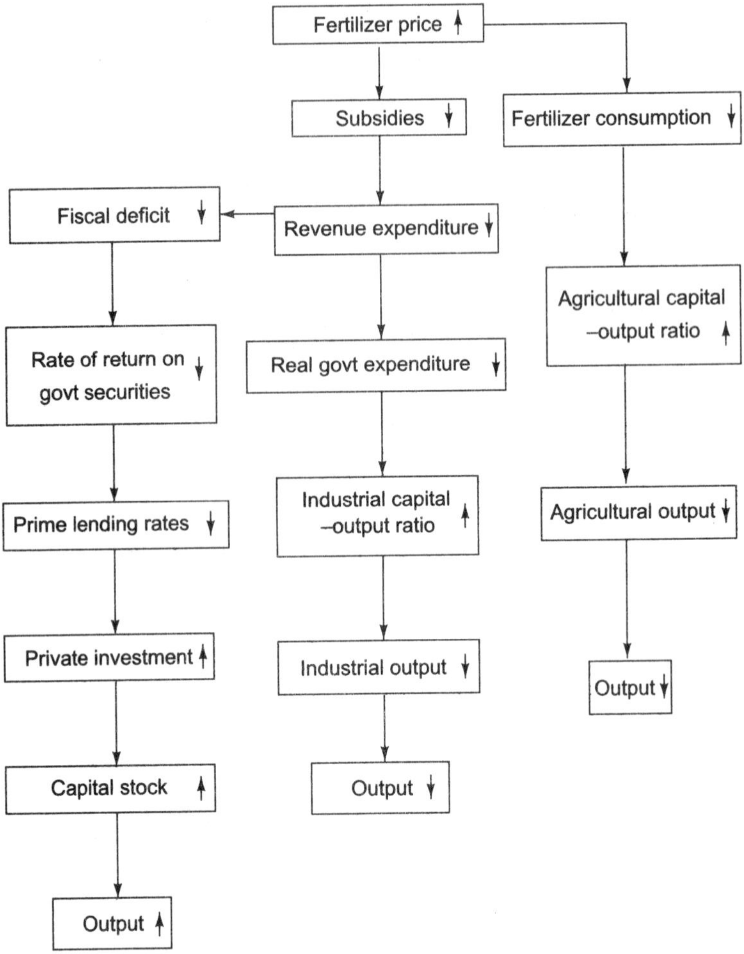

Figure 5.7 Effect of Changes in Fertilizer Price on Output.

Effects of a Change in Employment in Public Administration

An increase in the employment in public administration may lead to an increase in output by increasing the salaries and wages and hence GDP from public administration. However, an increase in the employment in public administration may lead to higher fiscal deficits and prime lending rates, bringing down investments and output. This is represented in Figure 5.8.

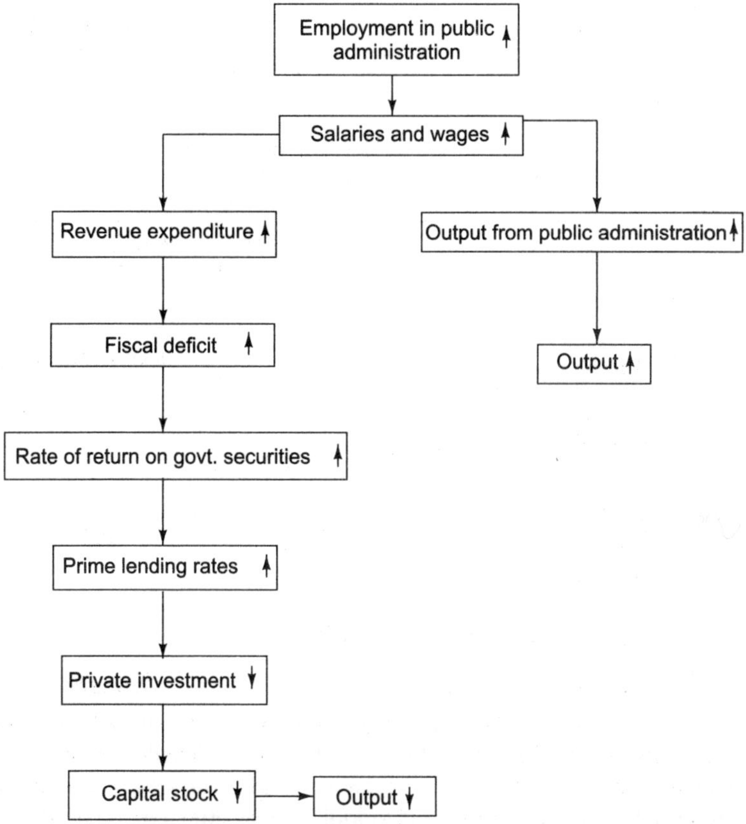

Figure 5.8 Effect of Changes in Employment in Public Administration on Output.

Growth–Inflation Trade-off

The model also manifests the growth–inflation trade-off that is well known in the macroeconomic literature. For example, an expansionary monetary policy (lower bank rate and CRR) will bring down the prime lending rate and hence investment and supply of output goes up. However, higher investments will also lead to higher aggregate demand. Moreover, due to lower prime lending rate, deposit rates will also go down and this will increase the levels of consumption. An increase in consumption also implies an increase in aggregate demand and this may lead to higher prices. Thus, there is a trade-off between growth and inflation and this is represented in Figure 5.9.

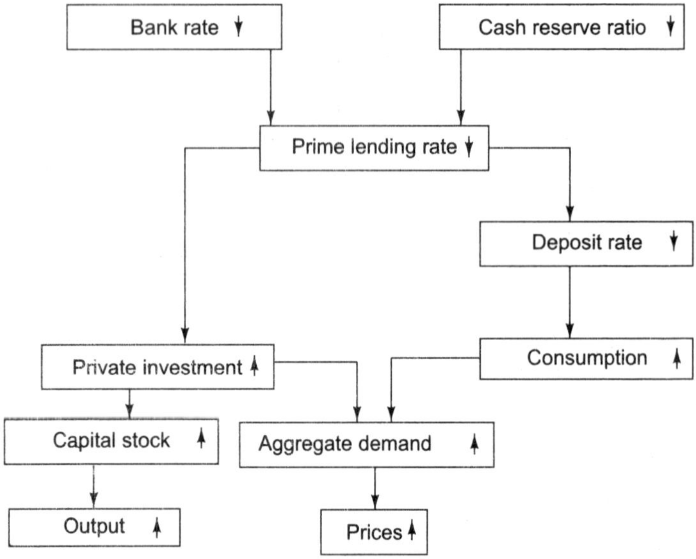

Figure 5.9 Growth–Inflation Trade-off.

VALIDATION OF THE MODEL

In the previous chapter and first part of this chapter, we have presented and discussed various aspects of a macroeconometric model representing the Indian economy. The interlinkages between the various sectors and the resultant policy implications have also been presented. It is now important to look at how effective the model is in explaining the Indian economy. Clearly any model is only as good as its performance. In statistical terms, this implies that the difference between the stimulated and actual values of the endogenous variables, that is the error, should be as low as possible. In other words, it is important to validate the model by using statistical measures based on these error terms. Once the model is validated, it can be profitably used to carry out counterfactual simulations.

Errors are an inherent aspect of any modelling process and no modelling activity can be entirely free from them. A prudent practice is to be aware of such errors and carefully consider them during any activity that is undertaken on the basis of the model (for example, ex ante forecasting, etc.) Here, we shall denote some of the reasons that may lead to such errors in our macroeconometric model.

- The behavioural equations in the model are determined by the use of regression techniques that have an inherent stochastic component, representing the random nature of the variables, giving rise to estimation errors.
- The macromodel is essentially a simultaneous equation system where the errors of individual variables multiply rather than adding up. This implies that a large model (like the present one) with more equations would be more prone to errors than smaller models.
- The forecasting method used in solving the model is dynamic, that is, present values of endogenous variables are forecasted on the basis of forecasted values of the past rather than actual values of the past. This process leads to cumulating of past errors and hence increases the errors compared to static forecasting methods.
- The macromodel is a non-linear system and hence does not have an unique solution. The solution is found by using the Gauss–Seidel method based on Newton's iterative procedure and a stopping rule that specifies that the percentage change in each solved variable during an iteration is less than 0.0001. This process is itself prone to errors.

The sources of error listed above are all due to the techniques that have been used in constructing and solving the model. There are some other sources of error that arise due to the gap between theoretical constructs and the actual working of the economy. Some of these sources that are relevant for our macromodel are listed here.

- The behavioural equations are based on theoretical concepts like capital, wealth, permanent income, etc., that are not measurable. In practice, some approximate measures are used as proxies for these variables and this gives rise to errors.
- The behavioural equations are chosen on the basis of theories that have been developed in the context of advanced capitalist economies with well-established market structures. These theories may not be as appropriate for developing economies like India and this introduces an inherent source of error in the model.
- One particularly important source of error arises from the fact that the model is based on a free-market economy while a substantial part of the sample period experienced a regime of controls and rationing in most sectors of the economy. This might lead to larger errors in the periods with controls.

- A specific error comes up from the treatment of variables in the external sector. Here, the estimation is carried out in dollar terms and then converted to rupees using the exchange rate. Now the exchange rate used in the model is the annual rupee–dollar rate and this gives rise to two types of errors. The first kind of error comes from the fact that all external transactions are not carried out in terms of the US dollar. The second kind of error comes from taking the annual rate, which is an average rate, and not the actual rates used for daily transactions throughout the year.

  Finally, we come to two sources of errors that arise from the nature of the data used in the model.

- The CSO has changed the base year of national accounts data to 1993–4 and all previous data have also been changed using a conversion factor. However this does not account for the fact that the production boundary has also been redefined since 1993–4 and hence there are errors inherent in the values of earlier years based on a conversion factor.
- The data used for the model have been taken from various sources like the National Accounts, the Balance of Payments Accounts, the Fiscal Accounts, etc. These different sources use different concepts in the process of computing the data and this also introduces some error into the system.

A STATISTICAL ANALYSIS OF THE EXPOST SIMULATIONS

As we have mentioned in a previous chapter, the most important objective of a macroeconometric exercise is to generate simulations on the basis of the model and analyse various aspects of the economy on the basis of these simulations. The first set of simulations that is generated by our model is based on the actual values of the exogenous variables and covers the period from 1978 to 1998. We call these the 'base run' simulations. These simulations (for which the actual values of the variables are available) are also known as expost forecasts. Before we start an analysis of the economy on the basis of the base run and other alternative scenario simulations, it is appropriate to analyse how well these simulations approximate the reality. In this section we present some rigorous statistical analysis to test how closely the base run simulation values approximate the actual values of the variables. This analysis is in terms of some statistical measures that are standard in the literature. The measures used are the root mean square error (RMSE), Theil's inequality statistics (TIS), mean absolute error (MAE), and the mean absolute percentage error (MAPE). All the statistical measures used in our analysis are described in Table 5.1.

Table 5.1 Statistical Measures of Validation.

Root Mean Square Error (RMSE) Measures the degree of absolute correspondence between the forecasted and the actual series	$RMSE = \sqrt{\frac{1}{h+1}\sum_{t=s}^{s+h}(\hat{y}_t - y_t)^2}$
Theil's Inequality Statistics (TIS) Measures the accuracy of turning point predictions	$TIS = \frac{\sqrt{\frac{1}{h+1}\sum_{t=s}^{s+h}(\hat{y}_t - y_t)^2}}{\sqrt{\frac{1}{h+1}\sum_{t=s}^{s+h}\hat{y}_t^2} + \sqrt{\frac{1}{h+1}\sum_{t=s}^{s+h}y_t^2}}$
Mean Absolute Error (MAE) Measures the absolute deviation between forecasted and actual series	$MAE = \frac{1}{h+1}\sum_{t=s}^{s+h}\lvert \hat{y}_t - y_t\rvert$
Mean Absolute Percentage Error (MAPE) Measures the absolute deviation between forecasted and actual series in percentage terms	$MAPE = \frac{1}{h+1}\sum_{t=s}^{s+h}\left\lvert\frac{\hat{y}_t - y_t}{y_t}\right\rvert$

It may be noted that in Table 5.1, $\hat{y}_t$ is the forecasted value, y_t is the actual value, s is the standard deviation, r is the correlation between the forecasted and actual values, and h denotes the number of observations. The first step involved in analysing the forecasts in terms of these statistical measures is to look at the frequency distribution of these measures. In Table 5.2, present the frequency distribution of the RMSE, TIS, and MAPE.

Table 5.2 Frequency Distributions of Various Statistical Measures of Validation.

Range	Number of variables (Dynamic simulation)		
	RMSE	TIS	MAPE
0–0.01	17	60	18
0.01–0.05	75	60	45
0.05–0.1	25	16	21
0.1–0.5	65	31	22
0.5 and above	35	40	102
Total	217	217	217

Theoretically, the lowest value of RMSE is zero and this implies that the simulated values coincide with actual values for all periods. The upper limit is undefined, and hence there is no test of significance of RMSE. Another aspect of RMSE is that it does not distinguish between overestimations and underestimations. If we compare the sectoral average of the RMSE values for the major endogenous variables, presented in Appendix 3, it appears that the forecasts of 'aggregate supply' including real GDP as well as its components show the best results closely followed by the 'price' sector. These are followed by the 'monetary' and 'fiscal' sectors in terms of performance, while the 'external' and the 'aggregate demand' sectors have the highest average RMSE.

If the model predicts the yearly changes perfectly, both in magnitude and direction, then the value of TIS will be zero. TIS will be unity, if the naïve 'no change' model is valid. If the value of TIS is greater than unity, the model performance can be regarded as unsatisfactory, as it performs worse than the naïve 'no change' model. The sectoral average of the TIS values for the major endogenous variables, presented in Appendix 3, show that in dynamic predictions, turning points were predicted most accurately for the 'aggregate supply' and the 'price' sector. These are followed by the 'external', 'fiscal', 'monetary', and the 'aggregate demand' sectors in terms of their performance in predicting the turning points.

A complete list of the values of all these statistics for all the endogenous variables of the macromodel is provided in a tabular form in Appendix 1. We shall now present an analysis of the performance of the ex post forecasts of the variables in each sector. The analysis will be based on both subjective assessments of the 'goodness of fit' of the forecasts and objective assessments based on statistical measures like RMSE and TIS. The subjective assessment is based on a comparison of the forecast and actual value of each variable corresponding to the 'base run' simulations, and characterizes the 'goodness of fit' in terms of overestimation, underestimation, good fit, and so on.

VALIDATION OF THE MODEL AT THE SECTORAL LEVEL

In the aggregate supply sector, for actual and forecasted values of real GDP (GDPCN) shows that the model is a very good fit and this is supported by very low values of RMSE and TIS, which are 0.007 and 0.003, respectively (see Appendix 3). As far as the sectoral components of real GDP are concerned, the services sector shows a much better fit as compared to agriculture, industry, and public administration. The value for RMSE and Theil's coefficient statistics for this sector are 0.012 and 0.006 whereas those for agriculture, industry, and public administration are 0.016 and 0.008, 0.019 and 0.009, and 0.018 and 0.009, respectively (see Appendix 3). The forecasts of aggregate real GDP show a little overestimation after 1993. Among the sectoral components, the agricultural sector has shown underestimation from 1987 onwards. In case of industry, overestimation is noticed in the years 1987–93, and underestimation in the years 1995–98. The services sector shows no systematic underestimation or overestimation. The public administration sector shows overestimation in the years 1978, 1981, 1988, and 1996. The estimates of aggregate real GDP as well as the sectoral components have all been able to capture turning points reasonably well throughout the period under consideration.

In the aggregate demand sector, the forecasts of GDPMP (nominal GDP at market prices) shows an almost perfect fit, which is again supported by low values of RMSE and Theil's coefficient which are 0.005 and 0.017 respectively. Other variables in this sector that are good fits (and their corresponding RMSE and Theil's statistics) are nominal GDP at factor cost (0.014 and 0.007), exports of goods and services in rupees (0.011 and 0.011), nominal consumption (0.027and 0.013), imports of goods and services in rupees (0.027and 0.013), non-salaries and wages (0.036 and 0.018), and salaries and wages (0.062 and 0.032) (Refer to Appendix 1). Evidently, the RMSE and TIS values are quite low for these variables. The total nominal private investments also show low values of RMSE and TIS, which are 0.045 and 0.023 respectively. The forecasts of nominal consumption show overestimation from 1992–7 and underestimation after that period (Appendix A8.6). RSW (salaries and wages) shows underestimation from 1986 onwards. NSW (Non-salaries and wages) forecasts have shown underestimation during 1981–91. The forecasts of imports and exports are described in the external sector. The forecasts of GDPMP have shown underestimation during 1996–8, whereas the forecast of nominal private investment shows underestimation during 1984–91 and overestimation in 1994. The forecasts of GDPMP (nominal GDP at market prices) as well as its broad components have all been able to capture the turning points throughout the period.

The forecast of total private investment has shown an almost perfect fit with RMSE and Theil's Statistics of 0.044 and 0.006 respectively (Appendix 1). Among the sectoral components, forecasts of private investment in the services sector show a relatively better fit—the values of RMSE and Theil's Statistics are 0.082 and 0.015—than those in industry (– 0.055 and 0.0270) and agriculture (– 0.064 and 0.032). The forecasts of IVACN (real private investment in agriculture) have shown overestimation during 1980–7, and underestimation during 1990–3. IVSCN (real private investment in industry) forecasts have shown underestimation during 1978–82, 1984–6, 1988–90, and 1996–8. IVSCN (real private investment in services) forecasts show underestimation throughout, except for overestimation in the years 1983–7. IV7CN (total private real investment) forecasts show underestimation in the years 1978–82, 1984–6, 1988–91, 1991–3, and 1996–8. The forecasts for total real private investment along with its sectoral components have been able to capture the turning points throughout with the exception of those in the services sector that have not been able to capture the turning points of 1982–3, 1985, 1992, and 1997–8.

Next, looking at the prices (see Appendix 1), the forecasts of PIGDP (general price GDP deflator) show that it is an almost perfect fit, with low values of RMSE and TIS that are 0.013 and 0.004, respectively. As far as the sectoral prices are concerned, the agricultural deflator (0.019 and 0.005) gives a relatively better fit followed by industry (0.013 and 0.0007), services (0.026 and 0.01), and public administration (0.037 and 0.015) respectively. The investment and consumption deflators exhibit relatively weaker fits, compared to the rest of the prices. The forecast of IEDEF (investment deflator) shows underestimation in the years 1980–92 and 1996–8 while there is overestimation during 1992–6. PIGDP (GDP deflator) forecasts have shown underestimation from 1996–8, PIAGR (agricultural price) forecast has shown overestimation during the years 1980–2, 1985–7, 1991–2 while PIIND (industrial price) forecasts have shown overestimation from the 1990s. PISVS (service deflator) forecasts have shown overestimation from 1978–90 and 1991–8, whereas PIGOV (deflator for public administration) forecasts have shown underestimation from 1994–8 and overestimation during 1987–93. CPDDEF (consumption deflator) forecasts have shown overestimation during 1985–97. The estimates of aggregate prices as well as sectoral prices have been able to capture the turning points well throughout the period.

In the monetary sector, the forecasts of M37WS (nominal money supply growth rate) show that the model is a good fit and this is supported by the low RMSE and TIS values, which are 0.006 and 0.001 respectively. Other variables in this sector that are good fits (and their corresponding RMSE and Theil's statistics) are nominal money supply (0.016 and 0.006), deposit rate (1–3 years) (0.050 and 0.012), average rate of interest on public debt (0.046 and 0.018), rate of return on government securities (average of the range 1–5 years) (0.132 and 0.029) and prime lending rate (0.026 and 0.044). For M37WS (nominal money supply growth rate), the forecasted values are very close to the actual values. The forecasts of MO7WS (nominal money supply) show underestimation during 1989–93 and 1996–8. The forecasts for R13RN (deposit rate for 1–3 years) show overestimation during 1978–87, and underestimation during 1991–8. LNDRN (prime lending rate) forecasts show overestimations for 1980, 1991, and 1995 and protracted underestimations during 1980–9 and 1996–8. RORGS (rate of return on government securities (average of the range 1–5 years)) forecasts show alternate episodes of overestimations and underestimations. AVR (average rate of interest on public debt) forecasts show consistent underestimations throughout the period, with the exception of overestimation in the period 1980–4. The estimates of M07WS (nominal reserve money) and M37WS (nominal money supply) capture the turning points reasonably well. R13RN (deposit rate (1–3 years) captures the turning points though it overreacts in 1990s. LNDRN (prime lending rate) does not capture the turning points in the year 1997. Similarly, RORGS (rate of return on government securities) does not capture the turning points in the years 1979, 1983, 1987, 1988, 1996, and AVR (average rate of interest on public debt) does not capture the turning points in 1981, 1983, and 1986.

In the fiscal sector, the forecasts of total expenditure (see Appendix 1) are an almost perfect fit with low values of RMSE and TIS (0.014 and 0.0016). Other variables in this sector that are good fits (and their corresponding RMSE and TIS) are fiscal deficit (0.028 and 0.001), revenue deficit (0.049 and 0.002) and public debt (0.007 and 0.003). The forecasts of both total expenditure and public debt are very close to their actual values, while the forecasts of revenue deficit show periods of both underestimation and overestimation. The forecasts of fiscal deficit show underestimation in the years 1983–9 and 1993–4 and overestimation in the years 1990–3 and 1994–7. The estimates of total expenditure as well as all other components have been able to capture the turning points reasonably well, with the exception of revenue deficit, which does not capture the turning point in 1997. Forecasts of interest payments (0.047 and 0.022) and subsidies (0.057 and 0.026) are also reasonably good fits. The forecasts for RIP (interest payments) show underestimations during 1986–8 and RSUB (subsidies) show overestimations during 1989–98. Both interest payments and subsidies have been able to capture the turning points.

Forecasts of direct taxes show a better fit (0.043 and 0.017) compared to the income taxes (0.039 and 0.003) and corporate taxes (0.077 and 0.034). The indirect taxes also show a good fit with RMSE and TIS of 0.045 and 0.022. Other variables in this sector that are good fits (and their corresponding RMSE and TIS) are the components of indirect taxes such as excise (0.036 and 0.011), customs (0.066 and

0.032), and sales tax (0.083 and 0.041). The forecasts of the direct and indirect taxes as well as their components are close to their actual values. Direct tax forecasts show overestimation in 1993, while indirect tax forecasts show underestimation in 1985 and total tax forecasts show underestimation during the period 1987–98. On the whole, all the taxes have successfully been able to capture the turning points reasonably well throughout the period.

In the external sector, the forecasts of exports show a reasonably good fit with RMSE and TIS of 0.194 and 0.012. Other variables in this sector that are reasonably good fits (and their corresponding RMSE and TIS) are imports (0.054 and 0.019), non-oil imports (0.041 and 0.020) as well as oil imports (0.145 and 0.070). Exports forecasts are overestimated during 1978–88 and during 1990–5, while imports are underestimated during 1978–87 and overestimated from 1987 onwards. The forecasts of exports and imports as well as the components of imports have been able to capture the turning points quite well. The forecasts of trade balance are a relatively weaker fit with RMSE and TIS being 0.276 and 0.135. The components of the CAB like private transfer receipts in dollars (0.084 and 0.005), net invisibles in dollars (0.037and 0.008), non-factor services receipts in dollars (0.066 and 0.012) and non-factor services payment in dollars (0.128 and 0.060) have shown much better fits. The forecasts of trade balance are underestimated until 1980s and during 1995–8, and overestimated during the period in between. The forecasts of current account balance are overestimated in the years 1980–3 and underestimates in the year 1995–6. Among its components, non-factor services payments shows underestimation throughout, while net invisibles show underestimation during 1978–87, and overestimation during 1988–92. The trade balance estimates and its components are able to capture the turning points reasonably well.

The forecasts for the capital account balance are a good fit with RMSE and TIS of 0.013 and 0.002. Other variables in this sector that are reasonably good fits (and their corresponding RMSE and TIS) are foreign direct investment (0.15 and 0.004), other commercial borrowings (0.3 and 0.017), and NRI deposits (0.206 and 0.031). The exchange rate (0.022 and 0.006) and the foreign exchange reserves in dollars (0.014 and 0.007) show remarkably good fits. The capital account balances are overestimated in 1979–80 and 1993–4 and underestimated in the years 1983–5, 1986, and1988. Except for other commercial borrowings, all other variables here have been able to capture the turning points.

6

Structural Changes and Policy Options

Macroeconometric exercises are useful to policy makers in a number of ways. However, they are mostly utilized for two purposes, (i) for a counterfactual analysis of the past and (ii) for a forecast of the future. In this chapter we shall undertake a study of the past, while the next chapter deals with the future of the Indian economy. Our analysis of the past will be based on simulating and comparing actual and counterfactual scenarios for the Indian economy for the 1980s and the 1990s. The objective of this exercise is to evaluate the contribution of certain policies and external shocks towards the economic performance witnessed during these two decades. During this period, two major structural changes took place in the economy. The first of these is the partial liberalization of imports together with the debt deficit syndrome that manifested itself from the mid-1980s and led to the crisis in the early 1990s. The second is the move towards complete liberalization initiated from the early 1990s. In order to evaluate the efficacy of various policies undertaken during these regimes, we have solved the model counterfactually, that is, based on various alternative assumptions about the relevant exogenous variables. We shall first take up the simulations corresponding to the 1980s and subsequently present those based on the 1990s.

THE 1980s

Impact of Lower Monetized Borrowing

One of the major causes of debt-induced economic crisis in the early 1990s was a rise in fiscal deficit triggered by excessive monetized borrowing. The rate of government borrowing from the RBI (as a ratio to GDP at market prices) increased sharply during the second half of the 1980s. During the same period, the GDP growth rate was also high, led mainly by an industrial and services boom. It may be interesting to examine the marginal contribution of the monetized deficit in stimulating growth and inflation during this period. In order to evaluate this, we have constructed four alternative scenarios. In scenario S1, the net RBI credit ratio (that is, the ratio between net RBI credit to the government (CRBI) and the nominal GDP) is reduced by 0.5 per cent for the period 1984 to 1990, compared to the values of the variable in the base run. In this scenario, there is no fall in the government expenditure corresponding to this credit cut, implying that the fall in CRBI is made up by an equivalent increase in the government's borrowing from the market (CRM). In scenario S2, the CRBI is reduced by the same amount and for the same period as in scenario S1 and this reduction is accompanied by an equal reduction in the non salaries and wages (NSW) expenditure of the government. Since the NSW is part of the government's consumption expenditure, this scenario envisages a lower level of monetized expenditure by achieving a lower level of government's consumption. In scenario S3, the CRBI is again reduced by the same amount and this is accompanied by an equal reduction in other revenue expenditure (REO) of the government, implying that the cut in the monetized deficit is at the cost of the overhead expenditure of the government. In scenario S4, the CRBI is again reduced by the same amount as in S1 and this is accompanied by an equal reduction in government investment expenditure. Clearly, the four simulations represent the effect of the same monetary policy (that is cut in monetized deficit) affecting the economy through different fiscal channels. Table 6.1, describes the simulations in a schematic manner.

Table 6.1 Counterfactual Simulations of Monetized Deficits, 1980s.

Simulation	Counterfactual policy stimulus	Adjustment mechanism	Implication
S1	CRBI to nominal GDP ratio falls by 0.5% compared to base run	Government borrowing from market	Lower monetized deficits and higher government's market borrowing
S2	CRBI to nominal GDP ratio falls by 0.5% compared to base run	Government consumption expenditure	Lower monetized deficits and lower government consumption

(*Contd.*)

Table 6.1 (*Contd.*)

Simulation	Counterfactual policy stimulus	Adjustment mechanism	Implication
S3	CRBI to nominal GDP ratio falls by 0.5% compared to base run	Other revenue expenditures of the government	Lower monetized deficits and lower government's overhead expenditure
S4	CRBI to nominal GDP ratio falls by 0.5% compared to base run	Public investments	Lower monetized deficits and lower public investments

In order to understand the differential impact of the various simulations on different parts of the economy, we shall compare their effect on (i) the rate of growth of aggregate output, (ii) the rate of growth of money supply, (iii) the fiscal deficit ratio, and (iv) the inflation rate. In each case, we shall compare the average value (for the period 1984 to 1990) for the base run (B) to the average values (for the same period) corresponding to the four simulations. The values are graphically represented in Figures 6.1, 6.2, 6.3, and 6.4.

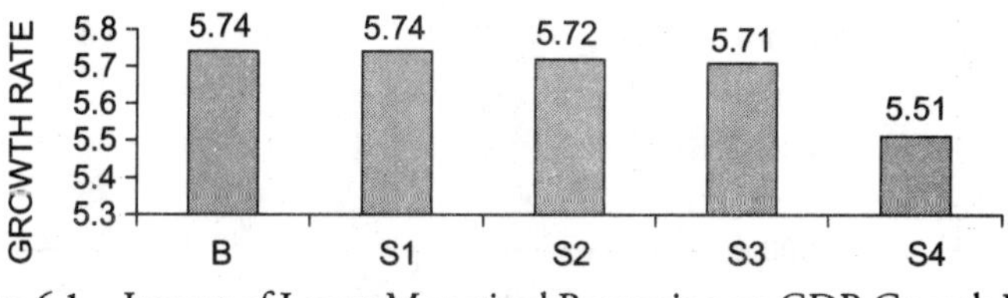

Figure 6.1 Impact of Lower Monetized Borrowing on GDP Growth Rate.

Note: The values are averages for the period 1984–5 to 1990–1.

Let us first look at the effect on aggregate GDP growth rate. As is evident from Figure 6.1, the simulations, B and S1 give rise to identical growth rates implying that the effect of the deficit on the growth rate does not depend on the mode of financing the deficit (whether printing money or borrowing from the market). S2 and S3 have very little difference in terms of growth rates compared to the base run, but growth falls distinctly corresponding to S4 when the cut in monetized deficit is achieved through lower investment rates. This clearly brings forth the fact that more than the levels of government deficits, it is the share of the components (government consumption, public investment, etc.) that determines the impact on the growth of the economy. This is due to the fact that while government consumption and overhead expenditures affect the growth rate only through the demand side, investments have both demand and supply side effects.

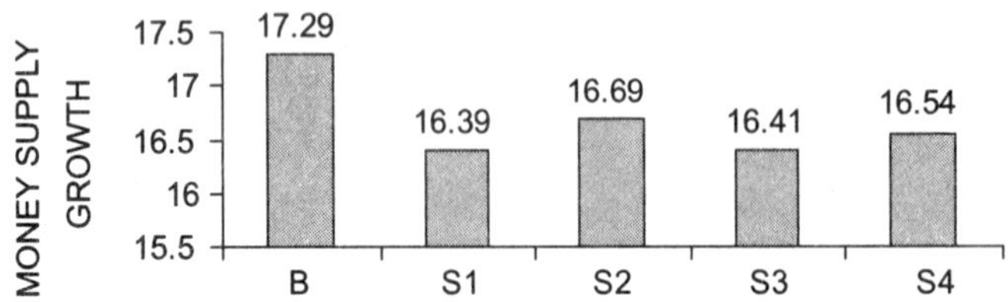

Figure 6.2 Impact of Lower Monetized Borrowing on Money Supply Growth.

Note: Same as for Figure 6.1.

In the monetary sector, the average rate of growth of money supply corresponding to the base run was 17.29 per cent. As Figure 6.2 shows, a cut in CRBI results in lower money supply growth rate corresponding to all four simulations. Clearly this is due to the fact that in all these cases, the amount that needs to be financed by printing money has been reduced, either by increasing the borrowing or decreasing the total public expenditure.

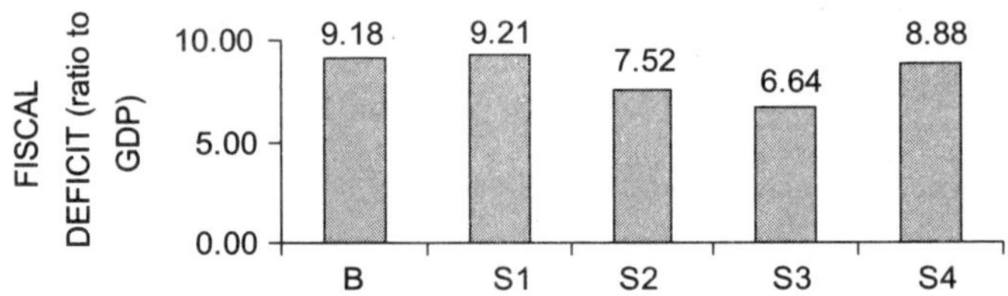

Figure 6.3 Impact of Lower Monetized Borrowing on Fiscal Deficit.

Note: Same as for Figure 6.1.

In the fiscal sector, since simulation S1 has no accompanying reduction in expenditure, the ex ante fiscal deficit ratio is the same as in the base run. However, there is a slight increase in the ex post fiscal deficit rate compared to the base run due to higher interest rates which are a result of lower monetary growth. Simulations S2, S3, and S4 all have lower fiscal deficit ratios compared to the base run, although the fall is less sharp in S4. This is due to the fact that a cut in fiscal deficits through lower investment expenditure also brings down GDP growth significantly.

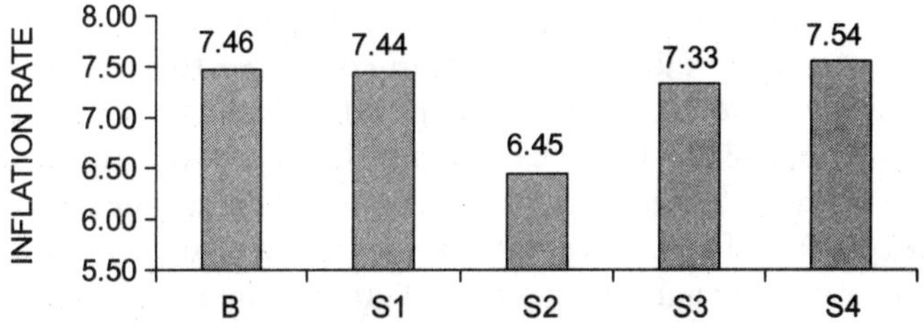

Figure 6.4 Impact of Lower Monetized Borrowing on Inflation.

Note: Same as for Figure 6.1.

Finally we look at the inflationary impact of the cut in monetized deficit. From Figure 6.4, it is clear that compared to the base run, there is almost no change in inflation rate corresponding to S1. We find a lower rate of inflation corresponding to S2 and S3 due to a fall in aggregate demand, with the impact being most significant in the case of S2. Interestingly, there is an increase in the inflation rate corresponding to S4 as a result of the cut in the monetized deficit. This counter-intuitive result is due to the fact that a cut in investment leads to a lower rate of growth of supply of output.

Impact of Normal Rainfall in 1986 and 1987

During the period 1984 to 1987, the economy experienced less than normal rainfall. The low rainfall was particularly acute in 1986 and 1987 and this affected the agricultural and aggregate growth rates adversely. In this simulation, we look at the possible effects of normal rainfall in these two years on different sectors of the economy. This implies that instead of taking the values 87 and 81 for these years, the rainfall index is 100 for both the years. Table 6.2 gives the annual average values of key macroeconomic variables for the period 1986 to 1990, corresponding to the base run and counterfactual scenario.

Table 6.2 Impact of Normal Rainfall, 1986 and1987.

Variable	Base run	Counterfactual
GDP growth	6.24	6.32
Agriculture growth	4.12	4.03
Industrial growth	7.65	7.83
Services growth	7.57	7.65
Inflation rate	8.03	8.11

Note: The values are averages for the period 1986–7 to 1990–1.

It is clear from Table 6.2 that with normal rainfall in these two years, the growth rate would have gone up compared to the base run. Surprisingly however, the increase in growth rate does not come from the agricultural sector, which has a slightly lower growth rate, but from the industrial and services sectors that grow at a higher rate compared to the base run. This counter-intuitive result is due to the fact that, in the base run, although the agricultural growth rate is low for the two years, it shoots up to a very high 15 per cent in the third year and this more than makes up for the steady rate of growth corresponding to the counterfactual scenario. The implication of this result is that in the long run, the agricultural performance has become largely imperious to rainfall shocks. The inflation rate is also slightly higher, corresponding to the counterfactual simulation indicating a trade-off.

Impact of Lower Interest Rates

As we have mentioned earlier, the net RBI credit to the government increased sharply during the second half of the 1980s and this resulted in a higher rate of growth of the monetary base. In order to keep a check on the rate of growth of money supply, the monetary authorities also maintained a high bank rate and CRR during this period. In this simulation, we look at the possible impact of a lower bank rate and CRR during this period. The counterfactual scenario assumes that the bank rate is the same as that in the base run till the year 1983 (that is, 10 per cent) after which it falls by one percentage point in each year, to reach 5 per cent in 1988 and remains at this level till 1990. Similarly, it assumes that the CRR is the same as that for the base run till 1983 (that is, 12 per cent) after which it falls by one percentage point each year, coming down to 5 per cent in 1990. Table 6.3 gives the annual average values of key macroeconomic variables for the period 1984 to 1990 for the base run and the counterfactual scenario.

Table 6.3 Impact of Low CRR and Bank Rate, 1980s.

Variable	Base run	Counterfactual
GDP growth	5.74	5.83
Agriculture growth	3.28	3.39
Industrial growth	7.27	7.37
Services growth	7.18	7.25
Inflation rate	7.46	6.85
Investment rate	20.60	20.95
Money supply growth	17.29	18.07

Note: The values are averages for the period 1984–5 to 1990–1.

From the table, we find that with a decrease in the values of CRR and bank rate, the money supply growth rate would have gone up and this expansionary monetary impact would have led to higher investments and a correspondingly higher growth rate. The higher growth is the result of higher growth in agriculture, industry, and services sectors. Interestingly, the higher money supply growth rate does not lead to higher rates of inflation. Here, there is no trade-off between growth and inflation due to the fact that the supply side effects of higher investments are stronger than their demand side effects.

Impact of Lower Growth in Government Employment

One of the biggest components of the Indian government's revenue expenditure is the salaries and wages bill of the government employees. Consequently, the high rate of growth in government employment has led to higher revenue and fiscal deficits for the economy. In this simulation, we look at the possible effects of a lower rate of growth in government employment during the second half of the 1980s. The alternative scenario assumes that the rate of growth of government employment was 1 per cent per year, during the period 1984 to 1990. Table 6.4 presents the annual average values of some important macroeconomic variables for the above period, corresponding to the base run as well as the alternative scenario.

We find that as expected, the revenue expenditure as a ratio to GDP would have gone down with lower government employment growth. This would have led to lower levels of revenue deficits and fiscal deficits as well. In the real sector, there would be a marginal decline in the growth rate mainly due to a fall in the growth rate of GDP from public administration and defence.

Table 6.4 Impact of Low Growth in Government Employment.

Variable	Base run	Counterfactual
GDP growth	5.74	5.68
Agriculture growth	3.28	3.27
Industrial growth	7.27	7.25
Services growth	7.18	7.16
Public administration growth	7.12	6.40
Inflation rate	7.46	7.33
Revenue expenditure ratio	22.16	21.87
Revenue deficit ratio	2.85	2.51
Fiscal deficit ratio	9.18	8.89

Note: Same as for Table 6.3.

Impact of Lower Fertilizer Subsidy

Subsidies are another significant component of the revenue expenditures and a large expenditure on subsidies has often adversely impacted the revenue and fiscal deficits. The subsidy on fertilizers is one of the major components of the subsidy bill. The objective of this subsidy is to keep a check on the rise in fertilizer prices. Hence, this component of the revenue expenditure is inversely related to the price of fertilizers. In this simulation, we look at the possible effects of a lower fertilizer subsidy. In order to do this, we generate a counterfactual simulation assuming that during the period 1984–5 to 1990–1, the rate of growth of fertilizer prices followed the rate of growth of oil prices more closely than they did historically. Table 6.5 gives the actual and counterfactual fertilizer price growth rates as well as the actual growth rate of oil prices, for the above period.

Table 6.6 presents the annual average values of some important macroeconomic variables for the above period, corresponding to the base run as well as the alternative scenario.

The simulation results indicate that with a lower fertilizer subsidy, the aggregate growth rate would have been lower. This is largely due to a fall in the agricultural growth rate, which depends significantly on fertilizer consumption. The rate of growth of the industrial and services sectors would have been largely unaffected. The inflation rate would have risen slightly due to the supply side effects of the lower growth rate. In the fiscal sector, the lower subsidy would have given rise to a lower revenue deficit and fiscal deficit ratio.

Table 6.5 Actual and Counterfactual Fertilizer Price Growth Rate.

Year	1984–5	1985–6	1986–7	1987–8	1988–9	1989–90	1990–1
Fertilizer price growth rate (Actual)	0.0	9.9	– 62.6	– 2.8	– 5.7	0.0	0.0
Fertilizer price growth rate (Counter-factual)	5.0	9.9	– 45.0	10.0	– 5.7	13.0	28.0
Oil price growth rate (Actual)	10.9	3.8	– 44.0	21.8	– 3.9	26.4	56.9

Table 6.6 Impact of Low Fertilizer Subsidy.

Variable	Base run	Counterfactual
GDP growth	5.74	5.65
Agriculture growth	3.28	3.06
Industrial growth	7.27	7.24
Services growth	7.18	7.16
Inflation rate	7.46	7.51
Revenue deficit ratio	2.85	2.7
Fiscal deficit ratio	9.18	9.04

Note: Same as for Figure 6.3.

THE 1990s

IMPACT OF ABSENCE OF SHOCKS REFORMS

The Indian economy experienced its biggest crisis during the early years of the 1990s, mostly in terms of a rising deficit in the external accounts of the economy. This crisis led to a paradigm change in development policy and to the adoption of the market reforms. Subsequently, there was a long debate on whether the crisis was due to long run structural problems in the economy or whether it was simply the outcome of external shocks like a hike in oil prices or a drought. The proponents of the latter argument maintained that in the absence of these shocks, there would have been no crisis and hence the market reforms would not have been necessary. It would be interesting to look at the veracity of some of these arguments. In order to do this, we have run three counterfactual simulations and compared them to the base run. In scenario S1, we assume that there was no oil shock in 1990. This implies that instead of going up by about 57 per cent in that year, the international oil prices are assumed to have gone up by 10 per cent. In the second simulation S2, we assume that there was neither any oil shock in 1990 nor any rainfall shock in 1991 and 1992 (that is, the rainfall index is assumed to be 100 instead of 91 and 93 in these two years). In the third scenario S3, we assume that not only were the external shocks absent but more importantly, there were no reforms initiated during this period. Clearly, by comparing S1 and S2 with

S3 and the base run, we will be able to answer some of the issues posed by the debate mentioned above. We compare the effect of these counterfactual scenarios on (i) the growth rate of aggregate output, (ii) the inflation rate, (iii) the fiscal deficit ratio, and (iv) the CAB. The values are graphically represented in Figures 6.5, 6.6, 6.7 and 6.8.

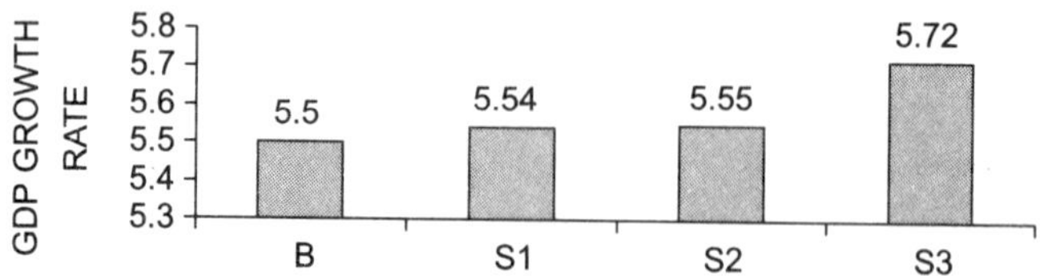

Figure 6.5 Impact of Absence of Shocks and Reforms on GDP Growth Rate.

Note: The values are averages for the period 1990–1 to 2000–1.

We start by looking at the aggregate growth rate. As Figure 6.5 shows, there would have been only marginal increases in the growth rate compared to the base run in the absence of the oil and rainfall shocks. Surprisingly however, there would have been an increase in the growth rate if there was no market reform as well. This counter-intuitive result is possibly due to the following reasons. As a part of the process of market reforms, the government has attempted to bring down public consumption expenditure and subsidies, etc. This may have had a dampening impact on growth in two ways. First, this directly decreases the growth in GDP from public administration. Second, by bringing down the total public expenditure, it may adversely affect industrial growth through the demand side. Of course, the magnitudes of these effects are not very large and hence the aggregate growth rates with and without reforms are not very different.

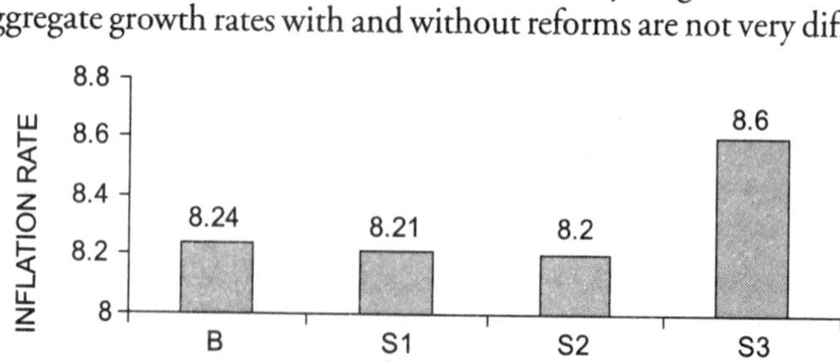

Figure 6.6 Impact of Absence of Shocks and Reforms on Inflation.

Note: Same as for Figure 6.5.

Next, we shall consider the inflation rates based on the wholesale prices. Here, we find (see Figure 6.6) that in the absence of the shocks, the inflation rates are marginally lower. This is easy to understand as the oil price hike affects the inflation rate through its effects on industrial prices, while low rainfall levels leads to higher agricultural inflation due to supply shortages. Interestingly, the absence of the shocks as well as market reforms leads to a higher rate of inflation. This is probably due to two reasons. First, reforms in the trade regime have resulted in competitive inputs and this has kept prices in check in the post-reform period. Second, the reform in investment sector has allowed foreign direct investments to come in and compete with the domestic producers and this again keeps a check on prices. Clearly, in the absence of these reforms, the inflation rates would have been higher.

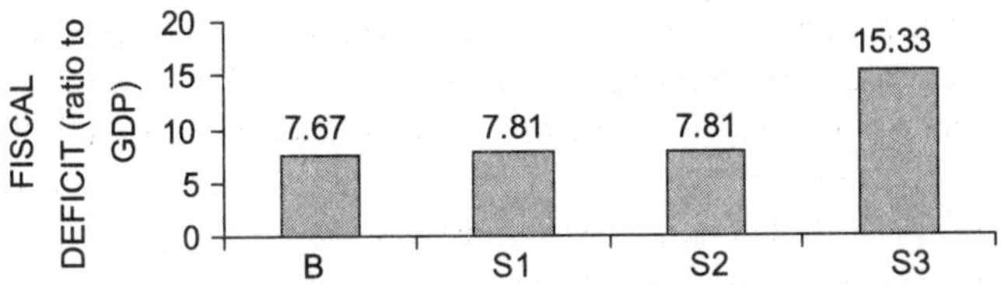

Figure 6.7 Impact of Absence of Shocks and Reforms on Fiscal Deficit.

Note: Same as for Figure 6.5.

Looking at the fiscal sector, we find that the reforms made a much more significant impact (see Figure 6.7) in this case. Thus, while the fiscal deficit is almost unchanged corresponding to the oil and rainfall shocks, it almost doubles in the absence of the market reforms. This is clearly due to the fact that a major thrust of the reform (most significantly during the early years) was to bring down public consumption and other expenditures in order to correct the fiscal imbalance that was generated during the 1980s.

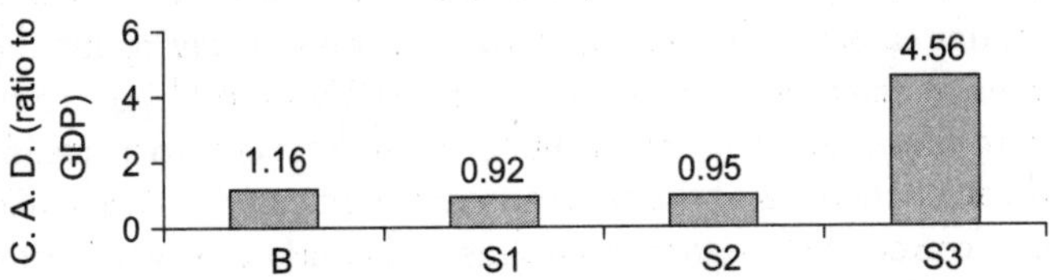

Figure 6.8 Impact of Absence of Shocks anf Reforms on Current Account Deficit.

Note: Same as for Figure 6.5.

Finally we look at the external sector and the current account deficit corresponding to the various scenarios. Here again, we find that the reform has been extremely successful in keeping the current account deficit within a reasonable range. This is amply demonstrated by the simulations which show that the current account improves marginally in the absence of the oil price and rainfall shocks, but becomes more than four times its value in the base run, corresponding to the case of no reforms. This is due to a number of changes that have been introduced in the external sector as a part of the reform process, of which, the most significant is the move from a fixed to a floating exchange rate regime. This acts as an automatic stabilizer by making imports more expensive and exports cheaper, in the face of rising external deficits.

Impact of Higher Monetized Borrowing

As we have already mentioned, the second half of the 1990s exhibited a slowdown in the economy with significantly lower rates of growth. One of the explanations given for this slowdown is the sharp reduction in the rate of government borrowing from the RBI as a ratio to GDP at market prices (CRBI ratio) during the second half of the 1990s. It may be interesting to examine the marginal contribution of this reduction in influencing growth and inflation during this period. In order to do this, we have constructed four alternative scenarios. In scenario S1, net RBI credit ratio or CRBI ratio is increased by 0.5 per cent of nominal GDP for the period 1995–6 to 2000–1, compared to the values of the variable in the base run, with no corresponding increase in the government expenditure. This implies that the rise in CRBI is made up by an equivalent fall in the government's borrowing from the market, CRM. In scenario S2, the CRBI is increased by the same amount and for the same period as in scenario S1. In this scenario, this increase is accompanied by an equal increase in the non salaries and wages (NSW) expenditure of the government, that is, this scenario envisages a higher level of monetized expenditure by achieving a higher level of government's consumption. In scenario S3, the CRBI is again increased by the same amount and this is accompanied by an equal increase in other revenue expenditure (REO) of the government, implying that the rise in the monetized deficit is due to a rise in the overhead expenditure of the government. In scenario S4, the CRBI is again increased by the same amount as in S1 and this is accompanied by an equal increase in government investment expenditure. Again, as in a previous section, the four simulations represent the effect of the same monetary policy (that is, a rise in monetized deficit) affecting the economy through different fiscal channels. Table 6.7 describes the simulations in a schematic manner.

Table 6.7 Counterfactual Simulations of Monetized Deficits, 1990s.

Simulation	Counterfactual policy stimulus	Adjusting variable	Implication
S1	CRBI to nominal GDP ratio rises by 0.5% compared to base run	Government borrowing from market	Higher monetized deficits and lower government's market borrowing
S2	CRBI to nominal GDP ratio rises by 0.5% compared to base run	Government consumption expenditure	Higher monetized deficits and higher government's consumption
S3	CRBI to nominal GDP ratio rises by 0.5% compared to base run	Other revenue expenditures of the government	Higher monetized deficits and higher government's overhead expenditure
S4	CRBI to nominal GDP ratio rises by 0.5% compared to base run	Public investments	Higher monetized deficits and higher public investments

In order to understand the differential impact of the various simulations on different parts of the economy, we shall compare their effect on (i) the rate of growth of aggregate output, (ii) the rate of growth of money supply, (iii) the fiscal deficit ratio, and (iv) the inflation rate. In each case, we shall compare the average value (for the period 1995–6 to 2000–1) for the base run to the average values (for the same period) corresponding to the four simulations. The values are graphically represented in Figures 6.9, 6.10, 6.11, and 6.12.

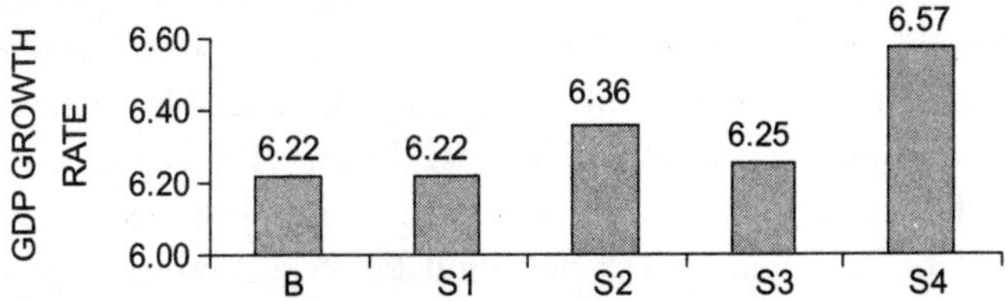

Figure 6.9 Impact of Higher Monetized Borrowing on GDP Growth Rate.

Note: The values are averages for the period 1995–6 to 2000–1.

Let us first look at the effect on aggregate GDP growth rate. As is evident from Figure 6.9, the simulations S1 and S3 have very little impact on the GDP growth rate compared to the base run. However, GDP growth rises distinctly corresponding to S2 when the rise in monetized deficit is achieved through higher government consumption. The GDP growth rate rises even more when the rise in monetized deficit is achieved through investment rates. This again underlines the fact that more than the levels of government deficits, it is the share of the components that determines the impact on the economy.

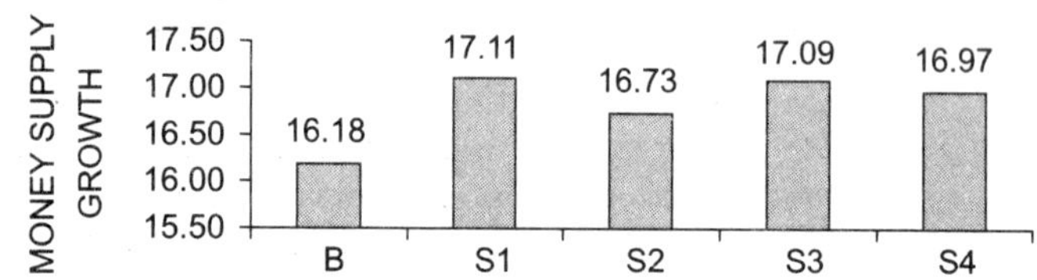

Figure 6.10 Impact of Higher Monetized Borrowing on Money Supply Growth.

Note: Same as for Figure 6.9.

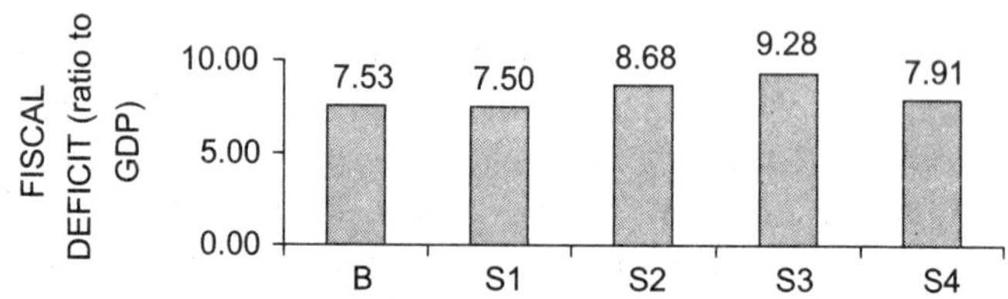

Figure 6.11 Impact of Higher Monetized Borrowing on Fiscal Deficit.

Note: Same as for Figure 6.9.

In the monetary sector, the average rate of growth of money supply corresponding to the base run was 16.18 per cent. As Figure 6.10 shows, a rise in CRBI results in higher money supply growth rate corresponding to all four simulations. However the growth rate is somewhat lower for S2, compared to the other simulations. In the fiscal sector (see Figure 6.11), since simulation S1 has no accompanying increase in expenditure, the ex ante fiscal deficit ratio is the same as in the base run. However, there is a slight decrease in the ex post fiscal deficit rate compared to the base run due to lower interest rates which are a result of higher monetary growth. Simulations S2, S3, and S4 all have higher fiscal deficit ratios compared to the base run, although the rise is less sharp in S4. This is due to the fact that a rise in fiscal deficit through higher investment expenditure also increases GDP growth significantly.

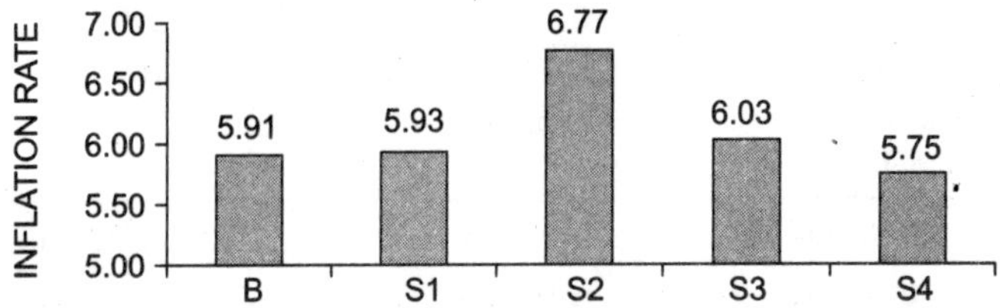

Figure 6.12 Impact of Higher Monetized Borrowing on Inflation.

Note: Same as for Figure 6.9.

Finally we look at the inflationary impact of the rise in monetized deficit. From Figure 6.12, it is clear that compared to the base run, there is a higher rate of inflation corresponding to S1, S2, and S3, with the impact being most significant in the case of S2. There is a decrease in the inflation rate corresponding to S4 as a result of the rise in the monetized deficit. This counter-intuitive result is due to the fact that a rise in investment leads to a higher rate of growth of supply of output.

Impact of Normal Rainfall in 1999 and 2000

As we have stressed in Chapter 4, agricultural growth (and hence aggregate growth) in India is highly sensitive to rainfall. Thus, one of the reasons for the slowdown is attributable the low rainfall and poor agricultural performance during the end of the 1990s. The extent of this 'rainfall effect' can be determined only by comparison with a season of normal rainfall during this period. Accordingly in this counterfactual scenario, we assume that rainfall was 'normal' for the years 1999 and 2000. This implies that instead of taking the values 96 and 92 for these years, the rainfall index is 100 for both the years. Table 6.8 presents the annual average values of some important macroeconomic variables for the above period, corresponding to the base run as well as the alternative scenario.

Table 6.8 Impact of Normal Rainfall, 1999 and 2000.

Variable	Base run	Counterfactual
GDP growth	5.78	6.36
Agriculture growth	0.95	2.68
Industrial growth	6.05	6.29
Services growth	7.9	8.02
Inflation rate	6.54	5.6
Fiscal deficit ratio	7.39	7.52

Note: The values are averages for the period 1999–2000 to 2000–1.

The simulations reveal that there is a significant increase in agricultural growth and aggregate growth, corresponding to normal rainfall in these years. The growth rate is also higher for industry and services, though the effect is marginal in these sectors. The strong supply side impact of this growth ensures that inflation rates are also lower compared to the base run. However, there is a slight increase in the fiscal deficit ratio.

Impact of Interest Rates

One of the important arguments that has been put forward to explain the low growth in the economy during the second half of the 1990s is based on high interest rates. According to the proponents of this argument, the normal interest rates during this period did not fall as much as the inflation rates, leading to higher real interest rates. In the context of this argument, it would be useful to look at the possible effect of lower interest rates during this period. Consequently, in the alternative scenario, we assume that the bank rate and CRR (during the period 1994–5 to 2000–1) fell at a faster rate compared to the base run. The counterfactual values are given in Table 6.9.

Table 6.9 Actual and Counterfactual Bank Rate and CRR.

Year	1994–5	1995–6	1996–7	1997–8	1998–9	1999–2000	2000–1
Bank Rate							
(Actual)	12	12	12	9	10	8	7
(Counter-factual)	12	10	9	8	7	6	5
CRR							
(Actual)	15	14	11	10	10.5	9	8
(Counter-factual)	15	10	9	8	7	6	5

Table 6.10 presents the annual average values of some important macroeconomic variables for the above period, corresponding to the base run as well as the alternative scenario.

Table 6.10 Impact of Low CRR and Bank Rate, 1990s.

Variable	Base run	Counterfactual
GDP growth	6.56	6.67
Agriculture growth	2.94	3.02
Industrial growth	7.31	7.47
Services growth	8.53	8.63
Inflation rate	6.86	6.54
Investment rate	24.52	24.81
Money supply growth	16.93	17.01

Note: The values are averages for the period 1994–5 to 2000–1.

Comparing the base run and the counterfactual scenario we find that with lower values of CRR and bank rate, there is an increase in the growth rate of the supply of money. This expansionary monetary impact leads to a marginally higher investment rate and growth rate. The increase in growth rates is due to high growth in all the sectors. In line with what we have found in the corresponding counterfactual simulation for the 1980s, the inflation rate comes down despite an expansionary monetary policy and hence, there is no trade-off between growth and inflation in this scenario.

Impact of Procurement Prices

As we have mentioned earlier, apart from the slowdown in growth during the latter half of the period, the other problem that cropped up during the 1990s is the increasing size of the fiscal imbalance. In the next few simulations, we shall focus on this aspect. One of the most important factors behind the deterioration in the fiscal balance has been the rise in the procurement prices which, on an average, grew at 10 per cent per year during the 1990s. In this simulation, we look at the effect of a lower rate of growth of procurement prices during this period. Accordingly, in the counterfactual scenario, we assume that procurement prices grew at 5 per cent annually for the 1990s.

Table 6.11 presents the annual average values of some important macroeconomic variables for the above period, corresponding to the base run as well as the alternative scenario.

Table 6.11 Impact of Low Growth of Procurement Prices.

Variable	Base run	Counterfactual
GDP growth	5.51	5.43
Agriculture growth	2.92	2.69
Industrial growth	6.08	6.04
Services growth	6.98	7.03
Inflation rate	8.25	8.15
Revenue expenditure ratio	22.87	22.74
Revenue deficit ratio	4.54	4.34
Fiscal deficit ratio	7.67	7.48

Note: The values are averages for the period 1990–1 to 2000–1.

The results indicate that this would lead to a somewhat lower growth rate in the agricultural sector through its effects on agricultural prices. The industrial and services sector growth is almost unchanged and hence there is only a small decrease in the aggregate growth rate. The fall in the growth rate of procurement prices also brings down the inflation rates even though there is no explicit relationship between the two built into the model. There are no surprises on the fiscal front, where the lower growth rate of the procurement prices leads to lower revenue and fiscal deficits as a result of lowering of expenditure on subsidies.

Impact of Tax Reforms

Chapter 4, describing the structural equation of the model, pointed out that a dummy variable representing the tax reforms initiated during the early 1990s had a negative coefficient. This implies that these reforms and their reduction in tax rates had adversely affected the government's capacity to raise tax revenue. Clearly, this would also aggravate the fiscal problem by choking the growth in revenue incomes earned by the government. Here, we carry out a counterfactual exercise, which assumes that there were no tax reforms (including a cut in tax rates) during this period.

Table 6.12 Impact of No Tax Reforms.

Variable	Base run	Counterfactual
GDP growth	5.51	5.41
Inflation rate	8.25	7.79
Direct tax ratio	2.83	3.29
Indirect tax ratio	11.98	13.11
Total tax ratio	14.82	16.4
Revenue deficit ratio	4.54	3.17
Fiscal deficit ratio	7.67	6.29

Note: Same as for Figure 6.11.

Comparing this to the base run, we can assess the extent to which this reform contributed to the fiscal problems during this period. Table 6.12 presents the annual average values of some important macroeconomic variables for the 1990s, corresponding to the base run as well as the alternative scenario. The results indicate that there would be a marginal decrease in the growth and inflation rates. However, in the fiscal sector, there is an increase in tax revenue from direct taxes (income and corporate taxes) as well as indirect taxes (excise taxes). This leads to increases in both direct tax to GDP ratio and indirect tax to GDP ratio. Consequently, there is a significant fall in the revenue deficit and the fiscal deficit.

Impact of Fifth Pay Commission

Another significant contributor to the worsening of the fiscal imbalance during the late 1990s has been the Fifth Pay Commission. Its recommendations that were implemented from the year 1997–8. As a result of this implementation, the average growth rate of the salaries and wages expenditure of the government jumped up to almost 25 per cent for the years 1997–8 and 1998–9, compared to about 14 per cent for the rest of the decade. Here, we shall consider the impact of this pay commission by comparing it to a counterfactual scenario, which assumes that there was no hike in salaries and wages during this period.

Table 6.13 Impact of No Fifth Pay Commission Hike.

Variable	Base run	Counterfactual
GDP growth	5.51	5.38
Industrial growth	6.08	6.01
Inflation rate	8.25	8.06
Revenue expenditure ratio	22.87	22.51
Total expenditure ratio	27.3	26.96
Revenue deficit ratio	4.54	4.15
Fiscal deficit ratio	7.67	7.28

Note: Same as for Figure 6.11.

Table 6.13 presents the annual average values of some important macroeconomic variables for the 1990s, corresponding to the base run as well as the alternative scenario. The simulation results indicate that without the pay hike, the aggregate growth rate falls slightly. This is a result of the fall in the growth rate of GDP from public administration (which is a function of the government wage bill) as well as the growth rate of industry (which is affected by the pay hike due to demand side factors). The lower growth rate is accompanied by lower inflation rates as well, indicating a trade-off between the two in this context. Of course, without the pay hike, the fiscal imbalance gets reduced with a reduction in the revenue expenditure to GDP ratio and the total expenditure to GDP ratio. This results in a fall in the revenue deficit as well as the fiscal deficit.

INFERENCES

During the 1980s, the Indian economy exhibited distinctly higher rates of growth than in the past. It was also the period during which the fiscal balances deteriorated to a large extent. A number of economic factors have been thought to be responsible for these outcomes. These included natural factors like low rainfall as well as policy-induced factors like high monetized deficits, high interest rates, high growth in government employment, high levels of fertilizer subsidy, etc. We have tested the efficacy of these arguments by generating counterfactual simulations. From the model simulations we find that the high monetized borrowing definitely played a role in the high growth rates, largely through the public investments that it financed but also marginally through the government's consumption and overhead expenditures. The drought played only a marginal role in bringing down growth rates during the 1980s, as the agricultural sector seems to have become resilient to such shocks in the long run. However, there was some spillover effect of the drought on the industrial and services sectors. The high interest rates during this period definitely dampened the growth impetus. Moreover they were quite unnecessary as part of a tight monetary policy, as lower interest rates would not have been inflationary in this context. As far as fiscal deficits are concerned, the high rates of monetized borrowings that financed the high rates of government expenditure did lead to greater fiscal imbalance. Lowering the growth rate of government employment would have reduced the fiscal imbalance but it would have also brought down the growth rate, mainly through a fall in the public administration sector growth. Similarly, a lower agricultural subsidy would have brought down the fiscal deficit but at the cost of the agricultural and aggregate growth rates.

The 1990s started off disastrously for the Indian economy with the country facing its worst external crisis. This was followed by the adoption of a package of market friendly reforms leading to a period of high rates of growth. During the second half of the decade however, the high growth petered out and the economy experienced a slowdown. The decade also experienced an improvement in the fiscal imbalances during the first half of the decade and a corresponding deterioration during the second half. Various natural and policy-induced factors have been suspected to be responsible for the performance of the economy during this period and our model simulation tries to test some of these hypotheses. We find that the oil price hike and the drought at the beginning of the decade did not have any significant impact on the growth rates, inflation rates, or the fiscal deficit. This again underlines the resilience of the economy to such shocks. Next we study the impact of the regime change and adoption of market friendly reforms on the performance of the economy. The overall growth show no significant upturn during the 1990s as a result of reforms. However, they have been very successful in keeping a check on inflation rates and the fiscal and external deficits. The slowdown during the second half of the decade has sometimes been associated with the reduction in borrowing from the RBI, the poor rains during the end of the decade, or the high interest rates during this period. The simulations indicate that in the absence of the reduction in borrowings from RBI, the growth rate would have been higher, particularly if the borrowings had financed higher public investments. Poor rainfall also had a role to play in the slowdown, as did a high interest rate regime. Significantly, a lower interest rate regime would not have been inflationary in this case. The fiscal balance, as we have already mentioned, was kept in check by the reforms. However a higher rate of growth of procurement prices, reduction in tax rates, and a hike in salaries by the fifth pay commission all resulted in a rising fiscal deficit; although in all these cases, these factors also had a small but positive impact on growth rates.

Some broad conclusions can be drawn about the Indian economy on the basis of the analysis of the 1980s and 1990s. First, most growth-oriented policy packages have tended to achieve their goal but also resulted in imbalances in the other sectors. Moreover, packages like higher government expenditure have exhibited very different degrees of success in giving a boost to growth depending on the composition of these expenditures. Public investments in particular give rise to much higher rates of growth than other forms of government expenditure. As far as the reforms are concerned, it seems that their principal utility lies in keeping a check on macroeconomic imbalances. Lastly, the goods news for the economy is that it is increasingly becoming more and more resilient to exogenous shocks.

7

Resilience to Shocks and Prospects for the Future

The Indian economy attained an impressive average growth rate of about 5.6 per cent in the last two decades of the twentieth century. Behind these average growth rates, however, lies the story of significant growth fluctuations. On the one hand, there are periods that experienced growth meltdowns as a result of domestic and external shocks. Two episodes of such shock-induced meltdown stand out in particular. These are: (i) the fall in the growth rate from 5 per cent in 1978 to – 5.2 per cent in 1979 and (ii) the fall in the growth rate from 5.5 per cent in 1990 to 1.3 per cent in 1991. On the other hand, there are periods of very high growth, for example, during the mid-1990s, when the economy grew by more than 7 per cent per annum. These varied growth experiences throw up two important questions.

- What is the degree of resilience of the economy to internal and external shocks?
- What is the probable (future) rate of growth of the Indian economy, in the absence of such shocks?

In this chapter, we shall deal with these two issues. The first part of the chapter presents a modified version of the earlier model that will be used for the analysis in this chapter. The second part of the chapter deals with the impact of shocks. The third part presents some short and long run analysis of future growth prospects of the Indian economy, in the absence of any shocks.

THE MODEL

In Chapters 4 and 5, we have presented a very large and disaggregated macroeconometric model of the Indian economy. The strength of that model is that it gives an in-depth insight into the structure of the Indian economy. The large size of the model, however, is not very useful when the objective is to generate simulations and forecasts. In this chapter we will present a modified version of the macromodel that is much smaller in size but much more useful from the point of view of simulations and forecasts. The modifications involve two kinds of changes—changes in the theoretical structure of the model as well as a change in the database (resulting in changes in the coefficients of the estimated equations of the model). Why do we make these modifications in our model? First, our simulation and forecasting exercise is going to focus on a more aggregated level of activity and this enables us to use a smaller and more aggregated model. Keeping this in mind, we modified the theoretical structure of the structural model, making it more aggregated and smaller in size. The reason for re-estimating the model using a different database is that the CSO came out with a new database after the original model was already estimated. Since it is important to take into account all new information in order to generate better forecasts of the future, we estimated this model using the new database. In this section, we present the modified model.

The Indian economy is heterogeneous in terms of production, investment, and price behaviour. Hence we have divided the economy into three parts namely, the agricultural sector, the industrial sector, and the tertiary sector (which includes services sectors and public administration) and for each sector we have an output, private investment, and price function (GDP deflator). To incorporate dynamic behaviour and to distinguish between the short and long run effects, we have incorporated lagged dependent variables in the estimation of all these functions. In the case of output, this would represent the generalized distributed lag behaviour between output and capital. In the case of investment this would represent the discrepancy between the desired and actual investment behaviour. In the case of prices, the lagged dependent variable will incorporate the adaptive expectations in price formation. It may be noted that in our model presented below, figures in parenthesis are standard errors. Number of *s on the right side of regressors indicates the level of significance of the coefficients (* denotes 10 per cent, ** denotes 5 per cent, and *** denotes 1 per cent level of significance). Dw and Dh gives the Durbin watron and Durbin's h statistic.

We postulate that agricultural output (XA) is constrained by supply side factors like capital stock in agriculture (KA) and rainfall (RF). The agricultural output function has an irregular dummy DUMXA (representing the extreme drought effect of 1979) and a structural dummy D80S (to take care of the secular fall in agricultural growth since the 1980s).

$$\begin{aligned} XA = EXP(&-8.16 + 1.43{*}LOG(KA)^{***} + 0.27{*}LOG(RF)^{***} \\ &\ (1.31) \quad\ (0.24) \qquad\qquad\qquad (0.05) \\ &- 0.12{*}D80S^{***} - 0.14{*}DUMXA^{***} + 0.10{*}LOG(XA(-1))) \\ &\ (0.03) \qquad\qquad\quad (0.03) \qquad\qquad\qquad (0.14) \end{aligned}$$

$$R^2 = 0.99 \qquad Dh = -1.06 \qquad (7.1)$$

The results indicate that capital stock in agriculture and rainfall affects agricultural output significantly. The relatively low value of the lagged dependent variable shows that capital formation in agriculture does not have a strong long run impact on output in this sector.

Industrial sector output (XI) and tertiary sector output (XT) are postulated to be functions of the productive capacity in these sectors and the capacity utilization rates. The productive capacity is determined by the capital stock (KI and KT) since large pools of unemployed labour ensure that there are no labour constraints in these sectors. Consistent with some recent theoretical and empirical studies on India, we postulate that output and capacity utilization in industry and the tertiary sector are sensitive to changes in demand. In the industrial output function (see Equation 7.2), domestic and external demand are represented by the autonomous expenditure (RAE), which is the sum of government expenditure and exports of goods and services. Industry also depends on agricultural demand. Moreover, industrial output is negatively related to industrial price (PI), again reflecting the demand-constrained nature of this sector. The industrial output function has two structural dummies, DPLIB (representing the partial liberalization of the economy in the mid-1980s) and D95 (representing the peak effect of liberalization in 1995 following large deregulation of the economy in 1994). In the tertiary sector, the demand constraints are captured by the commodity output (XCOM), that is, the sum of the output in the other two sectors. The tertiary output function (Equation 7.3) has two dummies DPLIB (partial liberalization) and DUMPAY (representing the impact of large hikes in the salaries and wages of public administration that inflate the value added in the tertiary sector).

$$XI = EXP(-2.57 + 0.08*LOG(KI) + 0.34*LOG(XA)^{***}$$
$$\quad (0.83) \quad (0.09) \quad (0.07)$$
$$+ 0.18*LOG(RAE)^{***} - 0.06*LOG(PI) + 0.02*DPLIB$$
$$(0.05) \quad (0.04) \quad (0.01)$$
$$+ 0.6*LOG(XI(-1))^{***} + 0.04*D95^{**})$$
$$(0.06) \quad (0.01)$$
$$R^2 = 0.99 \qquad Dh = -1.32 \qquad (7.2)$$

$$XT = EXP(-5.06 + 0.67*LOG(KT)^{***} + 0.13*LOG(XCOM)^{**}$$
$$\quad (1.02) \quad (0.17) \quad (0.05)$$
$$+ 0.01*DUMPAY^{*} + 0.02*DPLIB^{**} + 0.52*LOG(XT(-1))^{***})$$
$$(0.006) \quad (0.008) \quad (0.09)$$
$$R^2 = 0.99 \qquad Dh = -1.54 \qquad (7.3)$$

The results indicate that demand side factors like agricultural output and autonomous expenditure are the crucial determinants of industrial output. Capital stock has a small impact on current period output but the lagged dependent variable indicates that capital has a strong long-term impact on industrial output. The output in the tertiary sector is largely determined by capital stock, which has an impact on current as well as future services output. The demand factor, that is, the output from the commodity producing sectors also affects the output in this sector.

The capital stock in each of the three sectors is the sum of past capital stock in that sector (adjusted for depreciation) and private and public investments in that sector. The private investment functions are postulated to be a synthesis of a Flexible Accelerator Theory and a Keynesian investment function (represented by interest rate). It may be noted that due to institutional constraints, non-agriculturalists cannot invest in agriculture. Hence the agricultural investment function is based on agricultural output whereas the same in industry and tertiary sectors are dependent on aggregate GDP. The components of government expenditures also plays a crucial role in investments. We have postulated that public investment (IGA, IGI, and IGT) plays a positive role by crowding-in private investments, reflecting the fact that the Indian economy is still constrained by physical infrastructure, etc. On the other hand, other government expenditures (ORGE)—including government consumption and transfers—loosely representing the fiscal profligacy of the government, crowd-out private investment by using up scarce resources. Agricultural investments (IPA) have a structural dummy D80S (representing a secular fall since the 1980s). The industrial and tertiary sector investment functions (IPI and IPT) have an irregular dummy D95 (peak liberalization effect).

$$\begin{aligned}IPA = &-4714.17 + 0.05*XA^{***} + 0.44*IGA^{**} - 2700.76*D80S^{***}\\ &(1704.33)\quad(0.01)\qquad(0.2)\qquad(706.1)\\ &+0.28*IPA(-1)^{**}\\ &(0.13)\end{aligned}$$

$R^2 = 0.9$ Dh = – 1.81 (7.4)

$$\begin{aligned}IPI = &-25029.76 + 0.20*XGDP^{***} + 0.71*IGI^{**} - 0.56*ORGE^{***}\\ &(10074.05)\quad(0.04)\qquad(0.3)\qquad(0.13)\\ &-649.003*RPLR - 939.56*IFR + 41506.12*D95^{***}\\ &(696.28)\qquad(791.82)\qquad(7846.02)\\ &+0.22*IPI(-1)^{*}\\ &(0.11)\end{aligned}$$

$R^2 = 0.96$ Dh = – 0.91 (7.5)

$$\begin{aligned}IPT = &-33116.9 + 0.08*XGDP^{**} + 0.71*IGT - 663.11*RPLR\\ &(12348.49)\quad(0.04)\qquad(1.1)\qquad(590.26)\\ &-2920.68*DFEMRPLR^{*} + 0.45*IPT(-1)^{**}\\ &(1628.1)\qquad(0.19)\end{aligned}$$

$R^2 = 0.86$ DW = 2.07 (Dh not computable) (7.6)

The results indicate that the accelerator plays a strong role in determining private investment in all three sectors. Further, public investment crowds-in investment in the agricultural and the industrial sectors, but not in the tertiary sector. Similarly, other government expenditures crowd-out investment only in the industrial sector. The real interest rates (RPLR) have no impact on private investment in agriculture and a weak impact on industrial and tertiary sector investment. In the industrial sector, this is partly due to the fact that investors are worried about inflationary tendencies (IFR).

As far as public investment is concerned, it is assumed that the government exogenously determines their nominal values in all three sectors.

The demand side of the economy is largely determined by private consumption, while the other components are government consumption and investment, private investment, and net exports. Private consumption (RCP) is postulated to be a function of private disposable income (RPDI). The private consumption function has a lagged dependent variable representing long run adjustments of consumption to income and a structural dummy DWTO (representing the effect of higher consumption of imported goods following the opening up of trade under the WTO agreement).

$$\begin{aligned} RCP = EXP(&\underset{(0.33)}{2.89} + \underset{(0.06)}{0.65}*LOG(RPDI)^{***} + \underset{(0.01)}{0.03}*DWTO^{***} \\ &+ \underset{(0.08)}{0.11}*LOG(RCP(-1))) \end{aligned}$$

$R^2 = 0.99$ Dh = 1.74 (7.7)

The results show that like in many other developing economies, private consumption is largely determined by private disposable income. The low significance of the lagged dependent variable indicates that income does not have strong long run effect on consumption.

Private disposable income is equal to nominal output at factor cost (YGDP) plus government transfers minus taxes. The nominal output at factor cost is estimated to have a unitary elasticity with nominal output at market prices (GDPMP).

$$YGDP = EXP(\underset{(0.03)}{-0.08} + \underset{(0.002)}{0.99}*LOG(GDPMP)^{***}) + [AR(1)=\underset{(0.12)}{0.66}^{***}]$$

$R^2 = 0.99$ DW = 2.05 (7.8)

The aggregate GDP deflator is assumed to be a weighted average of the sectoral deflators, the weights being the share of the sectors in real output in the base year (1993). Agricultural prices (PA) are determined by both demand and supply factors. Agricultural output determines the supply in this sector while private disposable income (PDI) determines demand for agricultural output. The agricultural price function has an outlier dummy DUMPA (that takes care of the unusually high agricultural prices in 1973 and 1974 as a result of severe drought conditions in those years).

$$\begin{aligned} PA = EXP(&\underset{(1.71)}{4.002} - \underset{(0.15)}{0.71}*LOG(XA)^{***} + \underset{(0.08)}{0.59}*LOG(PDI)^{***} \\ &+ \underset{(0.02)}{0.12}*DUMPA^{***} + \underset{(0.14)}{0.31}*LOG(PA(-1)^{**})) \end{aligned}$$

$R^2 = 0.99$ Dh = 1.29 (7.9)

The industrial sector is assumed to have mark-up pricing and hence cost factors determine industrial prices (PI). The cost factors include agricultural prices, tariff rates (TRF), and import prices of oil (PMO) and non-oil commodities (PMN) separately.

$$\begin{aligned} PI = EXP(&-0.20 + 0.37{*}LOG(PA)^{***} + 0.05{*}LOG(PMO)^{***} \\ &(0.06)\quad (0.05) \qquad\qquad\qquad (0.009) \\ &+ 0.01{*}LOG(PMN) + 0.53{*}LOG(PI(-1)^{***}) \\ &(0.014) \qquad\qquad\qquad (0.05) \\ &+ 0.06{*}LOG(TRF)^{***}) \\ &(0.013) \end{aligned}$$

$R^2 = 0.99$ Dh = 0.61 (7.10)

The tertiary sector prices (PT) are assumed to adjust to agricultural and industrial prices.

$$\begin{aligned} PT = EXP(&\,0.11 + 0.16{*}LOG(PA)^{***} + 0.42{*}LOG(PI)^{***} \\ &(0.01)\quad (0.02) \qquad\qquad\qquad (0.04) \\ &+ 0.39{*}LOG(PT(-1)^{***})) \\ &(0.04) \end{aligned}$$

$R^2 = 0.99$ Dh = 0.61 (7.11)

The results indicate that both the demand and the supply factors are equally important in the determination of agricultural prices. Industrial prices are found to be strongly affected by agricultural prices, tariff rates, and import prices of oil but the import prices of non-oil commodities have no impact on them. The tertiary sector prices are strongly affected by prices in the other two sectors.

In the monetary sector, we assume that the demand and supply of money determine the interest rate, which in our model is the prime lending rate of commercial banks. The demand for money in real terms (RM3) is estimated to be a function of real output and real interest rates. The function has an irregular dummy DUMM3 and a structural dummy DWTO (representing higher consumption demand for money corresponding to the rise in consumption in that period).

From the results, we find that the coefficient of real interest rates has the wrong sign (positive) but shows the right sign (negative) with a slope dummy DFEMRPLR for financial and external sector liberalization. This is due to the fact that the monetary sector was stringently controlled before the liberalization of the economy and hence the positive relation between interest and money before liberalization actually represents the money supply function. In other words, the market determined interest rate is a post-liberalization phenomenon.

$$\begin{aligned}
RM3 = EXP(&-9.801 + 1.68{*}LOG(XGDP)^{***} + 0.008{*}RPLR^{***} \\
&\quad (0.5) \quad (0.03) \qquad\qquad\qquad (0.002) \\
&- 0.01{*}DFEMRPLR^{***} + 0.19{*}DUMM3^{***} \\
&\quad (0.004) \qquad\qquad\qquad (0.03) \\
&- 0.07{*}DWTO^{*}) \\
&\quad (0.03)
\end{aligned}$$

$$R^2 = 0.99 \qquad DW = 1.52 \qquad (7.12)$$

Given the demand for money, the interest rate is determined by the supply for money, which is assumed to be a function of the reserve money in the economy and the money multiplier. We postulate that the money multiplier is a function of interest rate and two monetary policy instruments namely, the bank rate (BR) and the CRR. In the model, we invert the supply function of money by estimating interest rate (PLR) as a function of money supply (M3), reserve money (M0), and the monetary policy variables.

$$\begin{aligned}
PLR = &\ 0.49 + 1.65e-05{*}M3^{***} - 7.2e-05{*}M0^{***} + 0.43{*}CRR^{***} \\
&(1.42) \quad (3.9e-06) \qquad\quad (1.7e-05) \qquad (0.09) \\
&+ 1.13{*}BR^{***} \\
&\quad (0.21)
\end{aligned}$$

$$R^2 = 0.88 \qquad DW = 2.45 \qquad (7.13)$$

The results indicate that interest rates are strongly affected by money supply, reserve money, and the monetary policy variables. It may be noted that the reserve money has two main components—monetized debt of the government net of non-monetary liabilities and foreign exchange reserves.

In the fiscal sector, government expenditure is equal to government consumption, investments, and transfers, all of which are assumed to be exogenous variables. The revenue side consists of tax and non-tax revenue, of which the latter is assumed to be exogenous. Tax revenue (TAX) is estimated as a function of nominal output (GDPMP). The tax function has two dummies DLIB (representing the effects of lowering of domestic tax rates as a part of the liberalization process) and DWTO (representing effects of lowering customs duties following India joining the WTO).

$$\begin{aligned} TAX = EXP(&-2.95 + 1.08^{*}LOG(GDPMP)^{***} - 0.104^{*}DLIB^{***} \\ &\;\;(0.18)\quad(0.01)\qquad\qquad\qquad\qquad(0.02) \\ &- 0.11^{*}DWTO^{***}) \\ &\;\;(0.02) \end{aligned}$$

$$R^2 = 0.99 \qquad DW = 1.906 \qquad (7.14)$$

The difference between the revenue earned and the expenditure gives the gross fiscal deficit.

In the external sector, the CAB is the sum of net exports and remittances, etc. Exports (EGS) are postulated to be a function of the volume of world trade (WT)—which is proxied in our model by world imports—and the depreciation in the real exchange rate. The export function has three structural change dummies—D80S (representing the beginning of export promotion policies since the 1980s), DFEM (representing the effect of trade and exchange rate deregulation in 1993), and DWTO (representing the positive effect on exports of joining the WTO). It also has an irregular dummy DUMEGS.

$$\begin{aligned} EGS = EXP(&-6.62 + 1.02^{*}LOG(WT)^{***} + 0.34^{*}LOG(REXR)^{**} \\ &\;\;(1.13)\quad(0.05)\qquad\qquad\qquad(0.14) \\ &+ 0.09^{*}D80S + 0.12^{*}DFEM^{*} + 0.14^{*}DWTO^{**} \\ &\;\;(0.05)\qquad\quad(0.06)\qquad\quad(0.05) \\ &+ 0.23^{*}DUMEGS^{***}) \\ &\;\;(0.05) \end{aligned}$$

$$R^2 = 0.99 \qquad DW = 1.49 \qquad (7.15)$$

The results show that world trade is the most important determinant of exports although the depreciation in real exchange rate is also found to boost exports.

Imports are divided into two parts, oil imports and non-oil imports. It may be noted that oil imports were extremely volatile before 1985 due to the two oil shocks as well as the discovery and extraction of large volumes of oil since the beginning of the 1980s. Hence we have estimated the oil import function post-1985. We postulate that oil imports (MGSO) are strongly related to commodity production (the tertiary sector is much less oil intensive), import price of oil (PMO), domestic prices (PGDP), and exchange rate (EXR)(the last three determining the relative price of oil). It also has an irregular dummy DUMMGSO.

$$\begin{aligned} MGSO = EXP(&-3.26 + 0.43^{*}LOG(XCOM)^{*} \\ &\;\;(2.09) \quad (0.21) \\ &+ 1.005^{*}LOG(PMO)^{***} + 0.55^{*}LOG(PGDP)^{**} \\ &\;\;(0.02) \qquad\qquad (0.2) \\ &- 0.69^{*}LOG(EXR)^{***} + 0.05^{*}DUMMGSO^{***}) \\ &\;\;(0.1) \qquad\qquad (0.01) \end{aligned}$$

$R^2 = 0.99$ DW = 1.85 (7.16)

The non-oil imports (MGSN) are postulated to be a function of output, price of non-oil imports (PMN), domestic prices, exchange rate, and tariff rates. The non-oil import function also has two structural dummies D95 (peak liberalization effect) and DWTO (effect of joining WTO).

$$\begin{aligned} MGSN = EXP(&-10.22 + 1.37^{*}LOG(XGDP)^{***} \\ &\;\;(2.29) \quad (0.2) \\ &+ 0.09^{*}LOG(PMN)^{**} + 1.36^{*}LOG(PGDP)^{***} \\ &\;\;(0.03) \qquad\qquad (0.1) \\ &- 1.34^{*}LOG(EXR)^{***} - 0.18^{*}LOG(TRF)^{***} \\ &\;\;(0.06) \qquad\qquad (0.03) \\ &+ 0.18^{*}D95^{***} + 0.05^{*}DWTO) \\ &\;\;(0.05) \qquad\quad (0.04) \end{aligned}$$

$R^2 = 0.99$ DW = 1.66 (7.17)

The results show that oil imports are largely determined by factors that affect its relative price, that is, import price of oil, domestic prices, and the exchange rate. Non-oil imports are also strongly affected by these three variables as well as the level of output and tariff rates.

The foreign exchange reserves are equal to the sum of past reserves, the CAB, and the capital account balance. The capital account balance is assumed to be an exogenous variable. The exchange rate (EXR) is hypothesized to be a function of the foreign exchange reserve (FER) as well as prices in the economy. We also postulate that the exchange rate adjusts to its past values. There is a dummy in the exchange rate equation DEV91 (representing a large devaluation undertaken in 1991).

$$\begin{aligned}EXR = EXP(&\underset{(0.1)}{0.39} - \underset{(0.01)}{0.07}*LOG(FER)^{***} + \underset{(0.04)}{0.27}*LOG(PGDP)^{***}\\ &+ \underset{(0.04)}{0.19}*DEV91^{***} + \underset{(0.06)}{0.69}*LOG(EXR(-1))^{***})\end{aligned}$$

$R^2 = 0.99$ Dh = – 1.17 (7.18)

The results indicate that the exchange rate is strongly influenced by the size of the foreign exchange reserve (FER), as well as prices in the economy. The exchange rate is also found to adjust to past values.

VALIDATION OF THE MODEL

The basic objective of building a macroeconometric model is to analyse and forecast macroeconomic variables. Before that however, it is important to look at how effective the model is in explaining the economy. A detailed investigation of error behaviour was presented in Chapter 5 in the context of the larger and disaggregated model using various measures such as the RMSE, TIS, MAE and MAPE. In this section we demonstrate the efficacy of the smaller (forecast) model simply by comparing the actual and forecast values of some of the important variables. Table 7.1 presents the average annual values of historical data and base run simulations of eighteen key endogenous variables covering the period 1997 to 2003.

From this table it is clear that the model has simulated the Indian economy fairly accurately. It may be noted that while our regressions (and hence our model) are based on a far longer period (1970–2003), the validation is for a much smaller period that we have chosen for the counterfactual scenarios (1997–2003). This validation therefore shows that although the economy underwent significant structural changes during the period after 1994 due to liberalization of the economy, the model takes care of these changes and represents the economy quite accurately.

Apart from the table, graphical representations of base run simulations and historical values of growth and inflation rates (for the simulation period) are presented in Appendix 9. These show that apart from approximating the historical long-run average values of the endogenous variables quite accurately, the simulations also predict the annual values of these variables reasonably well.

Table 7.1 Actual and Base Run Simulation Values (annual averages for 1997–2003).

Variables	GDP growth	Agricultural growth	Industrial growth	Tertiary growth	Investment rate	Inflation rate
Actual	5.6	2.4	4.7	7.9	23.8	4.8
Base run	5.9	2.6	5.7	8.0	24.1	4.9
Variables	Agricultural inflation	Industrial inflation	Money growth	Interest rate	Tax ratio	Government expenditure ratio
Actual	5.0	4.7	16.2	12.0	14.2	28.4
Base run	4.8	4.7	16.4	11.4	14.3	29.0
Variables	Gross fiscal deficit ratio	Exports	Imports	Current account balance	Foreign exchange reserves	Exchange rate
Actual	10.5	62.8	67.4	– 0.5	55.0	44.1
Base run	11.0	63.3	68.1	– 0.7	58.6	45.1

Note: All rates (except the exchange rate) and ratios are in percentage terms. The external sector variables are in billion US dollars. The exchange rate is in rupees/dollar.

Now that the model has been validated we shall use it to (i) evaluate the impact of shocks on the growth rates of the Indian economy and (ii) evaluate the future growth prospects of the economy in the absence of shocks. We shall analyse the impact of the shocks by comparing the equilibrium values of growth rates and related variables under base run (normal) and alternate scenarios (with shocks). The analysis of future growth prospects in the absence of shocks is based on equilibrium values of growth rates under normal conditions in the short and long run.

SHOCKS AND THE INDIAN ECONOMY

Analysing the impact of shocks is of utmost importance, as the consequences of these shocks push millions of people into abject poverty and deprivation. In this study we look at the impact of three external shocks (oil price hike, world trade shock, and capital flow shock) and two domestic shocks (rainfall shortfall and fiscal profligacy) that affect the economy through various channels.

Shocks have a short run and a long run impact. In the model described above, the long run effects have been incorporated in terms of dynamic specifications of some behavioural equations using lagged dependent variables. In the shock simulations, we assume the shocks to impact the economy in the first two years of the chosen period, that is, 1997 and 1998. Correspondingly, the average performance in these two years will represent the short run impact of the shocks. The average performance for the whole period, that is, 1997 to 2003, will represent the long run impact of the shocks.

In the simulation exercises, we shall focus on five aspects of the impact of the shocks on growth. The first aspect is the actual impact of the shock on the aggregate growth rate, that is, whether the shock leads to a mild or large fall in growth rate (as a percentage over base run values). The second aspect is the sectoral distribution of the shock, which implies how much each of the three sectors (agriculture, industry, and tertiary) contributes to the negative impact of the shocks on growth rates. The third aspect is to find whether the shock leads to a stagflationary situation or not. This is particularly important from the policy point of view since non-stagflationary shocks can be mitigated by using demand management policies while stagflationary situations sometimes worsen with the use of such policies. The fourth aspect that we shall focus on is the effect of the shocks on the fiscal and external sectors. This is important because a large increase in the deficits in these sectors (in terms of rising fiscal deficit ratio and falling foreign exchange reserves) has the potential to destabilize future growth rates by affecting investor confidence in the economy. Thus it is important to look at the impact on the actual growth rate as well as these variables. The fifth and final aspect that we shall look into is the pervasiveness of the shock, that is, how much of the short run impact of the shock spills over to the long run. This is again important from the policy perspective, since a pervasive shock indicates that the economy is not very resilient to this shock, making counter-shock policies that much more important.

Oil Price Shock

The first scenario represents an oil price shock. We assume that the price index of oil imports rises by 100 per cent over actual values in 1997 and 1998. Thus, the price index goes up in 1997 from 540 to 1080 and in 1998 from 440 to 880, respectively. The average price during this period jumps by about 50 per cent over 1996. This may be compared to the oil shock in 1979–80 when the corresponding jump was about 125 per cent. Thus it is a plausible shock though not of the extreme nature as the first and second international oil price shocks. The results of the simulation together with the base run are given in Table 7.2.

Table 7.2 Effect of Oil Price Shock.

	Variables	GDP growth	Agricultural growth	Industrial growth	Tertiary growth	Aggregate inflation	Industrial inflation	Gross fiscal deficit ratio	Foreign exchange reserves
Short run	Base run	6.7	3.3	4.7	10.2	7.3	5.6	7.6	36.1
	Shock	6.5	3.2	4.3	9.9	8.4	8.4	8.0	26.9
	% change	– 3.0	– 3.0	– 8.5	– 2.9	15.1	50.0	5.3	– 25.5
Long run	Base run	5.9	2.6	5.7	8.0	4.9	4.7	11.0	58.6
	Shock	5.7	2.5	5.5	7.7	5.1	4.9	10.8	55.0
	% change	– 3.4	– 3.8	– 3.5	– 3.8	4.1	4.3	– 1.8	– 6.1

Notes: In the shock scenario, oil price index is assumed to be 1080 in 1997 instead of 540 (base run value), and in 1998 it is assumed to be 880 instead of 440 (base run value). The row showing % change measures percentage increases in value of variables in shock scenario over base run values. Thus for shock scenario values that are lower than base run values % change is negative.

The table indicates that in the short run there is a small decrease in the growth rate (3 per cent) as a result of this shock. This fall is largely due to a corresponding fall in the industrial growth rates, with the other sectors contributing much less to this fall. Inflation rises by 15 per cent as a result of a large rise in industrial inflation, leading to a slightly stagflationary situation. There is no instability to the growth process from the fiscal sector, but a significant fall in the foreign exchange reserves as a result of the shock, gives rise to some instability to growth from the external sector. In the long run, the growth falls by 3.4 per cent, which is slightly larger than the fall in the short run. This indicates that the impact of the shock is pervasive, that is, the impact does not become weaker in the long run. The fall in the long run growth rate is the result of similar fall in all the sectors. This indicates that the shock has greater long run impact on the growth of the agricultural and tertiary sectors. The rise in inflation is more muted and there is no instability from the fiscal or external sectors.

World Trade Shock

The second scenario represents a world trade shock. In this scenario, we assume that the rate of growth of world imports is zero in 1997 instead of an actual growth of about 3.3 per cent and it is assumed to be – 4 per cent in 1998 instead of an actual growth rate of – 1.4 per cent. Thus the average growth in world imports in this period is assumed to be about – 2 per cent, while the actual average growth was about 1 per cent, that is, a fall of about 3 per cent. This is comparable to an average fall of about 3 per cent in 1981 and 1982, the sharpest fall in world imports in the recent past. It may be noted that although stagnation in world trade can also lead to changes in prices of imports, this scenario does not assume any such changes in import prices. The results of the simulation together with the base run are given in Table 7.3.

Table 7.3 Effect of World Trade Shock.

	Variables	GDP growth	Agricultural growth	Industrial growth	Tertiary growth	Exports	Aggregate inflation	Gross fiscal deficit ratio	Foreign exchange reserves
Short run	Base run	6.7	3.3	4.7	10.2	47.5	7.3	7.6	36.1
	Shock	6.5	3.3	4.4	9.8	42.8	6.4	8.3	31.3
	% change	– 3.0	0.0	– 6.4	– 3.9	– 9.9	–12.3	9.2	– 13.3
Long run	Base run	5.9	2.6	5.7	8.0	63.3	4.9	11.0	58.6
	Shock	5.9	2.6	5.8	7.9	62.2	4.8	11.3	56.5
	% change	0.0	0.0	1.8	– 1.3	–1.7	–2.0	2.7	– 3.6

Note: In the shock scenario, rate of growth of world imports is assumed to be zero in 1997 instead of 3.3 per cent (base run value), and in 1998 it is assumed to be – 4 per cent instead of – 1.4 per cent (base-run value). The row showing '% change' measures percentage increases in value of variables in shock scenario over base run values.

The table shows that in the short run, there is a small fall in the growth rate as a result of this shock (three per cent). The world trade shock leads to a fall in exports demand and this brings down the industrial and tertiary growth rates, while agricultural growth rates are untouched. The fall in aggregate demand (as a result of the fall of exports demand) dampens the inflation rate and hence, there is no stagflationary situation in this case. The fiscal balance and external reserves deteriorate, bringing some instability to the growth process. In the long run, there is no effect on the growth rate, indicating that this shock is completely temporary and not pervasive at all. This is due to the fact that while the shock has no impact on agriculture and some negative impact on the tertiary sector, the industrial sector gets a positive boost from this shock in the long run due to a fall in inflation rates (since industrial output is inversely related to price) and this more than makes up for the fall in growth rates in the tertiary sector. There is no instability in the long run from the fiscal or external sectors.

Capital Flow Shock

The third scenario represents a capital flow shock. It may be noted that the initial years of the simulation period saw the incidence of global financial market instability and the resultant East Asia crisis. Although India was left largely untouched by this shock, it would be worthwhile to see what would have happened if it did have an impact. In this scenario, we assume that the capital account balance is zero in both 1997 and 1998 instead of actual values of 10 billion dollars and 8.2 billion dollars respectively. The results of the simulation together with the base run are given in Table 7.4.

The table shows that the shock has a very small impact on the growth rate in the short run. This is due to the fact that the shock leaves the agricultural sector completely untouched and even gives a boost to industrial growth rates in the short run by bringing down inflation rates. Thus it is only the negative impact on the tertiary sector that gives rise to the fall in GDP growth rates. The fall in inflation rates ensures that the situation is not stagflationary. There is no instability to the growth process from the fiscal sector but a sharp fall in the foreign exchange reserves as a result of the shock gives rise to some instability to growth from the external sector. In the long run, the percentage fall is small (1.7 per cent) but it is larger than the short run impact, indicating the pervasive nature of this shock. The fall in growth is completely due to the tertiary sector, while the other two sectors have no long run impact. There is no instability in the long run from the fiscal or external sectors.

Table 7.4 Effect of Capital Flow Shock.

	Variables	GDP growth	Agricultural growth	Industrial growth	Tertiary growth	Aggregate inflation	Gross fiscal deficit ratio	Foreign exchange reserves
Short run	Base run	6.7	3.3	4.7	10.2	7.3	7.6	36.1
	Shock	6.6	3.3	4.9	9.7	7.2	7.6	25.5
	% change	– 1.5	0.0	4.3	– 4.9	– 1.4	0.0	– 29.4
Long run	Base run	5.9	2.6	5.7	8.0	4.9	11.0	58.6
	Shock	5.8	2.6	5.7	7.7	5.0	10.8	54.3
	% change	– 1.7	0.0	0.0	– 3.8	2.0	– 1.8	– 7.3

Note: In the shock scenario, capital account balance is assumed to be zero in both 1997 and 1998 instead of 10 billion dollars and 8.2 billion dollars respectively (base run values). The row showing '% change' measures percentage increases in value of variables in shock scenario over base run values.

Rainfall Shock

The fourth scenario represents a rainfall shock. Here, the rainfall index is assumed to be 80 in both 1997 and 1998, whereas the actual values were 102 and 106 respectively. It may be noted that the index is 100 in case of normal rainfall, and a value of 80 has given rise to drought conditions in 1979, 1987, and more recently in 2002. It may also be noted, that although such conditions are usually accompanied by government intervention, this scenario does not assume any reaction to the drought by the government. The results of the simulation and the base run are given in Table 7.5.

Table 7.5 Effect of Rainfall Shock.

	Variables	GDP growth	Agricultural growth	Industrial growth	Tertiary growth	Aggregate inflation	Agricultural inflation	Gross fiscal deficit ratio	Foreign exchange reserves
Short run	Base run	6.7	3.3	4.7	10.2	7.3	9.0	7.6	36.1
	Shock	4.3	– 1.7	0.7	10.1	11.7	16.2	6.5	35.3
	% change	– 35.8	– 151.5	– 85.1	– 1.0	60.3	80.0	–14.5	– 2.2
Long run	Base run	5.9	2.6	5.7	8.0	4.9	4.8	11.0	58.6
	Shock	5.3	2.0	4.5	7.6	5.9	6.1	10.0	59.7
	% change	– 10.2	– 23.1	– 21.1	– 5.0	20.4	27.1	– 9.1	1.9

Note: In the shock scenario, rainfall index is assumed to be 80 in both 1997 and 1998 instead of 102 and 106, respectively (base run values). The row showing '% change' measures percentage increases in value of variables in shock scenario over base run values.

The table indicates that there is a substantial fall in growth rate (almost 36 per cent) in the short run, as a result of this shock. This is due to a debilitating impact on the agricultural growth rates, which also has a significant spillover onto the industrial growth rates. The tertiary sector is almost unaffected by this shock in the short run. There is a large increase in the inflation rates (about 60 per cent) largely due to high agricultural inflation, leading to an acute stagflationary situation. There are no significant changes in the fiscal and external situation. The long run growth also falls significantly (by about 10 per cent) but it is a much smaller fall compared to the short run, indicating that the resilience of the economy to this shock makes it less pervasive. The fall in long run growth rates is again almost entirely due to the agricultural and industrial sectors, while the tertiary sector is much less affected. The inflation rates also rise significantly leading to a long run stagflationary situation. There is no instability in the long run from the fiscal or external sectors.

Fiscal Profligacy

The fifth scenario represents a case of fiscal profligacy. There is no objective definition of fiscal profligacy though it is loosely used to describe unproductive expenditure of the government. For our study, we have assumed fiscal profligacy to mean an increase in the state's revenue expenditure, which is financed (at least partly) by cutting back capital expenditure. In this scenario it is assumed that both government transfer and government consumption are 1 per cent (of nominal GDP) higher than in the base run in both 1997 and 1998. Simultaneously, public investment is assumed to be 1 per cent (of nominal GDP) lower than the base run in both the years. Since the cut in public investments does not fully cover the increase in revenue expenditure, this implies an increase in fiscal deficit. The results of the simulation together with the base run are given in Table 7.6.

The table indicates a significant fall in growth rates (about 13 per cent) in the short run corresponding to the shock. This is largely due to a fall in agricultural and industrial growth rates which result from the cut in public investments in these sectors. There is not much impact on the inflation rate or the external sector, but the fiscal deficit goes up significantly, contributing some instability to the growth process. In the long run, the percentage fall in growth rate is very similar to that in the short run, indicating that this shock is pervasive. Moreover, the rise in inflation is proportionately more in the long run leading to a stagflationary situation. There is no instability in the long run from the fiscal or external sectors.

It is interesting to note that, in the period that we have considered for the simulation exercise, the government was actually increasing its revenue expenditure at the cost of capital expenditure. Thus the base run itself exhibited fiscal profligacy. It is of interest to examine the possible impact of a reversal of this policy (that is, a positive shock) during this period. In order to do this we have run a simulation (simulation B) that assumes both government transfer and government consumption are 1 per cent (of nominal GDP) lower than in the base run in both 1997 and 1998 and public investment is 1 per cent (of nominal GDP) higher than the base run in both the years. The results of simulation B, together with the base run are given in Table 7.7. We have also included the fiscal profligacy shock simulation from Table 7.6 (here we call it simulation A) for comparison.

Table 7.6 Effect of Fiscal Profligacy.

	Variables	GDP growth	Agricultural growth	Industrial growth	Tertiary growth	Aggregate inflation	Gross fiscal deficit ratio	Foreign exchange reserves
Short run	Base run	6.7	3.3	4.7	10.2	7.3	7.6	36.1
	Shock	5.8	1.4	3.9	9.6	8.2	9.0	36.2
	% change	– 13.4	– 57.6	– 17.0	– 5.9	12.3	18.4	0.3
Long run	Base run	5.9	2.6	5.7	8.0	4.9	11.0	58.6
	Shock	5.1	1.6	4.2	7.6	6.0	10.8	59.6
	% change	– 13.6	– 38.5	– 26.3	– 5.0	22.4	– 1.8	1.7

Note: In the shock scenario, government transfer and government consumption are both assumed to be 1 per cent (of nominal GDP) higher than in the base run in both 1997 and 1998. Simultaneously, public investment is assumed to be 1 per cent (of nominal GDP) lower than the base run in both the years. The row showing '% change' measures percentage increases in the value of variables in shock scenario over base run values.

The table indicates that in the short run, Simulation B would not only have given rise to higher growth than in the base run but that this increase would have been proportionately more (about 25 per cent) than the loss in growth due to the Simulation A (about 13 per cent), where the policies are reversed. This underlines the non-linearity in the model. This asymmetry is present in the long run as well, although it is more muted. An important conclusion that can be drawn from this table is that the during the period under study, the economy was actually facing a fiscal profligacy shock that brought down the growth rate during this period to 5.9 per cent (compared to the 7 per cent growth rate in the period 1994 to 1996) and in the absence of this shock (that is, a situation corresponding to Simulation B), growth rates could have been similar to those in the previous period.

Table 7.7 Effect of Alternative Fiscal Policies.

	Variables	GDP growth	Agricultural growth	Industrial growth	Tertiary growth	Aggregate inflation	Gross fiscal deficit ratio	Foreign exchange reserves
Short run	Base run	6.7	3.3	4.7	10.2	7.3	7.6	36.1
	Simulation A	5.8	1.4	3.9	9.6	8.2	9.0	36.2
	% change (A)	– 13.4	– 57.6	– 17.0	– 5.9	12.3	18.4	0.3
	Simulation B	8.4	5.3	7.8	10.7	4.8	11.6	36.5
	% change (B)	25.4	60.6	66.0	4.9	– 34.2	52.6	1.1
Long run	Base run	5.9	2.6	5.7	8.0	4.9	11.0	58.6
	Simulation A	5.1	1.6	4.2	7.6	6.0	10.8	59.6
	% change (A)	– 13.6	– 38.5	– 26.3	– 5.0	22.4	– 1.8	1.7
	Simulation B	7.0	3.6	7.4	8.6	3.5	13.0	57.2
	% change (B)	18.6	38.5	29.8	7.5	– 28.6	18.2	– 2.4

Note: Simulation A has the same assumptions as in the case of fiscal profligacy. In Simulation B, government transfers and government consumption are both assumed to be 1 per cent (of nominal GDP) lower than in the base run in both 1997 and 1998. Simultaneously, public investment is assumed to be 1 per cent (of nominal GDP) higher than the base run in both the years. The row showing '% change (A)' measures percentage increases in value of variables in Simulation A over base run values. Similarly '% change (B)' is for Simulation B.

We have now completed presenting the impact of the five individual shocks. Before going on to a simulation of multiple shocks affecting the economy simultaneously, it would be worthwhile to summarize the results of the individual shocks. This will help to compare between the individual shocks as well as provide an adequate background to understand the impact of the multiple shocks. Table 7.8 presents the percentage change in growth, inflation, and foreign exchange reserves corresponding to the five shocks, both for the short and the long run. The last column gives the sum total of each of the percentage changes corresponding to the shocks. While these values do not correspond to a particular simulation, it is analytically useful to compare them with the corresponding values in the simulation of multiple shocks, as this will indicate whether the impact of a multiple shocks is more or less severe than the sum of the impact of the individual shocks.

The table shows that rainfall and fiscal profligacy shocks have a stronger growth retarding effect compared to the oil price hike, capital flow shock, and world trade shock, both in the short as well as the long run. Furthermore, the rainfall shock and fiscal profligacy is stagflationary in the long run, while the other three shocks are not. We also find that the oil price hike, the capital flow shock, and fiscal profligacy show strong pervasiveness, while the economy is much more resilient to the rainfall shock and the world trade shock in the long run. Finally, the external shocks give rise to some instability in the external sector in the short run, but in the long run none of the shocks have any significant negative impact on this sector.

Table 7.8 Summary of the Impact of Individual Shocks.

	Impact of the shocks	Oil price shock	World trade shock	Capital flow shock	Rainfall shock	Fiscal profligacy	Total
Short run	% change in GDP growth	– 3.0	– 3.0	– 1.5	– 35.8	– 13.4	– 56.7
	% change in inflation	15.1	– 12.3	– 1.4	60.3	12.3	74.0
	% change in forex reserves	– 25.5	– 13.3	– 29.4	– 2.2	0.3	– 70.1
Long run	% change in GDP growth	– 3.4	0.0	– 1.7	– 10.2	– 13.6	28.9
	% change in inflation	4.1	– 2.0	2.0	20.4	22.4	46.9
	% change in forex reserves	– 6.1	– 3.6	– 7.3	1.9	1.7	– 13.4

Multiple Shocks

One of the objectives of this chapter is to examine the impact of multiple shocks. In the next simulation we do this by assuming that all the five shocks that we have discussed earlier impact the economy simultaneously. This will test the resilience of the economy to shocks and provide an idea about the worst possible performance by the economy under such conditions. The period under study is the same as in the earlier simulations, 1997 to 2003. The results of the simulation together with the base run are given in Table 7.9.

The table shows that there is about 64 per cent fall in the growth rate in the short run. This is due to both the agricultural and industrial sectors showing retrogression (negative growth) during this period. Despite the multiple shocks, the services sector continues to grow at almost 9 per cent and this keeps the aggregate economy from sinking into retrogression. The inflation rates almost double, making for a stagflationary situation. The external sector also deteriorates leading to an unstable growth process. In the long run, the proportionate fall in growth is much smaller than in the short run (about 30 per cent), indicating that the economy is resilient to a multiple shock and its impact is not very pervasive. The rise in inflation is substantial even in the long run leading to a persistent stagflationary situation. There is no instability in the long run from the fiscal or external sectors. Next, comparing the values in Table 7.9 with the last column of Table 7.8, we find that both in the short and the long run, the impact of multiple shocks is more severe than the sum of the impact of the individual shocks, in terms of lower growth rates as well as higher inflation rates. Finally, the most important conclusion that can be drawn from this table is that even in the worst possible scenario, the economy will continue to show a long-run growth of more than 4 per cent, which is a reasonable performance even in ordinary circumstances.

We have completed describing the short and long run impacts of five shocks that we believe might have affected the growth of the Indian economy. We shall now classify these shocks according to their impact on various aspects of the growth process. These aspects include (i) the magnitude of the impact on growth rates, (ii) the pervasiveness of the shocks in the long run, (iii) the capability of the shock to give rise to stagflationary situations, and (iv) the capability of the shock to give rise to instability in the fiscal or external sectors. It is important to classify the shocks according to what effect they have on these aspects of the growth process.

Table 7.9 Effect of Multiple Shocks.

	Variables	GDP growth	Agricultural growth	Industrial growth	Tertiary growth	Aggregate inflation	Gross fiscal deficit ratio	Foreign exchange reserves
Short run	Base run	6.7	3.3	4.7	10.2	7.3	7.6	36.1
	Shock	2.4	– 3.5	–1.9	8.7	14.4	4.8	12.6
	% change	– 64.2	– 206.1	– 140.4	– 14.7	97.3	– 36.8	– 65.1
Long run	Base run	5.9	2.6	5.7	8.0	4.9	11.0	58.6
	Shock	4.1	0.9	2.8	6.6	7.7	8.0	53.0
	% change	– 30.5	– 65.4	– 50.9	– 17.5	57.1	– 27.3	– 9.6

Note: In the shock scenario, all the assumptions of the five individual shock scenarios hold simultaneously. The row showing '% change' measures percentage increases in value of variables in shock scenario over base run values.

The primary focus in this study is the effect of shocks on the aggregate growth rates. In this context, it is fair to say that realistic rainfall and fiscal profligacy shocks have a stronger growth retarding effect compared to realistic scenarios of the other three shocks, both in the short as well as the long run. Thus the two domestic shocks are the comparatively big shocks both in the short and long run.

The second issue of interest is the pervasiveness of the shocks, that is, their long run persistence. Here we find that the oil price hike, the capital flow shock, and fiscal profligacy show strong pervasiveness, while the economy is much more resilient to the rainfall shock and the world trade shock in the long run.

The third issue that is of interest from the policy point of view is whether the shock leads to a stagflationary situation or not. This is because demand management policies can be used in non-stagflationary situations while stagflationary situations sometimes worsen with the use of such policies. We find that the rainfall shock and fiscal profligacy is stagflationary in the long run, while the oil price hike, capital flow shock, and world trade shock are not stagflationary in the long run.

The fourth and final point of interest is to study whether the shock leads to some instability in the growth process by enlarging the disequilibrium in the fiscal or the external sectors. As we have mentioned, a large increase in the deficits in these sectors has the potential to destabilize future growth rates by affecting investor confidence in the economy. We find from our study that the oil shock, world trade shock, and the capital flow shock (the external shocks) give rise to some instability in the external sector in the short run. Similarly, the fiscal profligacy shock and the world trade shock give rise to some short run instability in the fiscal sector. However, in the long run we find that none of the shocks have any significant negative impact on either the fiscal deficit or the external reserves.

PROSPECTS FOR THE FUTURE

Macromodelling exercises have been found to be particularly useful for forecasting the performance of various parts of the economy corresponding to alternative policy options. In fact, economists and policy makers use them extensively for this purpose. In this part of the chapter, we shall present some forecasts made by our macromodel, for the Tenth Plan as well as the Eleventh Plan period.

THE SHORT RUN

The short run focuses on the Tenth Plan period (2002–3 to 2006–7). We will present a simulation of the Tenth Plan period based on current trends and under the assumption that there will be no shocks destabilizing the economy. However, to put this simulation in perspective, we shall compare it with the Planning Commission's targets for the Tenth Plan (Approach Paper for the Tenth Five Year Plan).

Macro Targets of the Tenth Five Year Plan

In order to double the per capita income over the next decade, the Indian economy needs to grow at a rate in excess of 8 per cent per annum. This has been the motivating factor behind the Tenth Five Year Plan, which has fixed an ambitious target of 8 per cent growth rate for the planned period. Is this a feasible rate of growth? The Planning Commission looks into this issue (in its approach paper to the Tenth Five Year Plan) and maintains that it is indeed a feasible growth rate given that the investment rate for the planned period is targeted to be 32.6 per cent, while the ICOR is targeted to be 4.08. These rates will, of course, not be achievable with a 'business as usual' approach. As far as the ICOR is concerned, a number of reforms have to be successfully implemented in order to bring the value down to 4.08. The high investment rate, on the other hand, will necessitate a high savings rate. The Tenth Plan targets a domestic saving rate of 29.8 per cent, which will be augmented by a foreign savings rate of 2.8 per cent. In order to achieve this domestic saving rate, the Plan targets 4.6 per cent savings in the public sector, 5.8 per cent in the private corporate sector and 19.4 per cent in the household sector. The Tenth Plan's targeted values for major macro variables are presented in Table 7.10.

Table 7.10 Planning Commission's Tenth Plan Targets.

Variables		Target Rates
GDP growth rate		8.0
Gross investment rate		32.6
Incremental capital–output ratio (ICOR)		4.08
Gross domestic saving rate	Public sector	4.6
	Private corporate sector	5.8
	Household sector	19.4
	Total	29.8
Current account deficit ratio (foreign saving)		2.8
Consolidated fiscal deficit ratio		3.3
Consolidated revenue deficit ratio		0.8

Source: Planning Commission Approach Paper to the 10th Plan.

Apart from the GDP growth rate, the Plan also undertakes to bring down the governments deficits. The target for the consolidated fiscal deficit is 3.3 per cent of GDP of which, the deficit of the centre is 1.8 per cent and that of the states is 1.5 per cent. Similarly, the target for the consolidated revenue deficit is 0.8 per cent of GDP, of which the deficit of the centre is 0.5 per cent and that of the states is 0.3 per cent.

The Tenth Plan Forecasts

The Tenth Plan simulation assumes that during this period there will be no new structural changes apart from the ongoing reform process.

Thus the liberalization dummies will continue. Rainfall is calibrated from information available till 2005 and assumed to be normal in 2006. A standard depreciation rate is adopted for all the three sectors for the whole period. In the fiscal sector, nominal public investment is assumed to rise in all the three sectors. The average tariff rate is brought down from more than 16 per cent in 2002–3 to 15 per cent by 2006–7 due to the requirements of the WTO agreement. The government transfer payments as a percentage of GDP at market prices come down from around 12 per cent in 2002 to less than 11 per cent by 2006. We also assume that there will be no pay hike during this period. In the monetary sector, it is assumed that the bank rate comes down from 6.5 in 2002 to 6 for the rest of the Plan period while the CRR rises from 4.75 in 2002 to 5 from 2004 onwards. In the external sector, the world trade growth is around 8 per cent in 2002 and goes up to around 10 per cent in 2006. There is a gradual increase in non-oil prices over the period while oil prices are assumed to rise sharply till 2004 and continue at this high level for the rest of the period.

The forecasts of major macroeconomic variables for the Tenth Plan period are presented in Tables 7.11, 7.12, and 7.13. These tables also present the actual values of the variables for the eighth and the ninth plan period. Together, these three Plan periods represent the post-liberalization period of the Indian economy.

Table 7.11 Tenth Plan Simulations for Growth, Investment, and Inflation.

Variables	Eighth Plan annual averages (1992–6)	Ninth Plan annual averages (1997–2001)	Tenth Plan annual averages (2002–6)
Aggregate GDP growth rate	6.69	5.50	6.78
Agricultural GDP growth rate	4.22	2.55	2.44
Industrial GDP growth rate	8.15	4.07	6.64
Tertiary GDP growth Rate	7.55	8.10	8.74
Private investment rate	15.31	16.06	21.91
Public investment rate	8.04	6.45	6.90
Total investment rate	24.82	24.00	27.51
Inflation rate (GDP deflator)	8.73	5.29	6.30

Note: Growth and inflation rates are in percentage terms. Investment rates are in percentage of GDP at current market prices.

These forecasts show that the average growth rate of aggregate output for the Tenth Plan period will be around 6.8 per cent. This is distinctly higher than the actual growth rate in the Ninth Plan, which is 5.5 per cent, and marginally higher than the 6.69 per cent growth rate during the Eighth Plan. However, in contrast to the Eighth Plan where the engine of growth was the agricultural and the industrial sector, the tenth plan growth is largely supported by the services sector. This high rate of growth is significantly due to an increase in the private investment rates (compared to the Eighth and Ninth Plan periods) that lead to high total investment rates in this period. As far as inflation (in terms of GDP deflator) is concerned, the rates are slightly higher for the Tenth Plan period compared to the Ninth Plan period, although significantly lower than the Eighth Plan period.

In the external sector, the average imports ratio is higher during the period compared to the average exports ratio, leading to deterioration in the average current account balance. The average foreign exchange reserves are expected to shoot up to three times the value for the Ninth Plan and six times the Eighth Plan. The rupee will slide continuously during the Plan period, giving an average value of 49.46 for this period.

Table 7.12 Tenth Plan Simulations for External Sector Variables.

Variables	Eighth Plan annual averages (1992–6)	Ninth Plan annual averages (1997–2001)	Tenth Plan annual averages (2002–6)
Exports ratio	9.99	12.32	17.96
Imports ratio (oil)	2.16	2.56	4.28
Imports ratio (non-oil)	8.67	11.02	16.18
Imports ratio (total)	10.84	13.58	20.47
Current account balance ratio	– 1.11	– 0.80	– 0.41
Foreign exchange reserves	20.48	39.26	121.69
Exchange rate	31.62	43.47	49.46

Note: All ratios are in percentage of GDP at current market prices. The foreign exchange reserves are in billion US dollars. The exchange rate is in rupees/dollar.

In the monetary sector, money supply growth rates in terms of broad money (M3) will be slightly lower in the Tenth Plan period compared to the Ninth Plan period. However, the reserve money growth is significantly higher than that in the Ninth Plan. As far as the prime lending rate is concerned, the model forecasts an average rate slightly higher than the average for the Ninth Plan period. Finally, in the fiscal sector, the average tax to GDP ratio shows improvement over the values in the Ninth Plan period and this helps to increase the average revenue income ratio for the same period. However, the average fiscal deficit is larger than that in the Ninth Plan and significantly larger than that in the Eighth Plan.

Table 7.13 Tenth Plan Simulations for Monetary and Fiscal Sector Variables.

Variables	Eighth Plan annual averages (1992–6)	Ninth Plan annual averages (1997–2001)	Tenth Plan annual averages (2002–6)
Money supply growth rate	17.07	16.59	16.44
Reserve money growth rate	15.26	11.09	16.74
Prime lending rate	16.80	12.55	13.41
Tax ratio	14.70	14.05	14.76
Govt revenue income ratio	18.38	17.54	19.22
Gross fiscal deficit ratio	7.63	9.99	10.46

Note: All rates are in percentage terms. All ratios are in percentage of GDP at current market prices.

The Long Run

The long run focuses on the Eleventh Plan period (2007–8 to 2011–12). We will present a simulation of the Eleventh Plan period based on current trends and under the assumption that there will be no shocks destabilizing the economy. The Eleventh Plan simulation again assumes a continuation of the ongoing reform process. Rainfall is assumed to be normal for the Eleventh Plan period. The depreciation rates adopted for all the three sectors are the same as those in the Tenth Plan period. On the fiscal front, nominal public investment continues to rise in all the three sectors. The average tariff rate remains at 15 per cent throughout the period. The government transfer payments, as a percentage of GDP remain fixed at 10.27 during this period. In the monetary sector, it is assumed that the bank rate is pegged at 6 while the CRR is pegged at 5 for the whole period. In the external sector, the world trade growth is

4.75 per cent throughout the Plan period. There is a gradual increase in non-oil prices over the period while oil prices continue at the high levels reached during the end of the Tenth Plan.

The forecasts of the major macroeconomic variables for the Eleventh Plan period, together with the Tenth Plan forecasts, are presented in Table 7.14. It may be noted that increasing the length of the period to be forecast increases forecast errors. Hence for a meaningful analysis of the Eleventh Plan, we shall focus only on the most important macroeconomic variables.

Table 7.14 Eleventh Plan Simulations for Major Macroeconomic Variables.

Variables	Tenth Plan annual averages (1992–6)	Eleventh Plan annual averages (2007–11)
Aggregate GDP growth rate	6.78	6.98
Agricultural GDP growth rate	2.44	2.82
Industrial GDP growth rate	6.64	5.81
Tertiary GDP growth rate	8.74	8.86
Total investment rate	27.51	29.65
Inflation rate (GDP deflator)	6.3	5.36
Current account balance ratio	– 0.41	– 1.64
Gross fiscal deficit ratio	10.46	9.60

Note: Growth and inflation rates are in percentage terms. Investment rate and ratios are in percentage of GDP at current market prices.

The forecasts indicate that the Indian economy will grow at about 7 per cent per annum during the Eleventh Plan period. This is slightly higher than the forecasted growth rate for the Tenth Plan period and is again the result of high aggregate investment rates and high growth rates in the services sector. The inflation rates are significantly low compared to past experiences and the fiscal deficits are also within acceptable limits. However, there is a significant deterioration in the CAB.

There are a number of conclusions that we can draw from these simulation results.

- It is clear that even in the absence of any shocks, the 8 per cent growth rate targeted in the Tenth Plan is unattainable under current conditions.
- The tertiary sector has become the engine of growth of the Indian economy with remarkably high growth rates.
- While the total investment in the Tenth Plan has increased, compared to the Eighth and Ninth Plan, the public investment rate has come down.
- As far as the Eleventh Plan is concerned, it seems that the economy is moving to a high growth trajectory of about seven per cent growth rate per annum.
- The only cause for worry for the Eleventh Plan period is the external sector, which shows a sharp deterioration in the external balances during the Eleventh Plan period.

INFERENCES

What are the inferences that we can draw from the results in this chapter? Let us start with the impact of the shocks. It is clear that any shock that affects the supply side, such as the rainfall shock, will have a big impact on GDP growth. The impact is pervasive because rainfall deficiency not only reduces agricultural output but also non-agricultural output via sectoral interlinkages. The long run impact of this shock depends on the magnitude of the accelerator. However, since rainfall moves in cycles, it has a tendency to restore balance in the long run and hence the long run impact is more muted than the short run impact. Second, the shocks affecting the demand side lower the output in the industrial sector (which is demand constrained) first and then in the tertiary sector through intersectoral linkages. The long run impact of demand-induced shocks again depends on the accelerator. Third, the fiscal profligacy shock affects both aggregate demand and supply. A rise in government expenditure may stimulate the industrial demand in the short run but has a marginal effect in the long run. However, a cut in public investment operates perversely through both aggregate demand and supply and thereby leads to a lasting long run impact. Fourth, in the case of the trade shock, the long run impact is neutralized by the exchange rate adjustment and hence this results in a marginal change in long run growth corresponding to this shock.

Clearly, the deregulation of exchange rate has introduced a built-in stability in the operation of this multiplier.

How does one interpret the overall impact of the multiple shocks? It may be noted that the Indian economy is comparatively stable among the developing countries in the world. During the last fifty-five years, the economy witnessed only three instances of negative annual GDP growth rates and every five-year average GDP growth rate has varied between 3.5 per cent and 6.4 per cent. Thus even a 2 percentage point decline in the long run growth rate (as in the multiple shock case) may be considered to be severe by Indian standards. However, it would be very mild compared to the experience of some Latin American and African economies, which have witnessed sharp fluctuations in the past. In international comparison, therefore, the Indian economy is far more resilient to domestic and external shocks.

On balance, it appears that the Indian economy has become more resilient to shocks. However, the lack of reforms in the fiscal sector—a failure to protect public investment—has lowered the long run growth prospects. This is supported by the results in the section on alternative fiscal policies. As far as counter shock policies are concerned, all major domestic and external shocks must be countered through contra-cyclical fiscal and monetary policies. In the short run, this may lead to higher inflation due to a trade-off between growth and inflation in case of certain shocks that are stagflationary. The long run effect of the counter shock policies will depend on their impact on investments. In this context our estimation results indicate that in spite of interest rate deregulation, the overall impact of interest rate or private investment is small, and hence monetary policy is not very effective as a long run counter shock policy. The alternative is therefore to go in for a more bold fiscal policy involving higher public investment financed by the lowering of other government expenditure.

Next, we focus on the long run growth in the absence of shocks. It is clear that even in the absence of these shocks, the 8 per cent growth rate targeted in the Tenth Plan is unattainable under current conditions, as it is significantly higher than the 6.78 per cent growth rate forecast for the period. This is partly due to the fact that the targeted investment rates are also very high and are unattainable during the Tenth Plan period. The tertiary sector has become the engine of growth with remarkably high growth rates, but the other sectors—particularly agriculture—are not doing that well. Any attempt at higher growth rates will be possible only if the agricultural and industrial sectors grow at a higher rate. Another issue that is of some concern is the fall in the public investment rate. Any growth-oriented strategy will have to focus on greater public investments, especially in sectors like infrastructure etc. It should be noted that even if the Tenth Plan growth rate is around 6.8 per cent instead of the targeted 8 per cent, it results in an average growth of about 6 per cent for more than a quarter of a century and very few nations have achieved this.

As far as the Eleventh Plan is concerned, it seems that the economy is moving to a high growth trajectory of about 7 per cent per annum. Moreover, the economy will achieve this with a low rate of inflation and manageable levels of fiscal deficit. The only cause for worry for the Eleventh Plan period is the external sector. It may be noted that the forecasts for the Eleventh Plan are based upon high international oil prices prevailing during 2004–5. The forecasts indicate a sharp deterioration in the external balances during the Eleventh Plan period. This negative CAB occurs despite optimistic assumptions regarding private transfers and capital flows. The broad conclusion that emerges is that unless the capital balance remains robust, the economy may not be able to sustain high oil prices in the long run.

APPENDIX 1

SUMMARY STATISTICS OF FORECAST ERRORS

Variable	RMSE	MPE	MAPE	THEIL
ACOR	0.0103	– 0.784	0.792	0.003
YGACN	0.016	1.245	0.0138	0.0084
YGAVP	0.196	0.419	0.568	0.099
YGAWN	0.032	2.744	0.027	0.016
YGAWNVP	0.087	– 0.204	0.137	0.058
FERVP	0.092	– 0.407	0.245	0.046
FERQI	0.010	0.051	0.007	0.005
INDCOR	0.012	– 0.067	0.034	0.006
YGICN	0.019	– 0.161	0.015	0.0096
YGIVP	0.246	1.450	0.366	0.121
YCICN	0.011	– 0.255	0.009	0.005
UTI	0.012	0.055	0.011	0.006
YGIWN	0.025	0.916	0.017	0.012
YGIWNVP	0.130	0.356	0.11	0.064
SVSCOR	0.007	0.008	0.006	0.003
YGSCN	0.012	– 0.329	0.008	0.006
YGSVP	0.197	– 1.599	0.199	0.099
RMAT	0.014	– 0.168	0.012	0.007
RMATVP	0.247	1.273	4.474	0.020
YCSCN	0.010	– 0.393	0.005	0.005
UTS	0.203	0.019	0.006	0.004
YGDVP	0.152	2.579	0.07	0.076
YGDCN	0.018	– 0.656	0.017	0.0092
YGNCN	0.008	– 0.291	0.006	0.102
GDPCN	0.007	0.212	0.006	0.003
GDPVP	0.164	– 0.228	0.193	0.082

(Contd.)

Variable	RMSE	MPE	MAPE	THEIL
GDPMP	0.017	– 0.990	0.011	0.008
GDPMPVP	0.085	– 1.119	0.075	0.042
GDPWN	0.014	– 0.478	0.009	0.007
GDPWNVP	0.091	– 0.937	0.081	0.045
NDPWN	0.016	– 0.522	0.010	0.008
DDWN	0.002	– 0.105	122.91	0.001
DDCN	0.002	– 0.131	0.002	0.001
YGNWN	0.022	– 1.965	0.020	0.011
YGNWNVP	0.092	– 1.157	0.080	0.046
ZCPDCN	0.199	0.885	0.200	0.099
CPDCN	0.012	– 0.982	0.011	0.006
CPDCNVP	0.187	0.511	0.205	0.094
CPDWN	0.027	0.872	0.0193	0.013
NWORTH	0.081	– 6.098	0.041	0.042
NWORTHVP	0.081	– 5.821	0.143	0.148
SCRH	0.137	– 8.036	0.059	0.072
SCRHCN	0.123	– 6.864	0.071	0.064
PDIWN	0.014	0.161	0.009	0.007
DYPP	0.087	– 0.677	0.072	0.043
PDICN	0.021	– 1.397	0.017	0.007
ZPDICN	0.313	2.636	0.312	0.151
PDICNVP	0.295	1.909	0.321	0.144
OTR	0.090	– 0.105	0.083	0.044
NFIA	0.012	– 0.458	0.03	0.006
PVTSAVPP	0.274	– 1.790	0.843	0.133
PVTSAV	0.629	– 168.832	0.585	0.458
IVACN	0.064	1.683	0.055	0.032
IVICN	0.055	– 0.792	0.067	0.027
IVSCN	0.082	– 3.091	3.078	0.015
IV7CN	0.044	– 1.300	1.76	0.006
IV7WN	0.045	– 1.714	0.055	0.023

(Contd.)

Variable	RMSE	MPE	MAPE	THEIL
I77CN	0.057	– 4.195	5.701	0.029
I77WN	0.047	– 4.154	0.081	0.024
IP7CN	0.125	– 11.307	0.120	0.065
INVGDP	0.088	– 7.040	0.77	0.045
INVGDPEO	0.087	– 6.950	0.078	0.044
IEACN	0.048	1.115	0.037	0.024
IESCN	0.064	– 1.160	0.056	0.032
IEICN	0.048	– 0.240	0.042	0.024
IE7CN	0.027	– 0.366	0.021	0.013
IE7WN	0.036	– 1.345	0.033	0.018
N7ACN	0.184	0.429	0.298	0.096
AGRST	0.024	– 1.257	0.023	0.012
N7ICN	0.305	– 4.590	0.603	0.159
INDST	0.075	– 8.000	0.076	0.038
N7SCN	0.467	– 11.654	0.592	0.219
SVSST	0.065	– 3.141	0.063	0.033
KEACS	0.005	0.399	0.004	0.002
KEICS	0.010	– 0.210	0.009	0.005
KESCS	0.009	– 0.396	0.005	0.004
K77CS	0.003	– 0.167	0.002	0.001
PVTCAP	0.104	– 7.848	0.052	0.054
PIAGRPP	0.148	– 0.549	0.466	0.075
PIAGR	0.019	1.408	1.164	0.005
RPAGR	0.017	1.553	0.015	0.008
PIINDPP	0.116	– 0.508	0.106	0.058
PIIND	0.013	0.555	0.341	0.0007
MGOPIA	0.044	– 0.163	0.047	0.021
MGOPEXR	0.048	– 0.247	3.727	0.024
MGOPPEXR	0.406	– 7.872	0.515	0.202
MGOPI	0.045	– 0.203	0.047	0.022
MGOPIPP	0.445	0.124	0.817	0.231

(Contd.)

Variable	RMSE	MPE	MAPE	THEIL
PISVSPP	0.187	– 2.071	0.202	0.095
PISVS	0.026	– 0.606	2.710	0.012
PIGOVPP	0.206	– 4.963	0.26	0.107
PIGOV	0.037	– 1.484	2.641	0.015
CPDDEFPP	0.248	– 2.235	0.22	0.126
CPDDEF	0.030	1.553	1.410	0.008
IEDEFPP	0.215	– 0.912	0.22	0.108
IEDEF	0.022	– 1.344	2.070	0.006
PIGDP	0.013	– 0.690	0.569	0.004
PIGDPPP	0.069	– 1.394	0.14	0.138
CPIPP	0.229	– 6.050	0.25	0.118
CPIPI	0.046	– 2.438	0.023	0.023
WPIPP	0.152	– 0.480	3.650	0.007
WPIPI	0.013	0.802	0.668	0.004
M37VP	0.053	– 0.004	1.241	0.007
M37WS	0.006	– 0.009	0.587	0.001
M37CS	0.029	– 1.693	0.023	0.014
VM	0.009	– 0.361	0.008	0.004
MYVP	0.058	0.089	0.105	0.117
M07WS	0.016	– 0.883	1.235	0.006
M07VP	0.11	– 0.243	8.837	0.027
FERWNR	0.031	– 1.752	1.072	0.016
FERWN	0.014	1.038	0.023	0.007
R13RN	0.050	– 1.613	1.987	0.012
REALR13	0.918	51.693	4.59	0.508
R13RN1	0.328	– 11.577	10.968	0.035
LNDRN	0.026	– 0.153	6.590	0.044
RLNDRN	0.354	0.199	7.775	0.019
RORGS	0.132	– 1.245	6.158	0.029
AVR	0.046	– 2.598	2.774	0.018
RVR	0.412	5.838	0.796	0.211

(*Contd.*)

Variable	RMSE	MPE	MAPE	THEIL
X77VP	0.194	– 2.017	0.29	0.099
X77WN	0.194	1.533	0.032	0.012
X77WNR	0.026	0.167	0.059	0.013
EXPGDP	0.031	3.783	0.062	0.063
EXPFOB	0.024	1.500	0.031	0.012
XGSWN	0.024	0.578	0.019	0.012
XGSWNR	0.011	0.184	0.038	0.011
IMPOILPP	0.258	5.103	1.041	0.133
IMPOIL	0.145	5.865	0.132	0.070
IMPNONOILVP	0.232	– 0.159	35.913	0.115
IMPNONOIL	0.041	– 0.147	0.044	0.020
M77WN	0.054	1.369	2.971	0.019
M77VP	0.246	2.184	0.41	0.121
M77WNR	0.045	3.269	0.037	0.022
IMPGDP	0.248	2.469	0.040	0.023
M77VPR	0.190	0.808	0.28	0.095
MGSWN	0.043	– 0.612	0.049	0.021
MGSWNR	0.027	1.011	0.030	0.013
M77CN	0.071	1.886	0.049	0.035
M77CP	0.495	8.285	0.478	0.233
IMPCIF	0.046	1.189	0.051	0.023
IMPMON	0.070	1.065	0.06	0.035
MNOILAVP	0.088	– 0.201	13.687	0.043
TRBAL	0.276	0.798	19.545	0.135
TRBALR	0.297	13.316	0.269	0.132
TRBALGDP	0.242	– 4.033	0.26	0.125
TTRADE	0.030	1.441	0.028	0.015
TTRADEVP	0.240	– 4.314	9.845	0.88
NFSREVP	0.30	0.720	0.91	0.145
NFSRE	0.066	– 3.001	4.103	0.012
NFSPTVP	0.210	– 5.517	0.52	0.105

(*Contd.*)

Variable	RMSE	MPE	MAPE	THEIL
NFSPT	0.128	– 13.719	14.492	0.060
PTRECVP	0.344	11.243	1.34	0.172
PTREC	0.084	– 0.363	1.764	0.005
NETINVS	0.037	– 2.031	4.16	0.008
TRBALM	0.025	– 0.766	0.025	0.012
CABWN	0.037	0.444	1.387	0.004
CABWNR	0.042	0.594	0.077	0.003
CABGDP	0.071	3.266	0.07	0.034
KABWN	0.013	0.581	0.822	0.002
KABWNR	0.013	0.385	0.039	0.006
KABGDP	0.042	2.743	0.04	0.020
NRI	0.206	3.033	21.45	0.031
FDI	0.15	0.852	7034.69	0.004
OCB	0.3	– 5.024	13.07	0.017
RINTPP	0.563	– 12.208	3.527	0.277
EXRPL	0.022	0.661	2.051	0.006
ZEXRPL	0.015	– 0.927	5.485	0.003
RDEXRPL	0.004	– 0.446	27.31	0.019
EXRPLVP	0.223	– 0.446	0.89	0.111
FERWN	0.014	1.038	0.023	0.007
ZFERWN	0.056	0.976	0.286	0.028
FERRE	0.023	0.555	0.024	0.011
FERPT	0.043	– 0.618	0.050	0.021
NETFERRE	0.643	115.49	0.823	0.415
TE	0.014	– 0.335	0.355	0.0016
TEGDP	0.005	0.368	0.010	0.005
TEVP	0.067	– 1.030	0.045	0.034
RTE	0.012	0.199	0.008	0.006
RTEVP	0.219	– 0.850	0.53	0.113
RE	0.017	– 0.415	0.011	0.008
REGDP	0.013	0.210	0.229	0.006

(*Contd.*)

Variable	RMSE	MPE	MAPE	THEIL
REOVP	0.204	0.699	12.23	0.101
REO	0.146	10.618	0.105	0.068
RSWVP	0.127	– 2..974	0.11	0.064
RSW	0.062	– 5.263	0.042	0.032
RSWCN	0.044	– 3.796	0.040	0.022
RSWVPR	0.562	1.879	0.620	0.274
NSWVP	0.191	– 1.725	0.206	0.097
NSW	0.036	– 2.547	0.052	0.018
RSUB	0.057	5.511	7.331	0.026
RSUBVP	0.220	1.238	0.30	0.110
RIP	0.047	– 4.742	5.199	0.022
RIPRR	0.050	1.676	0.040	0.024
RR	0.021	– 0.342	0.011	0.010
RRGDP	0.013	0.521	0.009	0.006
TAX	0.030	– 2.695	2.257	0.014
TAXGDP	0.018	– 1.398	0.014	0.009
DT	0.043	2.969	2.226	0.017
DTGDP	0.040	2.882	0.031	0.020
TITVP	0.252	– 0.752	0.38	0.129
TIT	0.039	0.969	1.645	0.003
TCTVP	0.168	0.991	0.39	0.085
TCT	0.077	5.380	4.445	0.034
IDT	0.045	– 4.038	3.205	0.022
IDTGDP	0.026	– 2.305	0.023	0.013
TEXVP	0.189	– 3.119	0.210	0.096
TEX	0.036	– 1.894	1.592	0.011
TSTVP	0.140	– 4.181	0.11	0.071
TST	0.083	– 7.824	5.714	0.041
TCMVP	0.187	– 2.191	0.20	0.094
TCM	0.066	– 6.059	4.964	0.032
NTAX	0.11	8.136	6.169	0.046

(*Contd.*)

Variable	RMSE	MPE	MAPE	THEIL
OTRECR	0.026	0.870	0.031	0.013
ONTXVP	0.197	1.091	17.72	0.100
ONTX	0.208	14.134	12.998	0.086
CR	0.025	– 0.321	0.024	0.012
CRM	0.037	– 0.026	0.051	0.018
CRE	0.026	0.451	0.031	0.013
CRHVP	1.612	25.604	2.58	0.570
CRH	0.079	– 1.846	0.143	0.040
FDGWN	0.028	– 0.369	0.798	0.001
FDGGDP	0.035	– 0.088	0.032	0.017
RD	0.049	– 0.787	7.685	0.002
RDGDP	0.088	– 2.291	0.170	0.044
PD	0.007	– 0.771	1.518	0.003
PDGDP	0.014	– 0.066	0.011	0.007

Notes: RMSE: Root Mean Square Error; MPE: Mean Percentage Error; MAPE: Mean Absolute Percentage Error; THEIL: Theil's Inequality Coefficient.

APPENDIX 2

CORRELATION AND COINTEGRATION BETWEEN ACTUAL AND FORECAST VALUES OF ENDOGENOUS VARIABLES

Variable	Correlation coefficient	Level of significance of correlation coefficient	Cointegration	ADF test
ACOR	1.000	**	NSM	**
YGACN	1.000	**	**	–
YGAVP	1.000	**	**	***
YGAWN	1.000	**	NSM	–
YGAWNVP	1.000	**	–	–
FERVP	1.000	**	NSM	**
FERQI	1.000	**	*	–
INDCOR	1.000	**	*	*
YGICN	1.000	**	*	–
YGIVP	1.000	**	**	***
INDCORP	1.000	**	NSM	–
YCICN	1.000	**	*	–
UTI	1.000	**	*	**
YGIWN	1.000	**	**	–
YGIWNVP	1.000	**	NSM	**
SVSCOR	1.000	**	*	–
YGSCN	1.000	**	*	–
YGSVP	1.000	**	NSM	**
RMAT	1.000	**	*	–
RMATVP	1.000	**	**	–
SVSCORP	1.000	**	NSM	–
YCSCN	1.000	**	**	–
UTS	1.000	**	**	–

(Contd.)

Variable	Correlation coefficient	Level of significance of correlation coefficient	Cointegration	ADF test
YGDVP	1.000	**	*	***
YGDCN	1.000	**	–	–
GDPCN	1.000	**	**	–
YGNCN	1.000	**	**	–
GDPMP	1.000	**	**	–
GDPMPVP	1.000	**	NSM	–
GDPWN	1.000	**	*	–
GDPWNVP	1.000	**	**	–
NDPWN	1.000	**	**	–
DDWN	1.000	**	**	**
DDCN	1.000	**	**	**
YGNWN	1.000	**	*	–
YGNWNVP	1.000	**	*	*
ZCPDCN	1.000	**	**	**
CPDCN	1.000	**	**	–
CPDCNVP	1.000	**	**	**
CPDWN	1.000	**	**	–
NWORTH	1.000	**	*	–
NWORTHVP	0.416	*	**	–
SCRH	1.000	**	*	–
SCRHCN	1.000	**	–	–
PDIWN	1.000	**	*	–
DYPP	1.000	**	**	–
PDICN	1.000	**	–	–
ZPDICN	1.000	**	**	**
PDICNVP	1.000	**	**	**
OTR	1.000	**	*	–
NFIA	1.000	**	*	–
PVTSAVPP	1.000	**	**	*
PVTSAV	1.000	**	–	–
IVACN	1.000	**	–	**

(*Contd.*)

Variable	Correlation coefficient	Level of significance of correlation coefficient	Cointegration	ADF test
IVICN	1.000	**	–	–
IVSCN	1.000	**	–	*
IV7CN	1.000	**	–	**
IV7WN	1.000	**	–	–
I77CN	1.000	**	–	–
I77WN	1.000	**	–	***
IP7CN	0.956	**	–	–
IP7WN	1.000	**	NSM	NSM
INVGDP	0.795	**	–	–
INVGDPEO	0.865	**	–	–
IEACN	0.933	**	–	–
IESCN	0.984	**	*	–
IEICN	0.993	**	–	–
IE7CN	0.996	**	–	**
IE7WN	0.998	**	–	–
N7ACN	0.981	**	–	**
AGRST	0.997	**	*	–
N7ICN	0.908	**	**	–
INDST	0.996	**	–	–
N7SCN	0.872	**	**	*
SVSST	0.989	**	–	*
KEACS	0.999	**	–	–
KEICS	0.999	**	*	–
KEDCS	1.000	**	NSM	NSM
KESCS	0.999	**	*	–
K77CS	0.999	**	*	*
PVTCAP	0.996	**	*	*
PIAGRPP	0.921	**	*	**
PIAGR	0.999	**	*	–
RPAGR	0.984	**	–	*
PIINDPP	0.898	**	**	**

(*Contd.*)

Variable	Correlation coefficient	Level of significance of correlation coefficient	Cointegration	ADF test
PIIND	0.999	**	*	–
MGOPIA	0.996	**	–	–
MGOPEXR	1.000	**	–	–
MGOPPEXR	1.000	**	–	–
MGOPI	1.000	**	*	–
MGOPIPP	1.000	**	*	–
PISVSPP	1.000	**	**	*
PISVS	1.000	**	*	*
PIGOVPP	1.000	**	–	–
PIGOV	1.000	**	*	*
CPDDEFPP	1.000	*	–	–
CPDDEF	1.000	**	*	–
IEDEFPP	1.000	**	**	***
IEDEF	1.000	**	*	–
PIGDP	1.000	**	*	–
PIGDPPP	1.000	**	*	***
CPIPP	1.000	**	–	–
CPIPI	1.000	**	*	*
WPIPP	1.000	**	–	***
WPIPI	1.000	**	–	–
M37VP	1.000	**	**	***
M37WS	1.000	**	*	–
M37CS	1.000	**	*	–
VM	1.000	**	*	–
MYVP	1.000	**	**	***
M07WS	1.000	**	**	–
M07VP	1.000	**	**	**
FERWNR	1.000	**	*	–
SCRBI	0.999	**	–	–
R13RN	1.000	**	–	–
REALR13	1.000	**	–	–

(*Contd.*)

Variable	Correlation coefficient	Level of significance of correlation coefficient	Cointegration	ADF test
R13RN1	1.000	*	–	–
LNDRN	0.959	**	–	*
RLNDRN	1.000	**	**	**
RORGS	1.000	**	*	*
AVR	1.000	**	–	–
RVR	1.000	**	*	**
X77VP	1.000	**	–	***
X77WN	1.000	**	–	–
X77WNR	1.000	**	**	–
EXPGDP	1.000	**	*	–
EXPFOB	1.000	**	–	–
XGSWN	1.000	**	–	–
XGSWNR	1.000	**	*	***
IMPOILPP	1.000	**	*	–
IMPOIL	1.000	**	–	–
IMPNONOILVP	0.955	**	**	**
IMPNONOIL	1.000	**	–	–
M77WN	1.000	**	–	–
M77VP	1.000	**	*	***
M77WNR	1.000	**	**	–
IMPGDP	1.000	**	–	–
M77VPR	1.000	**	*	***
MGSWN	1.000	**	–	–
MGSWNR	1.000	**	*	–
M77CN	1.000	**	–	–
M77CP	1.000	**	**	*
IMPCIF	1.000	**	–	–
IMPMON	1.000	**	–	–
PCNONOILAD	1.000	**	NSM	NSM
AVGTARVP	1.000	**	NSM	NSM
PCNONOILADVP	1.000	**	NSM	NSM

(*Contd.*)

Variable	Correlation coefficient	Level of significance of correlation coefficient	Cointegration	ADF test
MNOILAVP	1.000	**	–	***
TRBAL	1.000	**	–	–
TRBALR	1.000	**	*	***
TRBALGDP	1.000	**	–	–
TTRADE	1.000	**	–	–
TTRADEVP	1.000	**	*	*
NFSREVP	1.000	**	–	–
NFSRE	1.000	**	*	–
NFSPTVP	1.000	**	*	–
NFSPT	1.000	**	*	**
PTRECVP	1.000	**	**	–
PTREC	1.000	**	*	–
NETINVS	1.000	**	–	–
TRBALM	1.000	**	*	–
CABWN	1.000	**	*	**
CABWNR	1.000	**	*	**
CABGDP	1.000	**	*	–
KABWN	1.000	**	*	***
KABWNR	1.000	**	–	–
KABGDP	1.000	**	–	–
NRI	1.000	**	*	**
FDI	1.000	**	–	***
OCB	1.000	**	*	–
EXTB	1.000	**	NSM	NSM
RINTPP	1.000	**	*	–
EXRPL	1.000	**	–	–
ZEXRPL	1.000	**	**	*
RDEXRPL	1.000	**	–	***
EXRPLVP	1.000	**	–	***
ZFERWN	1.000	**	**	**
FERWN	1.000	**	–	–

(*Contd.*)

Variable	Correlation coefficient	Level of significance of correlation coefficient	Cointegration	ADF test
FERRE	1.000	**	–	–
FERPT	1.000	**	–	–
NETFERRE	1.000	**	–	–
TE	1.000	**	*	–
TEGDP	1.000	**	–	–
TEVP	1.000	**	*	–
RTE	1.000	**	–	*
RTEVP	1.000	**	**	***
RE	1.000	**	*	–
REGDP	1.000	**	–	–
REOVP	1.000	**	**	–
REO	1.000	**	–	–
RSWVP	1.000	**	*	***
RSW	1.000	**	*	***
RSWCN	1.000	**	*	–
RSWVPR	1.000	*	*	***
NSW	1.000	**	**	–
NSWVP	1.000	**	**	–
RSUB	1.000	**	–	–
RSUBVP	1.000	**	*	***
RIP	1.000	**	*	–
RIPRR	1.000	**	–	–
CE	1.000	***	NSM	NSM
RR	1.000	**	**	*
RRGDP	1.000	**	–	**
TAX	1.000	**	*	–
TAXGDP	1.000	**	–	–
DT	1.000	**	*	–
DTGDP	1.000	**	–	–
TITVP	1.000	**	**	*
TIT	1.000	**	*	*

(Contd.)

Variable	Correlation coefficient	Level of significance of correlation coefficient	Cointegration	ADF test
TCTVP	1.000	**	*	–
TCT	1.000	**	**	–
IDT	1.000	**	*	–
IDTGDP	1.000	**	–	–
TEXVP	1.000	**	*	–
TEX	1.000	**	–	–
TSTVP	1.000	**	**	**
TST	1.000	**	**	–
TCMVP	1.000	**	*	***
TCM	1.000	**	–	–
OIDT	1.000	**	NSM	–
NTAX	1.000	**	*	–
OTRECR	1.000	**	–	–
ONTXVP	1.000	**	**	***
ONTX	1.000	**	*	–
CR	1.000	**	*	***
CRM	1.000	**	*	**
CRE	1.000	**	–	–
CRHVP	0.278	*	**	***
CRH	1.000	**	*	*
FDGWN	1.000	**	*	***
FDGGDP	1.000	**	–	–
RD	1.000	**	**	***
RDGDP	1.000	**	–	–
PD	1.000	**	*	–
PDGDP	1.000	**	–	–
IPACN	1.000	**	–	–
IPICN	1.000	**	–	–
IPSCN	1.000	**	–	–
IEDCN	1.000	**	*	***
GINV	1.000	**	–	–

Notes: * in correlation and cointegration tables denotes significance at 10 per cent level;

** in correlation and cointegration tables denotes significance at 5 per cent level;

* in ADF test denotes significance at 10 per cent level;

** in ADF test denotes significance at 5 per cent level;

*** in ADF test denotes significance at 1 per cent level;

NSM : denotes near singular matrix.

APPENDIX 3

SECTORAL AVERAGES OF RMSE AND TIS

Sectors	RMSE	Sectoral average	TIS	Sectoral average
Fiscal				
REO	0.146		0.068	
RSW	0.062		0.032	
NSW	0.036		0.018	
RSUB	0.057		0.026	
RIP	0.047		0.022	
TCT	0.077	0.077	0.034	0.033
TIT	0.039		0.003	
TEX	0.036		0.011	
TST	0.083		0.041	
TCM	0.066		0.032	
ONTX	0.208		0.086	
External				
X77WN	0.025		0.012	
IMPOIL	0.145		0.070	
IMPNONOIL	0.041		0.012	
NFSRE	0.066		0.012	
NFSPT	0.128		0.060	
PTREC	0.084	0.117	0.005	0.022
FDI	0.151		0.004	
OCB	0.302		0.017	
NRI	0.206		0.031	
EXRPL	0.022		0.006	
Output				
GDPCN	0.007		0.003	
YGACN	0.016		0.008	

(Contd.)

Sectors	RMSE	Sectoral average	TIS	Sectoral average
YGICN	0.019	0.014	0.009	0.007
YGSCN	0.012		0.006	
YGDCN	0.018		0.009	
Price				
PIGDP	0.013		0.004	
CPIPI	0.046		0.023	
WPIPI	0.013		0.004	
PIAGR	0.019	0.023	0.005	0.009
PIIND	0.013		0.000	
PISVS	0.026		0.012	
PIGOV	0.037		0.015	
Demand				
CPDWN	0.027		0.013	
RSW	0.062		0.063	
NSW	0.036	0.210	0.008	0.157
IV7WN	0.045		0.023	
XGSWNR-MGSWNR	0.883		0.680	
Monetary				
M37WS	0.006		0.004	
LNDRN	0.026		0.048	
AVR	0.046	0.052	0.057	0.043
R13RN	0.050		0.008	
RORGS	0.132		0.099	

Note: For each sector, a set of variables have been included that the authors think are the most representative variables from that sector.

APPENDIX 4

MODEL I: THE MACROECONOMETRIC MODEL FOR STRUCTURAL ANALYSIS

AGGREGATE SUPPLY

AGRICULTURAL GDP

1. ACOR = 2.45 - 0.004 * RFAQI - 0.01 * FERQI - 0.005 * RPAGR(-1) + 0.06* DUMACOR
(25.28) (-14.69) (-13.24) (-5.14) (12.29)
Adj. R^2 = 0.97 DW=1.80

2. YGACN = KEACS(-1) / ACOR
3. YGAVP = (YGACN - YGACN(-1)) * 100 / YGACN(-1)
4. YGAWN = YGACN * 0.01 * PIAGR
5. YGAWNVP = (YGAWN - YGAWN(-1)) * 100 / YGAWN(-1)
6. FERVP = 4.82 + 0.31 * YGAVP - 0.18 * PCFERPP + 0.04 * PIAGRPP + 12.09 * DFERQI
(11.48) (9.15) (-21.79) (1.16) (34.96)
Adj. R^2=0.98 DW=2.35

7. FERQI = FERQI(-1) * (1 + 0.01 * FERVP)

INDUSTRIAL GDP

8. INDCOR = 2.58 - 0.007 * YGAVP(- 1) - 0.002 * RTEVP - 0.001 * M77CP + 0.55 *
(157.09) (- 4.99) (-2.07) (-2.31) (23.78)
D85QN + 0.50 * DUMINDCOR - 0.03 * D91QN
(21.16) (-1.42) Adj. R^2=0.97 DW=1.73
9. YGICN = KEICS(-1) / INDCOR
10. YGIVP = (YGICN - YGICN(-1)) * 100 / YGICN(-1)
11. INDCORP = EXP(0.758637 + 0.012316 * TREND)
12. YCICN = KEICS(-1) / INDCORP
13. UTI = (YGICN / YCICN) * 100
14. YGIWN = YGICN * 0.01 * PIIND
15. YGIWNVP = (YGIWN - YGIWN(-1)) * 100 / YGIWN(-1)

SERVICES GDP

16. SVSCOR = 4.79 - 0.002 * RMATVP - 0.003 * RMATVP(-1) - 0.09 * TREND + 0.04*
(360.13) (- 1.84) (- 2.24) (-135.90)
DUMSVSCOR Adj. R^2=0.99
(11.03)
17. YGSCN = KESCS(-1) / SVSCOR DW=1.83
18. YGSVP = (YGSCN - YGSCN(-1)) * 100 / YGSCN(-1)
19. SVSCORP = EXP(1.480829 - 0.02605 * TREND)
20. YCSCN = KESCS(-1) / SVSCORP
21. UTS = (YGSCN / YCSCN) * 100

PUBLIC ADMINISTRATION AND DEFENCE GDP

22. YGDVP = 2.23 + 0.58 * RSWVPR + 3.04 * DUMYGDVP -
(4.80) (9.31) (11.24)
0.35 * D91QN
(-0.70) Adj. R^2=0.91 DW=1.70

23. YGDCN = YGDCN(-1) * (1 + .01 * YGDVP)

AGGREGATE REAL GDP AND RELATED MEASURES AT FACTOR COST

24. GDPCN = YGACN + YGICN + YGSCN + YGDCN
25. GDPVP = (GDPCN - GDPCN(-1)) * 100 / GDPCN(-1)
26. YGNCN = GDPCN - YGACN
27. RMAT = GDPCN - YGSCN
28. RMATVP = 100 * (RMAT - RMAT(-1)) / RMAT(-1)

AGGREGATE DEMAND AND RELATED MEASURES AT CURRENT PRICES

GDP AT CURRENT MARKET PRICES

29. GDPMP = CPDWN + (RSW + NSW) + (IV7WN + IP7WN) + (XGSWNR - MGSWNR) + ERGDPMP + ADGDPMP
30. GDPMPVP = (GDPMP - GDPMP(-1)) * 100 / GDPMP(-1)

GDP AT CURRENT FACTOR COST

31. GDPWN = GDPMP - IDT + RSUB + ERGDPWN
32. GDPWNVP = (GDPWN - GDPWN(-1)) * 100 / GDPWN(-1)

NON-AGRICULTURAL GDP AT CURRENT FACTOR COST

33. YGNWN = GDPWN - YGAWN
34. YGNWNVP = (YGNWN - YGNWN(-1)) * 100 / YGNWN(-1)

PRIVATE CONSUMPTION

35. ZCPDCN = 5874.23 + 0.03 * ZNWORTH(-1) + 0.38 * ZPDICN
(4.62) (2.30) (12.53)
- 507.56 * REALR13 + 14633.22 * DUMZCPDCN
(-2.99) (15.50) Adj. R^2=0.96 DW=2.10

36. CPDCN = CPDCN(-1) + ZCPDCN
37. CPDCNVP = 100 * ZCPDCN / CPDCN(-1)
38. CPDWN = CPDCN * 0.01 * CPDDEF
39. NWORTH = M37CS + SCRHCN + PVTCAP
40. ZNWORTH = NWORTH - NWORTH(-1)
41. NWORTHVP = (NWORTH - NWORTH(-1)) * 100 / NWORTH(-1)
42. SCRH = SCRH(-1) + CRH
43. SCRHCN = SCRH * 100 / CPDDEF

DISPOSABLE INCOME AT CURRENT PRICES

44. PDIWN = NDPWN - GIEP - SNDE + RIP + RTR + OTR + NFIA - TCT - PVTSAV - GMR - TIT + ERPDIWN
45. DYPP = (PDIWN - PDIWN(-1)) * 100 / PDIWN(-1)
46. NDPWN = GDPWN - DDWN
47. DDWN = DDCN * 0.01 * PIDEP
48. DDCN = DEPR * 0.01 * K77CS(-1)
49. OTR = (PTREC + OTREC) * (EXRPL / 10) + OTRER
50. NFIA = NINV * (EXRPL / 10) + RESNFIA
51. PVTSAVPP = - 5.52 + 2.34 * YGIWNVP + 87.84 * DUMSAV
(-0.33) (2.18) (26.87) Adj. R^2=0.96 DW=1.88

52. PVTSAV = PVTSAV(-1) * (1 + 0.01 * PVTSAVPP)

DISPOSABLE INCOME AT CONSTANT PRICES

53. PDICN = (PDIWN / CPDDEF) * 100

54. ZPDICN = PDICN - PDICN(-1)

55. PDICNVP = (PDICN - PDICN(-1)) * 100 / PDICN(-1)

GROSS INVESTMENT

REAL PRIVATE INVESTMENT IN AGRICULTURE

56. IVACN = - 11256.52 + 0.03 * YGACN - 118.4435747 * LNDRN -42.11 * D93LNDRN
(-2.89) (-8.10) (-2.45) (-1.63)
+ 110.75 * RPAGR(-1) + 0.39 * IPACN + 0.17 * IVACN(-1)
(3.22) (3.28) (2.23)
+ 3301.15 * DUMIVACN + 0.18 * D91IVACN(-1)
(13.06) (3.84)

Adj. R^2=0.97 DW=2.34

57. D93LNDRN = D93QN * LNDRN

58. D91IVACN = D91QN * IVACN

REAL PRIVATE INVESTMENT IN INDUSTRY

59. IVICN = 24591.24 + 0.06 * GDPCN - 201.02 * RLNDRN -
(5.15) (6.30) (-1.75)
1098.68 * D93RLNDRN + 0.42 * IVICN(-1) + 33131.59 * DUMIVICN
(-3.09) (5.45) (12.59)

Adj. R^2=0.98 DW=2.10

60. D91IVICN = D91QN * IVICN

61. D93RLNDRN = D93QN * RLNDRN

REAL PRIVATE INVESTMENT IN SERVICES

62. IVSCN = - 3463.46 + 0.05 * GDPCN - 192.38 * RLNDRN -
(-1.31) (4.93) (-1.82)
170.11 * D93RLNDRN + 0.19 * IVSCN(-1) - 0.03 * D91IVSCN(-1)
(-0.59) (1.18) (-0.53)
+ 8608.02 * DUMIVSCN
(5.61)

Adj. R^2=0.94 DW=2.17

63. D91IVSCN = D91QN * IVICN

TOTAL PRIVATE INVESTMENT

64. IV7CN = IVACN + IVICN + IVSCN

65. IV7WN = IV7CN * 0.01 * IEDEF

66. IV7GDP = IV7WN * 100 / GDPMP

TOTAL PUBLIC INVESTMENT

67. IP7WN = GINV + PEINV

68. IP7CN = IP7WN * 100 / IEDEF

69. IP7GDP = IP7WN * 100 / GDPMP

TOTAL NOMINAL AND REAL INVESTMENT WITH ERRORS AND OMISSIONS

70. I77CN = IV7CN + IP7CN

71. I77WN = I77CN * 0.01 * IEDEF

72. INVGDP = 100 * I77WN / GDPMP

73. INVGDPEO = INVGDP + EOINV
74. INVGDPR = I77CN * 100 / (GDPMP * 100 / PIGDP)
75. INVGDPEOR = INVGDPR + EOINV
76. I77CNVP = 100 * (I77CN - I77CN(-1)) / I77CN(-1)

FIXED INVESTMENT

77. IEACN = IVACN + IPACN - N7ACN
78. IEICN = IVICN + IPICN - N7ICN
79. IESCN = IVSCN + IPSCN - N7SCN
80. IE7CN = IEACN + IEICN + IESCN + IEDCN
81. IE7WN = IE7CN * 0.01 * IEDEF

CHANGE IN STOCK

82. N7ACN = 972.96 - 0.03 * AGRST(-1) - 25.42 * PIAGRPP + 0.005 * YGACN
(1.92) (-2.39) (-1.84) (1.45)
+ 3027.39* DUMN7ACN
(10.62)
Adj. R^2=0.84 DW=1.80

83. AGRST = N7ACN + AGRST(-1)
84. N7ICN = 8337.38 - 0.02 * INDST(-1) - 48.54 * RLNDRN + 6682.59 * DUMN7ICN
(8.33) (-1.91) (-0.59) (9.12)
Adj. R^2=0.76 DW=2.12

85. INDST = N7ICN + INDST(-1)
86. N7SCN = - 1008.30 - 14.68 * RLNDRN + 4363.84 * DUMN7SCN + 482.76 * YGSVP
(-1.16) (-0.29) (9.24) (3.06)
Adj. R^2=0.75 DW=2.23

87. SVSST = N7SCN + SVSST(-1)

NET FIXED CAPITAL STOCK

AGRICULTURE

88. KEACS = KEACS(-1) + IEACN - DEPRA * KEACS(-1)

INDUSTRY

89. KEICS = KEICS(-1) + IEICN - DEPRI * KEICS(-1)

SERVICES

90. KESCS = KESCS(-1) + IESCN - DEPRS * KESCS(-1)

PUBLIC ADMINISTRATION AND DEFENCE

91. KEDCS = KEDCS(-1) + IEDCN - DEPRG

AGGREGATE NET FIXED CAPITAL STOCK

92. K77CS = KEACS + KEICS + KESCS + KEDCS
93. PVTCAP = PVTCAP(-1) + IV7CN - PVTDEPR * PVTCAP(-1)

SECTORAL PRICES

AGRICULTURAL DEFLATOR

94. PIAGRPP = - 1.11 + 0.71 * DYPP - 0.63 * YGAVP - 0.18 * YGAVP(-1) +
(-1.17) (6.94) (-9.39) (-4.79)
0.20 * PIGDPPP + 0.07 * PROCPP + 4.78 * DUMPIAGRPP
(1.45) (1.72) (8.06)
Adj. R^2=0.96 DW=2.10

95. PIAGR = PIAGR(-1) * (1 + 0.01 * PIAGRPP)

RELATIVE PRICE OF AGRICULTURE

96. RPAGR = (PIAGR / PIGDP) * 100

INDUSTRIAL DEFLATOR

97. PIINDPP = - 2.38 + 0.22 * LNDRN + 0.45 * PIGDPPP + 0.06 * PIAGRPP(-1) +
(-0.49) (1.96) (7.77) (2.22)
0.04 * MGOPPEXR + 0.02 * UTI(-1) + 3.72 * DUMPIND - 0.96 *D91QN
(4.43) (0.52) (9.37) (-2.15)
Adj. R^2=0.96 DW=1.92

98. PIIND = PIIND(-1) * (1 + 0.01 * PIINDPP)

IMPORT PRICE

99. MGOPI = 0.2788 * PCOIL + 0.7212 * PCNONOIL
100. MGOPIPP = (MGOPI - MGOPI(-1)) * 100 / MGOPI(-1)

IMPORT PRICE ADJUSTED FOR TARIFF

101. MGOPIA = MGOPI * (1 + AVGTAR)

IMPORT PRICE ADJUSTED FOR TARIFF AND EXCHANGE RATE DEPRECIATION

102. MGOPEXR = MGOPIA * (1 + RDEXRPL)

103. MGOPPEXR = (MGOPEXR - MGOPEXR(-1)) * 100 / MGOPEXR(-1)

SERVICES DEFLATOR

104. PISVSPP = 3.50 + 0.26 * PIGDPPP + 0.28 * CPIPP +
(3.34) (1.49) (2.36)
8.10 * DUMPISVS - 0.37 * D91QN
(10.85) (-0.42) Adj. R^2=0.86 DW=2.12
105. PISVS = PISVS(-1) * (1 + .01 * PISVSPP)

DEFLATOR FOR GDP FROM PUBLIC ADM

106. PIGOVPP = 2.50 + 0.72 * CPIPP + 7.64 * DUMPIGOV
(4.30) (12.69) (8.88) Adj. R^2=0.87 DW=1.58
107. PIGOV = PIGOV(-1) * (1 + .01 * PIGOVPP)

PRIVATE CONSUMPTION DEFLATOR

108. CPDDEFPP = 2.22 + 0.71 * CPIPP + 2.04 * DCPDDEF
(4.30) (12.69) (8.88) Adj. R^2=0.89 DW=1.99
109. CPDDEF = CPDDEF(-1) * (1 + 0.01 * CPDDEFPP)

GROSS INVESTMENT DEFLATOR

110. IEDEFPP = 2.84 + 0.67 * PIINDPP + 5.16 * DUMIEDEF
(2.80) (6.00) (4.57)
+ 0.06 * MGOPPEXR
(2.88) Adj. R^2=0.80 DW=2.35
111. IEDEF = IEDEF(-1) * (1 + 0.01 * IEDEFPP)

GENERAL PRICE

GDP DEFLATOR

112. PIGDP = (GDPWN / GDPCN) * 100
113. PIGDPPP = (PIGDP - PIGDP(-1)) * 100 / PIGDP(-1)

CONSUMER PRICE(INDUSTRIAL WORKERS)

114. CPIPP = 0.09 + 0.29 * PIAGRPP + 0.70 * PIINDPP +
(0.09) (3.92) (5.41)
7.31 * DUMCPI
(6.44) Adj. R^2=0.87 DW=2.04
115. CPIPI = CPIPI(-1) * (1 + 0.01 * CPIPP)

WHOLESALE PRICE

116. WPIPP = 0.18 + 0.24 * PIAGRPP + 0.73 * PIINDPP +
(5.35) (103.59) (172.73)
1.03 * DUMWPI
(196.37) Adj. R^2=0.99 DW=1.76

117. WPIPI = WPIPI(-1) * (1 + .01 * WPIPP)

MONEY SUPPLY AND VELOCITY OF MONEY

118. M37VP = 11.87 + 0.32 * M07VP - 0.17* ZCRR -
(19.57) (8.36) (-0.92)
1.001 * ZBNKRN + 0.003 * ZLNDRN + 0.75 * D93ZLNDRN
(-5.46) (0.02) (2.73) (10.00)
+ 5.31 * DUMM37VP
Adj. R^2=0.92 DW=2.37

119. M37WS = M37WS(-1) * (1 + .01 * M37VP)

120. M37CS = (M37WS / CPDDEF) * 100

121. VM = M37WS / GDPCN

GROWTH OF MONEY RELATIVE TO GROWTH OF OUTPUT

122. MYVP = M37VP - GDPVP

RESERVE MONEY

123. M07WS = SCRBI + FERWNR - NNML

124. M07VP = (M07WS - M07WS(-1)) * 100 / M07WS(-1)

125. FERWNR = FERWN * EXRPL / 10

126. SCRBI = SCRBI(-1) + CRBI

INTEREST RATE

127. R13RN = 1.51 - 0.02 * MYVP + 0.5 * R13RN(-1) +
(5.69) (-2.97) (12.71)
0.12 * D93R13RN(-1) + 0.14 * LNDRN + 0.03 * RORGS +
(12.07) (10.59) (2.51)
2.09 * DUMR13RN
(23.35) Adj. R^2=0.99 DW=1.76

128. D93R13RN = D93QN * R13RN

129. REALR13 = R13RN - CPIPP

130. R13RN1 = R13RN - LIBOR

131. LNDRN = 0.69 + 0.33 * BNKRN + 0.04 * CRR +
(0.87) (2.52) (0.67)
0.01 * RORGS - 0.09 * D93LNDRN(-1) + 0.70 * LNDRN(-1)
(0.46) (-5.63) (7.88)
+ 3.58 * DUMLNDRN
(7.59) Adj. R^2=0.95 DW=2.07

132. ZLNDRN = LNDRN - LNDRN(-1)

133. D93ZLNDRN = D93QN * ZLNDRN

134. RLNDRN = LNDRN - WPIPP

135. RORGS = 0.46 + 0.31 * FDGGDP + 3.46 *
(0.52) (2.03) (2.77) DUMRORGS
+ 0.71 * RORGS(-1) - 0.07 * D93RORGS(-1)
(6.02) (-1.29)
Adj. R^2=0.89 DW=2.24

136. D93RORGS = D93QN * RORGS

137. AVR = 0.00019 + 0.03 * RORGS + 0.03 * R13RN
(0.0007) (2.02) (0.63)
+ 0.94 * AVR(-1) + 1.20 * DUMAVR
(24.70) (7.76) Adj. R^2=0.99 DW=2.27

138. RVR = AVR - PIGDPPP

EXTERNAL TRANSACTIONS

FOREIGN TRADE

EXPORTS IN US DOLLARS MILLION

139. X77VP = 2.41 + 0.23 * EXRPLVP + 0.40 * D93EXRPLVP
(2.58) (3.54) (3.04)
+ 0.71 * MWTVP - 0.19 * WPIPP + 8.33 * DUMEXP
(12.30) (-1.87) (12.60)
Adj. R^2=0.95 DW=1.90

140. X77WN = X77WN(-1) * (1 + 0.01 * X77VP)

EXPORT (DGCIS) IN Rs CRORE

141. X77WNR = X77WN * EXRPL / 10

142. EXPGDP = X77WNR * 100 / GDPMP

143. EXPFOB = X77WN - EXPERR

EXPORTS IN GOODS AND SERVICES

144. XGSWN = X77WN + NFSRE

145. XGSWNR = XGSWN * EXRPL / 10

146. D93EXRPLVP = D93 * EXRPLVP

IMPORTS

OIL IMPORTS IN US DOLLARS MILLION

147. IMPOILPP = - 3.71 + 1.58 * GDPVP(-1) + 0.86 * PCOILPP
(-0.89) (2.31) (18.18)

- 0.62 * EXRPLVP + 33.98 * DUMIMPOIL -
(-2.56) (9.38)
0.28 * AVGTARVP - 0.23 * D93EXRPLVP
(-1.43) (-0.40) Adj. R^2=0.96 DW=1.74

148. IMPOIL = IMPOIL(-1) * (1 + 0.01 * IMPOILPP)

NON-OIL IMPORTS (DGCIS) IN US DOLLARS MILLION

149. IMPNONOILVP = - 1.72 + 1.77 * GDPVP - 0.07 *
(-0.75) (9.47) (-2.69)
PCNONOILPP + 0.87 * PIINDPP - 0.80 * EXRPLVP +
(4.71) (-10.77)

0.26 * D93EXRPLVP - 0.20 * AVGTARVP + 12.18 * DUMIMPNOIL
(1.66) (-4.24) (11.99)
Adj. R^2=0.97 DW=2.36

150. IMPNONOIL = IMPNONOIL(-1) * (1 + 0.01 * IMPNONOILVP)

TOTAL IMPORTS (DGCIS) IN US DOLLARS MILLION

151. M77WN = IMPOIL + IMPNONOIL
152. M77VP = (M77WN - M77WN(-1)) * 100 / M77WN(-1)

IMPORTS (DGCIS) IN Rs CRORE

153. M77WNR = (M77WN * EXRPL / 10)
154. IMPGDP = M77WNR * 100 / GDPMP
155. M77VPR = (M77WNR - M77WNR(-1)) * 100 / M77WNR(-1)

IMPORTS OF GOODS AND SERVICES IN US DOLLARS MILLION

156. MGSWN = M77WN + NFSPT

IMPORTS OF GOODS AND SERVICES IN Rs CRORE

157. MGSWNR = MGSWN * EXRPL / 10

REAL IMPORTS (DGCIS)

158. M77CN = (M77WN / MGOPI) * 100
159. M77CP = (M77CN - M77CN(-1)) * 100 / M77CN(-1)
160. IMPCIF = M77WN - IMPERR
161. IMPMON = (FERWN / M77WN) * 12
162. PCNONOILAD = PCNONOIL * (1 + AVGTAR)
163. AVGTARVP = (AVGTAR - AVGTAR(-1)) * 100 / AVGTAR(-1)
164. PCNONOILADVP = (PCNONOILAD - PCNONOILAD(-1)) * 100 / PCNONOILAD(-1)
165. MNOILAVP = PCNONOILADVP + EXRPLVP

TRADE BALANCE AND TOTAL TRADE

166. TRBAL = X77WN - M77WN
167. TRBALR = TRBAL * EXRPL / 10
168. TRBALGDP = TRBALR * 100 / GDPMP
169. TTRADE = X77WN + M77WN
170. TTRADEVP = (TTRADE - TTRADE(-1)) * 100 / TTRADE(-1)

MERCHANDISE TRADE

171. TRBALM = EXPFOB - IMPCIF + ADTRBALM

INVISIBLES RECEIPTS FROM FACTOR SERVICES

172. NFSREVP = - 1.61 + 1.06 * TTRADEVP + 22.34 * DUMNFSRE
(-0.71) (9.88) (12.89)
+ 0.08 * EXRPLVP + 0.87 * D93QN
(0.55) (0.40) Adj. R^2=0.89 DW=1.64

173. NFSRE = NFSRE(-1) * (1 + 0.01 * NFSREVP)

PAYMENTS FROM FACTOR SERVICES

174. NFSPTVP = 4.52 + 0.26 * TTRADEVP + 27.81 * DUMNFSPT
(2.08) (2.52) (15.45)
+ 2.09 * D93QN + 0.11 * EXRPLVP
(0.98) (0.79) Adj. R^2=0.90 DW=1.58

175. NFSPT = NFSPT(-1) * (1 + 0.01 * NFSPTVP)

176. PTRECVP = 21.94 - 2.54 * EXRPLVP + 0.14 * PCOILPP
(6.85) (-6.67) (3.60)
+ 153.06 * D91 + 62.57 * D93 + 83.27 * DUMPTREC
(9.74) (5.43) (10.39) Adj. R^2=0.89 DW=2.14

177. PTREC = PTREC(-1) * (1 + 0.01 * PTRECVP)

NET INVISIBLE

178. NETINVS = NFSRE - NFSPT + PTREC + OTREC + NINV + ADNETINVS

CURRENT ACCOUNT BALANCE

179. CABWN = TRBALM + NETINVS
180. CABWNR = CABWN * EXRPL / 10
181. CABGDP = CABWNR * 100 / GDPMP

CAPITAL ACCOUNT

182. KABWN = FDI + FPI + OCB + EXTB + NRI + RPDEBT + RESCAP + ADKABWN
183. KABWNR = KABWN * EXRPL / 10
184. KABGDP = KABWNR * 100 / GDPMP
185. NRI = 889.43 + 49.49 * GDPVP - 3.75 * EXRPLVP +
(5.81) (2.09) (-0.41)
122.66 * R13RN1 + 1092.35 * DUMNRI - 297.81 * D93QN
(4.89) (8.89) (-1.31) Adj. R^2=0.83 DW=1.78

186. FDI = - 3.26 + 39.66 * GDPVP(-1) + 1761.20 * D91QN -
(-0.04) (2.90) (18.64)

24.66 * EXRPLVP + 847.33 * DUMFDI
(-4.30) (12.25) Adj. R^2=0.95 DW=1.92

187. OCB = - 693.95 + 113.89 * LNDRN - 63.41 * LIBOR -
(-1.00) (2.38) (-1.25)

8.90 * EXRPLVP - 207.05 * D91QN + 60.76 * GDPVP +
(-0.53) (-0.57) (1.70)

1673.14 * DUMOCB
(8.02) Adj. R^2=0.75 DW=2.29

188. EXTB = CRED + EXTBAD
189. RINTPP = WPIPP - MGOPIPP

EXCHANGE RATE

190. EXRPL = EXRPL(-1) + ZEXRPL
191. ZEXRPL = - 0.53 - 5.14e-05 * FERRE + 0.0001 * FERPT
(-2.42) (-1.81) (3.36)
+ 5.39 * D91 + 3.80 * D93 + 0.02 * WPIPP(-1) + 1.38 * DUMZEXR
(11.54) (7.76) (1.79) (7.16)
Adj. R^2=0.92 DW=1.99

192. RDEXRPL = (EXRPL - EXRPL(-1)) / EXRPL(-1)
193. EXRPLVP = (EXRPL - EXRPL(-1)) * 100 / EXRPL(-1)

FOREIGN EXCHANGE RESERVES

RBI FOREIGN EXCHANGE RESERVES IN $ MILLION

194. ZFERWN = CABWN + KABWN + RESFERWN
195. FERWN = FERWN(-1) + ZFERWN

FOREIGN EXCHANGE RESERVES (SUPPLY RECEIPTS)

196. FERRE = X77WN + NFSRE + FDI + FPI + NRI + NINV + PTREC + OTREC
197. FERPT = MGSWN
198. NETFERRE = FERRE - FERPT

FISCAL BLOCK

TOTAL EXPENDITURE

199. TE = CE + RE
200. TEGDP = TE * 100 / GDPMP
201. TEVP = (TE - TE(-1)) * 100 / TE(-1)

REAL EXPENDITURE

202. RTE = (TE / PIGDP) * 100
203. RTEVP = (RTE - RTE(-1)) * 100 / RTE(-1)

CURENT EXPENDITURE

204. RE = RSW + NSW + RIP + RSUB + RTR + REO + ADRE
205. REVP = 100 * (RE - RE(-1)) / RE(-1)
206. REGDP = RE * 100 / GDPMP

OTHER REVENUE EXPENDITURE

207. REOVP = - 3.57 + 1.02 * REVP + 76.05 * DUMREOVP
(-0.68) (3.23) (21.97) Adj. R^2=0.95 DW=1.98
208. REO = REO(-1) * (1 + 0.01 * REOVP)
209. RSWVP = 9.93 + 1.26 * EMPGOVPP + 0.26 * CPIPP +
(7.69) (2.36) (3.40)

6.43 * D87 + 11.86 * D97 + 6.59 * DUMRSW
(2.76) (6.25) (4.53) Adj. R^2=0.76 DW=1.79
210. RSW = RSW(-1) * (1 + 0.01 * RSWVP)
211. RSWCN = (RSW / PIGOV) * 100
212. RSWVPR = (RSWCN - RSWCN(-1)) * 100 / RSWCN(-1)
213. NSWVP = 10.03 + 0.33 * RSWVP - 2.80 * D91QN +
(4.14) (2.20) (-1.75)
12.64 * DUMNSW
(12.25) Adj. R^2=0.84 DW=1.72
214. NSW = NSW(-1) * (1 + 0.01 * NSWVP)
215. RSUBVP = 18.97 - 0.22 * PCFERPP + 0.42 * PROCPP -
(9.06) (-4.02) (1.74)

18.80 * D91QN + 20.94 * DUMRSUB
(-7.65) (9.90) Adj. R^2=0.85 DW=2.37
216. RSUB = RSUB(-1) * (1 + .01 * RSUBVP)

INTEREST PAYMENTS

217. RIP = AVR * PD(-1) * .01
218. RIPRR = RIP * 100 / RR

CAPITAL EXPENDITURE

219. CE = GINV + OCE

CURRENT REVENUE

220. RR = TAX + NTAX
221. RRGDP = RR * 100 / GDPMP

TAX REVENUE

222. TAX = DT + IDT
223. TAXGDP = TAX * 100 / GDPMP

DIRECT TAX

224. DT = TIT + TCT + ODT
225. DTGDP = DT * 100 / GDPMP
226. TITVP = - 3.38 + 0.99 * YGNWNVP + 1.014 * D91YGNWNVP
(-0.72) (3.21) (3.00)
- 8.15 * DUMITRD + 15.88 * DUMTIT
(-1.42) (10.33) Adj. R^2=0.82 DW=2.39
227. D91YGNWNVP = D91QN * YGNWNVP
228. TIT = TIT(-1) * (1 + 0.01 * TITVP)
229. TCTVP = 1.22 + 0.69 * YGNWNVP + 0.35 * D91YGNWNVP
(0.28) (2.48) (1.02)
+ 15.80 * DUMTCT - 2.48 * DUMITRD
(10.63) (-0.43) Adj. R^2=0.87 DW=2.27
230. TCT = TCT(-1) * (1 + 0.01 * TCTVP)

INDIRECT TAX

231. IDT = TEX + TST + TCM + OIDT
232. IDTGDP = IDT * 100 / GDPMP
233. TEXVP = - 0.08 + 0.51 * YGIVP + 0.95 * PIINDPP +
(-0.03) (2.40) (5.33)
4.87 * D91QN + 16.35 * DUMTEX - 7.50 * DUMITRD
(1.49) (8.79) (-2.20) Adj. R^2=0.76 DW=2.27
234. TEX = TEX(-1) * (1 +0 .01 * TEXVP)
235. TSTVP = 9.40 + 0.45 * GDPVP + 0.64 * PIGDPPP +
(4.79) (2.41) (4.21)
6.50 * DUMTST - 1.36 * D91QN
(10.51) (-1.09) Adj. R^2=0.84 DW=2.12
236. TST = TST(-1) * (1 + 0.01 * TSTVP)

CUSTOMS

237. TCMVP = 1.31 + 0.83 * M77VPR + 1.08 * AVGTARVP -
(1.03) (14.21) (18.48)
12.34 * DUMTCM
(-4.34) Adj. R^2=0.92 DW=2.25
238. TCM = TCM(-1) * (1 + .01 * TCMVP)

OTHER INDIRECT TAXES

239. OIDTVP = 0.097 + 1.029 * GDPMPVP + 10.26 * DUMOIDT
(0.07) (11.11) (40.05)

- 0.43 * D91QN
(-0.63) Adj. R^2=0.98 DW=1.63

240. OIDT = OIDT(-1) * (1 + 0.01 * OIDTVP)

NON-TAX CURRENT REVENUE

241. NTAX = GIEP + GMR + OTRECR + ONTX
242. NTAXGDP = 100 * NTAX / GDPMP
243. OTRECR = OTREC * EXRPL / 10
244. ONTXVP = - 12.72 + 1.61 * YGNWNVP - 3.57 * D91QN +
(-1.23) (2.32) (-0.95)

135.72 * DUMONTX
(20.23) Adj. R^2=0.94 DW=2.27

245. ONTX = ONTX(-1) * (1 + 0.01 * ONTXVP)

CAPITAL RECEIPTS

246. CR = TE - RR
247. CRM = FDGWN - CRH - CRE - CRBI - CRO + ERCRM
248. CRE = CRED * EXRPL / 10
249. CRHVP = 100 * (CRH - CRH(-1)) / CRH(-1)
250. CRH = - 5340.32 + 0.01 * PDIWN + 728.73 * R13RN +
(-3.93) (20.30) (4.19)
7858.35 * DUMCRH
(11.33) Adj. R^2=0.98 DW=1.82

FISCAL DEFICIT, REVENUE DEFICIT, AND PUBLIC DEBT

251. FDGWN = CR - OCR
252. FDGGDP = (FDGWN / GDPMP) * 100
253. RD = RE - RR
254. RDGDP = (RD / GDPMP) * 100
255. PD = PD(-1) + FDGWN - CRO
256. PDGDP = PD * 100 / GDPMP

Appendix 5

VARIABLE LIST FOR MODEL I

Dummy Variables for Structural changes

D85QN: Structural changes in imports (1 from 1985); **D87:** IVth Pay Commission Effect (1 in 1987 only); **D91:** Liberalization dummy (1 in 1991 only); **D91IVACN:** Slope dummy for delicensing of investment in agriculture (1 from 1991); **D91IVICN:** Slope dummy for delicensing of investment in industry (1 from 1991); **D91IVSCN:** Slope dummy for delicensing of investment in services (1 from 1991); **D91GDPMPVP:** Slope dummy for growth rate of GDP at market prices; **D91QN:** Dummy for structural changes from 1991 (1 from 1991); **D91YGNWNVP:** Slope dummy for tax efforts from 1991; **D93:** Dummy for interest and exchange rate deregulation (1 in 1993 only); **D93EXRPLVP:** Slope dummy for exchange rate growth rate; **D93LNDRN:** Slope dummy for lending rate; **D93QN:** Dummy for structural changes on account of interest and exchange rate deregulation; **D93R13RN:** Dummy for deposit rate for 1–3 years; **D93RLNDRN:** Dummy for real lending rate; **D93RORGS:** Dummy for rate of return on govt. securities; **D93ZLNDRN:** Dummy for change in real lending rate; **D97:** Dummy for Fifth Pay Commission effect; **DCPDDEF:** Dummy for consumption deflator; **DFERQI:** Dummy for fertilizer index; **DRFAQI:** Dummy for rainfall index

Dummy Variables for Outliers and Irregular Changes

DUMACOR: Dummy for agricultural capital–output ratio; **DUMAVR:** Dummy for average rate of interest; **DUMCPI:** Dummy for consumer price; **DUMCPDCN:** Dummy for real consumption; **DUMCRH :** Dummy for government borrowings from households; **DUMDT:** Dummy for direct taxes; **DUMEXP:** Dummy for exports; **DUMEXRPL:** Dummy for exchange rate; **DUMGCONS:** Dummy for government consumption; **DUMIDTD:** Dummy for domestic indirect taxes; **DUMIEDEF:** Dummy for investment deflator; **DUMIEDEFP:** Dummy for deflator of public investment; **DUMIEDEFV:** Dummy for deflator of private investment; **DUMIMPNOIL:** Dummy for non-oil imports in dollars; **DUMIMPOIL:** Dummy for imports of oil in dollars; **DUMITRD:** Dummy for tax reform from 1993; **DUMIVACN:** Dummy for real private investment in agriculture; **DUMIVICN:** Dummy for real private investment in industry; **DUMIVSCN:** Dummy for real private investment in services; **DUMKABWN:** Dummy for capital account balance; **DUMLNDRN:** Dummy for prime lending rate; **DUMM37:** Dummy for nominal money supply; **DUMM37VP:** Dummy for nominal money supply growth rate; **DUMN7ACN:** Dummy for change in stocks in agriculture; **DUMN7ICN:** Dummy for change in stocks in industry; **DUMN7SCN:** Dummy for change in stocks in services; **DUMNFSPT:** Dummy for non factor services payments in dollars; **DUMNFSRE:** Dummy for non factor services receipts in dollars; **DUMNRI:** Dummy for NRI deposits; **DUMNSW:** Dummy for non salaries and wage expenditure; **DUMNTAX:** Dummy for non-tax revenues; **DUMOCB:** dummy for other commercial borrowings; **DUMONTX:** Dummy for other revenue of non-tax; **DUMPIAGRPP:** Dummy for agricultural price growth rate; **DUMPIGOV:** Dummy for public administration deflator; **DUMPIND:** Dummy for industrial price; **DUMPISVS:** Dummy for services price; **DUMPTREC:** Dummy for private transfers receipts in dollars; **DUMR13RN:** Dummy for deposit rate(1–3 years); **DUMREOVP:** Dummy for other revenue expenditure growth ratc; **DUMRORGS:** Dummy for rate of return on government securities; **DUMRSUB:** Dummy for subsidies; **DUMRSW:** Dummy for salaries and wages; **DUMSAV:** Dummy for private savings; **DUMSVSCOR:** Dummy for services capital–output ratio; **DUMTCM:** Dummy for customs tax; **DUMTCT:** Dummy for corporate taxes; **DUMTEX:** Dummy for excise tax; **DUMTIT:** Dummy for income tax; **DUMTST:** Dummy for sales tax; **DUMWPI:** Dummy for wholesale price; **DUMYGA:** Dummy for real agricultural growth rate; **DUMYGDVP:** Dummy for real public expenditure and defence growth rate; **DUMYGI:** Dummy for industrial growth rate; **DUMYGS:** Dummy for services growth rate; **DUMZCPDCN:** Dummy for change in real consumption; **DUMZEXR:** Dummy for change in exchange rate

OTHER EXOGENOUS VARIABLES

AVGTARVP*: Average tariff growth rate; **AVGTAR:** Average tariff; **BNKRN:** Bank rate; **CRE:** Govt external borrowings; **CRED:** Net government external borrowings from RBI in dollars; **CRO:** Non-debt fiscal deficit; **CRR:** Cash reserve ratio; **DEPR:** Depreciation rate in aggregate; **DKAR:** Depreciation rate of capital stock in agriculture; **DKGR:** Depreciation rate of capital stock in government; **DKIR:** Depreciation rate of capital stock in industry; **DKSR:** Depreciation rate of capital stock in services; **EMPGOVPP:** Employment growth rate in public administration and defence; **EOINV:** Errors and omissions in nominal investment; **EOINVCN:** Errors and omissions in real investment; **ERCRM:** Adjusted government borrowings; **EOINVR:** Errors and omissions in investment to GDPMP; **ERGDPMP:** Error in GDP at market prices identity, nominal; **ERGDPWN:** Error in GDP at factor cost identity, nominal; **ERGDPWNR:** Ratio of errors to GDPMP; **EXPERR:** Difference between exports and exports f.o.b; **ERPDIWN:** Adjustment variable in personal disposable income; **EXTBAD:** Adjusted government external borrowings; **FPI:** Foreign portfolio investment; **GIEP:** Income from entrepreneurship and property; **GMR:** Government miscellaneous revenue; **GINV:** Nominal government investment; **GRBI:** Net RBI credit to the government; **IEDCN*:** Real fixed investment in public administration and defence; **IMPERR:** Difference between imports and imports c.i.f,; **IPACN:** Real public investment in agriculture; **IPICN:** Real public investment in industry; **IPSCN:** Real public investment in services; **LIBOR:** London inter bank offer rate; **MWTVP:** World imports growth rate; **NINV:** Net investment income; **ODT:** Other direct taxes; **NNML:** Net non-monetary liabilities; **OCE:** Other capital expenditure; **OCR:** Other capital receipts; **OTREC:** Official transfer receipts; **OTRER:** Error in official transfer receipts; **PCFERPP:** Fertilizer price growth rate; **PCNOIL:** Price of non oil exports; **PCNOILPP:** The growth rate of price of non-oil exports; **PCOIL*:** Price of oil; **PCOILPP:** The growth rate of price of oil; **PEINV:** Nominal investment of departmental public enterprises; **PIGOV*:** Deflator for public administration; **PIDEP:** Depreciation deflator; **PROCPP:** Procurement price growth rate; **PTREC:** Private transfer receipts; **PVTDEPR:** Private capital depreciation rate; **RESCAP:** Net residual capital flows; **REVP:** Revenue expenditure growth rate; **RFAQI:** Rainfall Index; **RPDEBT:** Rupee debt service; **RESFERWN:** Monetary movements and errors and omissions in BOP account; **RESNFIA:** Exchange rate adjustment in net factor income from abroad; **RESPDIWN:** Errors and omissions in nominal disposable income; **RSUB*:** Subsidies; **RTR:** Fiscal transfer payments other than subsidies; **RTRR:** Ratio of fiscal transfer payments other than subsidies to GDPMP; **SNDE:** Savings of non-departmental enterprises; **ZBNKRN:** Change in the bank rate; **ZCRR:** Change in cash reserve ratio; **ZLNDRN:** Change in the prime lending rate; **ZNWORTH:** Change in net worth; **ZLNBNK:** Differences in changes in bank rate and lending rate

ENDOGENOUS VARIABLES

AVR: Average rate of interest; **CABWN:** Current account balance in dollars; **CABWNR:** Current account balance in rupees; **CE:** Capital expenditure; **CPDCN:** Real consumption; **CPDCNVP:** Real consumption growth rate; **CABGDP:** Current account balance – GDP ratio; **CPDDEF:** Consumption deflator; **CPDDEFPP:** Consumption deflator growth rate; **CPDWN:** Nominal consumption; **CPIPI:** Consumer price; **CPIPP:** Consumer price growth rate; **CR:** Capital receipts; **CRD:** Government domestic borrowing other than RBI (non-monetized domestic borrowing); **CRH:** Govt borrowings from households; **CRHVP:** Govt borrowings from households growth rate; **CRM:** Govt market borrowings; **DDCN:** Total real depreciation; **DDWN:** Total nominal depreciation; **DT:** Direct tax; **DTVP:** Direct tax growth rate; **DTGDP:** Direct tax–GDP ratio; **DYPP:** Nominal disposable income growth rate; **EXPFOB:**

Adjusted exports; **EXPGDP:** Exports-GDP ratio; **EXRPL:** Exchange rate(RS/ $); **EXRPLVP:** Exchange rate(RS/$) growth rate; **EXTB:** External commercial borrowings; **FDGWN:** Fiscal deficit; **FDGGDP:** Fiscal deficit-GDP ratio; **FDI:** Foreign direct investment; **FERPT:** Foreign exchange payments in dollars; **FERRE:** Foreign exchange receipts in dollars; **FERWN:** Foreign exchange reserves in dollars; **FERWNR:** Foreign exchange reserves in rupees; **FERQI:** Fertilizer index; **FERVP:** Fertilizer growth rate; **GCONS:** Government Consumption; **GCONSVP:** Government consumption growth rate; **GDPCN:** Real GDP at factor cost; **GDPMP:** Nominal GDP at market prices; **GDPMPCN:** Real GDP at market prices; **GDPMPVP:** Nominal GDP growth rate at market prices; **GDPVP:** Real GDP growth rate at factor cost; **GDPWN:** Nominal GDP at factor cost; **GDPWNVP:** Nominal GDP growth rate at factor cost; **I77CN:** Total real investment; **I77CNVP:** Total real investment growth rate; **I77WN:** Total nominal investment; **IDT:** Total indirect taxes; **IDTGDP:** Indirect tax–GDP ratio; **IDTD:** Domestic indirect taxes; **IDTDVP:** Domestic indirect taxes growth rate; **IEDEF:** Investment deflator; **IEDEFP:** Deflator of public investment; **IEDEFPP:** Investment deflator growth rate; **IE7CN:** Total fixed real investment; **IE7WN:** Total fixed nominal investment; **IEACN:** Real fixed investment in agriculture; **IEDEFV:** Deflator of private investment; **IEICN:** Real fixed investment in industry; **IESCN:** Real fixed investment in services; **IMPCIF:** Adjusted imports; **IMPGDP:** Imports–GDP ratio; **IMPMON:** Import coverage in months; **IMPNOIL:** Imports of non-oil in dollars; **IMPNOILVP:** Imports of non-oil growth rate in dollars; **IMPOIL:** Imports of oil in dollars; **IMPOILVP:** Imports of oil growth rate in dollars; **INVGDP:** Investment–GDP ratio; **INVGDPEO:** Investment–GDP ratio for errors and omissions; **INVGDPEOR:** Ratio of total investment to real GDP at market prices; **IP7CN:** Total public real investment; **IP7GDP:** Public investment as a ratio to GDP; **IP7WN:** Total public nominal investment; **IV7CN:** Total fixed private real investment; **IV7WN:** Total fixed private nominal investment; **IV7GDP:** Private investment as a ratio of GDP; **IVACN:** Real Private investment in agriculture; **IVICN:** Real Private investment in industry; **IVSCN:** Real private investment in services; **K77CS:** Total net fixed real capital stock; **KABWN:** Capital account balance in dollars; **KABWNR:** Capital account balance in rupees; **KEACS:** Net fixed real capital stock in Agriculture; **KEDCS:** Net fixed real capital stock in government; **KEICS:** Net fixed real capital stock in industry; **KESCS:** Net fixed real capital stock in services; **KG:** Growth rate of net fixed capital stock; **KGA:** Growth rate of net fixed capital stock in agriculture; **KGI:** Growth rate of net fixed capital stock in industry; **KGS:** Growth rate of net fixed capital stock in services; **LNDRN:** Prime lending rate; **M07VP:** Nominal reserve money (M0) growth rate; **M07WS:** Nominal reserve money (M0); **M37VP:** Nominal money supply growth rate; **M37WS:** Nominal money supply (M3); **M77CN:** Total real imports in dollars; **M77CP:**

Total real imports growth rate in dollars; **M77VP:** Total imports growth rate in dollars; **M77VPR:** Total imports growth rate in rupees; **M77WN:** Total imports in dollars; **M77WNR:** Total imports in rupees; **MGOPI:** Import price; **MGOPP:** Import price growth rate; **MGOPPA:** Import price change adjusted for tariff rate change and exchange rate depreciation; **MGSWN:** Imports of goods and services in dollars; **MGSWNR:** Imports of goods and services in rupees; **MYVP:** Relative growth rate of money and real output (excess money growth); **NDPWN:** Nominal net domestic product; **NETINVS:** Net invisibles in dollars; **NFIA:** Net factor income from abroad; **NFSPT:** Non factor services payments in dollars; **NFSRE:** Non factor services receipts in dollars; **NFSPTVP:** Non factor services payments growth rate in dollars; **NFSREVP:** Non factor services receipts growth rate in dollars; **NSW:** Non salaries and wages; **NSWVP:** Non salaries and wages growth rate; **NWORTH:** Net worth; **NWORTHVP:** Net worth growth rate; **NTAX:** Non tax current revenue; **NTAXVP:** Non-tax current revenue growth rate; **N7ACN:** Change in stocks in agriculture; **N7ICN:** Change in stocks in industry; **N7SCN:** Change in stocks in services; **NETFERRE:** Net foreign exchange receipts; **OCB:** Other commercial borrowings; **OTR:** Total transfer receipts; **ONTX:** Other revenue of non tax current revenue; **ONTXVP:** Other revenue of non tax current revenue growth rate; **OTRECR:** Official transfer receipts in rupees; **PD:** Public debt; **PDICN:** Real disposable income; **PDICNVP:** Real disposable income growth rate; **PDIWN:** Net nominal disposable income; **PIAGR:** Agricultural price; **PCNONOILAD:** Price of non-oil imports adjusted to average tariff; **PCNONOILADVP:** Adjusted price of non-oil imports growth rate; **PDGDP:** Public debt-GDP ratio; **PIAGRPP:** Agricultural price growth rate; **PIDEP:** Deflator for depreciation; **PIGDP:** GDP Deflator; **PIGDPPP:** GDP deflator growth rate; **PIIND:** Industrial price; **PIINDPP:** Industrial price growth rate; **PISVS:** Services price; **PISVSPP:** Services price growth rate; **PTREC:** Private transfers receipts in dollars; **PTRECVP:** Private transfers receipts growth rate in dollars; **PVTCAP:** Total private capital; **PVTSAV:** Private corporate savings; **PVTSAVPP:** Private corporate savings growth rate; **R13RN:** Deposit rate(1–3 years); **R13RN1:** Relative Interest Rate; **RD:** Revenue deficit; **RDEXRPL:** Change in the exchange rate; **RE:** Revenue expenditure; **REGDP:** Revenue expenditure to GDP ratio; **REALR13:** Real deposit rate; **REO:** Other revenue expenditure; **REOVP:** Other revenue expenditure growth rate; **REVP:** Revenue expenditure growth rate; **RGCONS:** Real government consumption; **RGCONSVP:** Real government consumption growth rate; **RINTPP:** Real interest rate; **RIP:** Interest payments; **RIPRR:** Interest payments to revenue receipts; **RLNDRN:** Real lending rate; **RMAT:** Real material output; **RMATVP:** Real material growth rate; **RORGS:** Rate of return on govt securities; **RPAGR:** Relative price; **RR:** Revenue receipts; **RRGDP:** Revenue receipts–GDP ratio; **RSUB:** Subsidies; **RSUBR:** Ratio of subsidies to gross domestic product at current market prices; **RSUBVP:** Subsidies growth rate; **RTE:** Real total expenditure; **RTEVP:** Real total expenditure growth rate; **RSW:** Salaries and wages; **RSWCN:** Real value of govt salaries and wages; **RSWVP:** Salaries and wages growth rate; **RSWVPR:** Growth in the real expenditure on salary and wages by the government; **RVR:** Real average rate of interest; **SGRBI:** RBI credit to Govt outstanding; **SCRH:** Govt nominal borrowings from households, outstanding stocks; **SCRHCN:** Govt real borrowings from households, outstanding stocks; **TAX:** Total taxes; **TAXGDP:** Tax–GDP ratio; **TCM:** Customs tax; **TCMVP:** Customs tax growth rate; **TCT:** Corporate taxes; **TCTVP:** Corporate taxes growth rate; **TE:** Total expenditure; **TEVP:** Total expenditure growth rate; **TEGDP:** Total expenditure to GDP ratio; **TEX:** Excise tax; **TEXVP:** Excise tax growth rate; **TIT:** Income tax; **TITVP:** Income tax growth rate; **TRBAL:** Trade balance in dollars; **TRBALM:** Trade balance (merchandise); **TRBALR:** Trade balance in rupees; **TRBALM:** Trade balance (merchandise); **TST:** Sales tax; **TSTVP:** Sales tax growth rate; **TTRADE:** Total trade in dollars; **TTRADEVP:** Total trade growth rate in dollars; **VM:** Money per unit of output;**WPIPI:** Wholesale price; **WPIPP:** Wholesale price growth rate; **X77VP:** Exports of goods in dollars growth rate; **X77WN:** Exports of goods in dollars; **X77WNR:** Exports of goods in rupees; **XGSWN:** Exports of goods and Services in dollars; **XGSWNR:** Exports of goods and services in rupees; **YGACN:** Real agricultural GDP; **YGAVP:** Real agricultural growth rate; **YGAWN:** Nominal agricultural GDP; **YGDCN:** Real govt output; **YGDVP:** Real govt growth rate; **YGDWN:** Nominal government output; **YGICN:** Real industrial GDP; **YGIVP:** Real industrial growth rate; **YGIWN:** Nominal industrial output; **YGNWN:** Nominal non-agricultural output; **YGNWNVP:** Nominal non-agricultural growth rate; **YGSCN:** Real services GDP; **YGSVP:** Real services growth rate; **YGSWN:** Nominal services output; **YGTCN:** Real Tertiary GDP; **YGTVP:** Real tertiary GDP growth rate; **ZBNKRN:** Change in bank rate; **ZCPDCN:** Change in real consumption; **ZCRR:** Change in cash reserve ratio; **ZEXRPL:** Change in exchange rate; **ZFERWN:** Change in foreign exchange reserves; **ZLNDBNK:** Change in difference of lending rate and bank rate; **ZLNDRN:** Change in lending rate.

APPENDIX 6

MODEL II: THE MACROECONOMETRIC MODEL FOR SIMULATION AND FORECASTING

GDP AT FACTOR COST

1. XGDP = XA + XI + XT
2. GR = 100* (XGDP - XGDP(-1))/ XGDP(-1)

3. XA = EXP(-8.16+ 1.43*LOG(KA)*** + 0.27*LOG(RF)*** - 0.12*D80S*** - 0.14*DUMXA***
(1.31) (0.24) (0.05) (0.03) (0.03)

+ 0.10*LOG(XA(-1)))
(0.14)
$R^2 = 0.99$ DW = -1.06

4. XAG = 100*(XA-XA(-1))/XA(-1)

5. XI =EXP(-2.57 + 0.08*LOG(KI) + 0.34*LOG(XA)*** + 0.18*LOG(RAE)*** - 0.06*LOG(PI)
(0.83) (0.09) (0.07) (0.05) (0.04)

+ 0.02*DPLIB + 0.6*LOG(XI(-1))*** + 0.04*D95**)
(0.01) (0.06) (0.01)

$R^2 = 0.99$ DW = -1.32

6. XIG = 100*(XI-XI(-1))/XI(-1)

7. XT =EXP(-5.06 + 0.67*LOG(KT)*** + 0.13*LOG(XCOM)** + 0.01*DUMPAY* + 0.02*DPLIB**
(1.02) (0.17) (0.05) (0.006) (0.008)
+ 0.52*LOG(XT(-1))***)
(0.09)
$R^2 = 0.99$ DW = -1.54

8. XTG = 100*(XT-XT(-1))/XT(-1)
9. XCOM = XA + XI
10. RAE = 100*(GE + EGSR)/PGDP

CAPITAL STOCK

11. K = KA + KI + KT
12. KA = KA(-1) *(1-DKAR) + IGA + IPA
13. KI = KI(-1) * (1-DKIR) + IGI + IPI

14. KT = KT(-1) * (1-DKTR) + IGT + IPT

PRIVATE INVESTMENT

15. IP = IPA + IPI + IPT
16. IPN = IP * PGDP*0.01+EIPN

17. IPA = -4714.17 + 0.05*XA*** + 0.44*IGA** - 2700.76*D80S*** + 0.28*IPA(-1)**
(1704.33) (0.01) (0.2) (706.1) (0.13)
R^2 = 0.9 DW = -1.81

18. IPI = -25029.76 + 0.20*XGDP*** + 0.71*IGI** - 0.56*ORGE*** - 649.003*RPLR - 939.56*IFR
(10074.05) (0.04) (0.3) (0.13) (696.28) (791.82)
+ 41506.12*D95*** + 0.22*IPI(-1)*
(7846.03) (0.11)
R^2 = 0.96 DW = -0.91

19. IPT = -33116.9 + 0.08*XGDP** + 0.71*IGT - 663.11*RPLR - 2920.68*DFEMRPLR*
(12348.49) (0.04) (1.1) (590.26) (1628.1)
+ 0.45*IPT(-1)**
(0.19)

R^2 = 0.86 DW = 2.07 (Dh not computable)

20. RPLR = PLR - IFR

PUBLIC INVESTMENT

21. IGA= 100*IGAN/PGDP
22. IGI = 100*IGIN/PGDP
23. IGT = 100*IGTN/PGDP
24. IG = IGA + IGI + IGT
25. IGN = IGAN + IGIN + IGTN + EIGN

TOTAL INVESTMENT

26. INV = IGN + IPN
27. INVR = 100*INV/GDPMP

AGGREGATE DEMAND

28. GDPMP = CP + GC + IGN + IPN + EGSR - MGSR + RESGDP
29. CP = RCP * PGDP*.01

30. RCP =EXP(2.89 + 0.65*LOG(RPDI)*** + 0.03*DWTO*** + 0.11*LOG(RCP(-1)))
(0.33) (0.06) (0.01) (0.08)
R^2 = 0.99 DW = 1.74

31. PDI = YGDP -TAX + GTR + OPDI
32. RPDI = PDI*100/PGDP

33. YGDP = EXP(-0.08 + 0.99*LOG(GDPMP)***) + (AR(1)=0.66***)
(0.03) (0.002) (0.12)

R^2 = 0.99 DW = 2.05

PRICE

34. PGDP=0.309*PA+0.26*PI+0.42*PT
35. IFR = 100*(PGDP - PGDP(-1)) / PGDP(-1)

36. PA =EXP(4.002 - 0.71*LOG(XA)*** + 0.59*LOG(PDI)*** + 0.12*DUMPA*** + 0.31*LOG(PA(-1)**))
(1.71) (0.15) (0.08) (0.02) (0.14)

R^2 = 0.99 DW = 1.29

37. PI = EXP(-0.20 + 0.37*LOG(PA)*** + 0.05*LOG(PMO)*** + 0.01*LOG(PMN) +
(0.06) (0.05) (0.009) (0.014)

0.53*LOG(PI(-1)***) + 0.06*LOG(TRF)***)
(0.06) (0.013)

R^2 = 0.99 DW = 0.61

38. PT =EXP(0.11 + 0.16*LOG(PA)*** + 0.42*LOG(PI)*** + 0.39*LOG(PT(-1)***))
(0.01) (0.02) (0.04) (0.04)

R^2 = 0.99 DW = 0.61

MONEY AND INTEREST

39. M3 = RM3*PGDP/100

40. RM3 =EXP(-9.801 + 1.68*LOG(XGDP)*** + 0.008*RPLR*** - 0.01*DFEMRPLR***
(0.5) (0.03) (0.002) (0.004)

+ 0.19*DUMM3*** - 0.07*DWTO*)
(0.03) (0.03)

R^2 = 0.99 DW = 1.52

41. PLR = 0.49 + 1.65e-05*M3*** - 7.2e-05*M0*** + 0.43*CRR*** + 1.13*BR***
(1.42) (3.9e-06) (1.7e-05) (0.09) (0.21)

R^2 = 0.88 DW = 2.45

42. M3G = 100*(M3 - M3(-1))/ M3(-1)
43. M0 = FERR + GSRBI - NNML
44. FERR = FER * EXR/10
45. GSRBI = GSRBI(-1) + MGFD

FISCAL SECTOR

46. GE = GC + IGN + GTR
47. RGE = GE *100/PGDP
48. ORGE = RGE - IG
49. GFD = GE - TAX - NTAX
50. GFDR = 100*GFD/GDPMP

51. TAX = EXP(-2.95 + 1.08*LOG(GDPMP)*** - 0.104*DLIB*** - 0.11*DWTO)***
(0.18) (0.01) (0.02) (0.02)

R^2 = 0.99 DW = 1.906

EXTERNAL TRANSACTIONS

52. FER = FER (-1) + CAB + KAB + RESFER
53. CAB = EGS - MGS + REM
54. CABR = 100*(CAB*EXR*0.1)/GDPMP

55. EGS =EXP(-6.62 + 1.02*LOG(WT)*** + 0.34*LOG(REXR)** + 0.09*D80S + 0.12*DFEM*
(1.13) (0.05) (0.14) (0.05) (0.06)

+ 0.14*DWTO** + 0.23*DUMEGS***)
(0.05) (0.05)

R^2 = 0.99 DW = 1.49

56. EGSR = EGS*EXR/10
57. MGS=MGSO+MGSN

58. MGSO =EXP(-3.26 + 0.43*LOG(XCOM)* + 1.005*LOG(PMO)*** + 0.55*LOG(PGDP)**
(2.09) (0.21) (0.02) (0.2)

- 0.69*LOG(EXR)*** + 0.05*DUMMGSO)***
(0.1) (0.01)

R^2 = 0.99 DW = 1.85

59. MGSN =EXP(-10.22 + 1.37*LOG(XGDP)*** + 0.09*LOG(PMN)** + 1.36*LOG(PGDP)***
(2.29) (0.2) (0.03) (0.1)

- 1.34*LOG(EXR)*** - 0.18*LOG(TRF)*** + 0.18*D95*** + 0.05*DWTO)
(0.06) (0.03) (0.05) (0.04)

R^2 = 0.99 DW = 1.66

60. MGSR = MGS*EXR/10
61. PM = 0.2788*PMO + 0.7212*PMN

62. EXR = EXP(0.39 - 0.07*LOG(FER)*** + 0.27*LOG(PGDP)***
(0.1) (0.01) (0.04)
+ 0.19*DEV91*** + 0.69*LOG(EXR(-1))***)
(0.04) (0.06)

R^2 = 0.99 DW = -1.17

63. REXR = 100*EXR/PGDP

Appendix 7

VARIABLE LIST FOR MODEL II

BR: Bank rate set by central bank; **CAB:** Current account balance; **CABR:** Capital account balance ratio; **CP:** Nominal personal consumption expenditure; **CRR:** Cash reserve ratio set by central bank; **D80S:** Dummy for structural changes since the 1980s; **D95:** Dummy for peak liberalization effect; **DEV91:** Dummy for large devaluation in 1991; **DFEM:** Dummy for financial and external market liberalization in 1993; **DFEMRPLR:** Slope dummy for effect of DFEM on RPLR; **DKAR:** Depreciation rate of agricultural capital stock; **DKIR:** Depreciation rate of industrial capital stock; **DKTR:** Depreciation rate of tertiary sector capital stock; **DLIB:** Dummy for liberalization in 1991; **DPLIB:** Dummy for partial liberalization in mid-1980s; **DUMEGS:** Outlier dummy for exports; **DUMM3:** Outlier dummy for money demand; **DUMMGSO:** Outlier dummy for oil imports; **DUMPA:** Outlier dummy for agricultural prices; **DUMPAY:** Dummy for pay hike in public administration; **DUMXA:** Outlier dummy for agricultural output; **DWTO:** Dummy for effect of joining WTO; **EGS:** Export of goods and services in dollars; **EGSR:** Export of goods and services in rupees; **EIGN:** Errors and omissions in IGN; **EIPN:** Errors and omissions in IPN; **EOINV:** Errors and omissions in INV; **EXR:** Exchange rate; **FER:** Foreign exchange reserves in dollars; **FERR:** Foreign exchange reserves in rupees; **GC:** Government consumption; **GDPMP:** Nominal GDP at market price; **GE:** Government expenditure; **GFD:** Nominal gross fiscal deficit; **GFDR:** Gross fiscal deficit ratio; **GR:** GDP growth; **GSRBI:** Central bank credit to government; **GTR:** Government transfer payments; **IFR:** Inflation rate based on GDP deflator; **IG:** Real public investment; **IGA:** Real public investment in agriculture; **IGAN:** Nominal public investment in agriculture; **IGI:** Real public investment in industry; **IGIN:** Nominal public investment in industry; **IGN:** Nominal public investment; **IGT:** Real public investment in tertiary sector; **IGTN:** Nominal public investment in tertiary sector; **INV:** Total nominal investment; **INVR:** Total real investment; **IP:** Real private investment; **IPA:** Real private investment in agriculture; **IPI:** Real private investment in industry; **IPN:** Nominal private investment; **IPT:** Real private investment in tertiary sector; **K:** Capital stock; **KA:** Capital stock in agriculture; **KAB:** Capital account Balance; **KI:** Capital stock in industry; **KT:** Capital stock in tertiary sector; **M0:** Nominal reserve money; **M3:** Nominal money supply; **M3G:** Nominal money supply growth rate; **MGFD:** Monetized gross fiscal deficit; **MGS:** Nominal imports of goods and services in dollars; **MGSN:** Nominal imports of non-oil goods and services in dollars; **MGSO:** Nominal imports of oil in dollars; **MGSR:** Nominal imports of goods and services in rupees; **NNML:** Net non-monetary liabilities; **NTAX** Non tax revenues; **ORGE:** Other real government expenditure (other than public investments); **PA:** Agricultural deflator; **PDI:** Nominal private disposable income; **PGDP:** GDP deflator; **PI:** Industrial deflator; **PLR:** Interest rate (prime lending rate); **PM:** Import price; **PMN:** Import price of non-oil products; **PMO:** Import price of oil; **PT:** Tertiary sector deflator; **RAE** Real autonomous expenditure; **RCP** Real personal consumption expenditure; **REM:** Remittances etc.; **RESFER:** Errors and omissions in BOP account; **RESGDP:** Errors in 'GDP at market prices' identity; **REXR:** Real exchange rate; **RF:** Rainfall index; **RGE:** Real government expenditure; **RM3:** Real money supply; **RMGS:** Real imports of goods and services in dollars; **RPDI:** Real private disposable income; **RPLR:** Real interest rate; **TAX:** Tax revenues; **TRF:** Average tariff rate; **XA:** Real agricultural output; **XAG:** Growth in agricultural output; **XCOM:** Real commodity output; **XGDP:** Real GDP; **XI** Real industrial output; **XIG:** Growth in industrial output; **XT:** Real tertiary sector output; **XTG:** Growth in tertiary output; **YGDP:** Nominal GDP at factor cost

Appendix 8

ACTUAL AND FORECASTS OF KEY MACRO VARIABLES FROM MODEL I

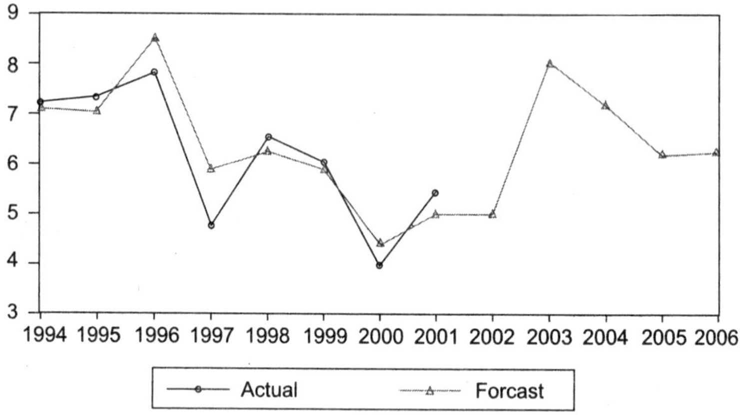

Figure A8.1 Growth Rate of GDP

Source: Computed using data from RBI's Handbook of Statistics on Indian Economy. Forecast data generated by solving Model I.

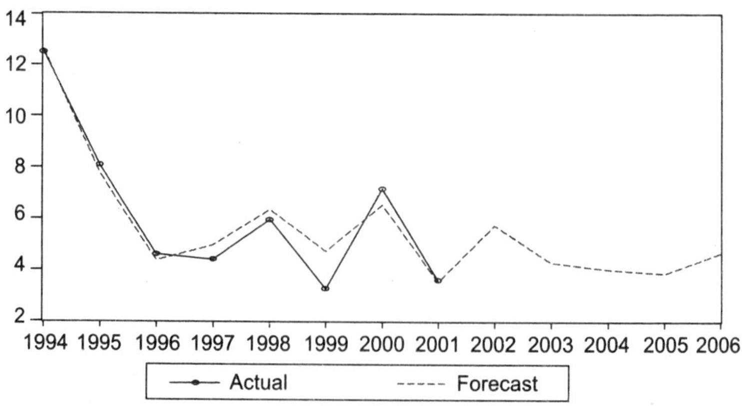

Figure A8.2 Inflation Rate From WPI

Source: Same as for Figure A8.1.

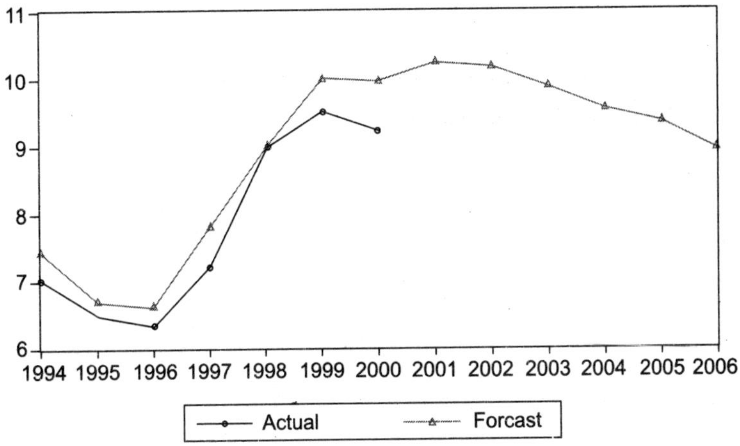

Figure A8.3 Gross Fiscal Deficit of Centre and States as Percentage of GDP

Source: Same as for Figure A8.1.

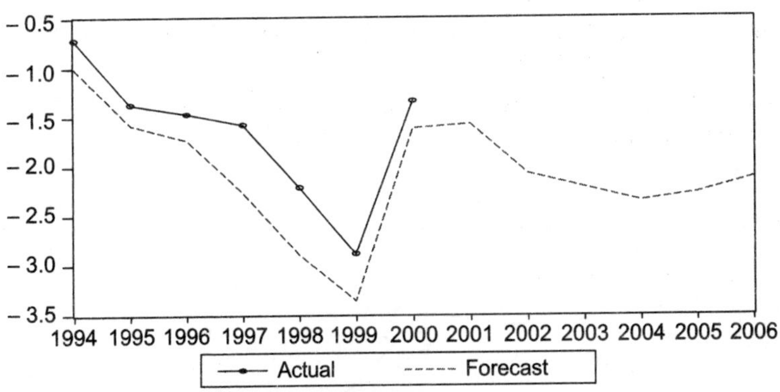

Figure A8.4 Trade Balance as Percentage of GDP

Source: Same as for Figure A8.1.

APPENDIX 9

ACTUAL AND FORECASTS OF KEY MACRO VARIABLES FROM MODEL II

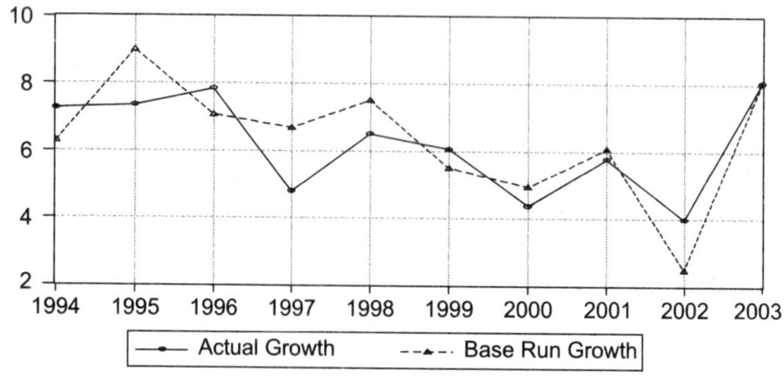

Figure A9.1 Base Run Simulation and Historical GDP Growth Rates (1994–2003)

Source: Computed using data from RBI's Handbook of Statistics on Indian Economy. Forecast data generated by solving Model II.

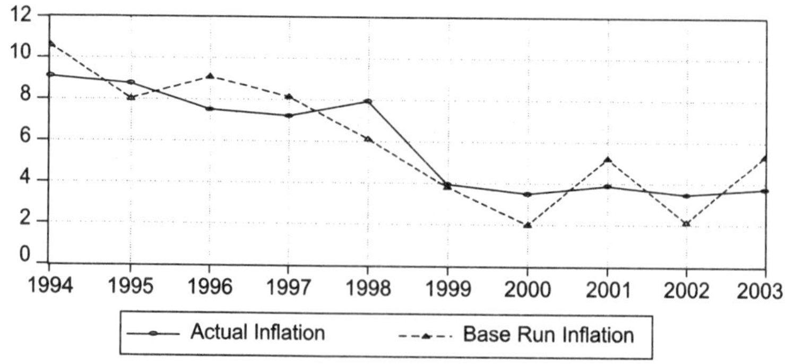

Figure A9.2 Base Run Simulation and Historical Inflation Rates (1994–2003)

Source: Same as for Figure A9.1.

Bibliography

Agarwala, R. (1970), *An Econometric Model of India*, 1948–61, Frank Class, London.

Ahluwalia, I.J. (1979), *Behaviour of Prices and Outputs in India : A Macroeconomic Approach*, Macmillan, New Delhi.

Ahluwalia, I.J. and C. Rangarajan (1986), 'Agriculture and Industry: A Study of Linkages, the Indian Experience', Vol. 8, World Economic Congress of International Association, December.

Balakrishnan, P. (1991), *Pricing and Inflation in India*, Oxford University Press, New Delhi.

Barro, R.J. and X. Sala-i-Martin (1995), *Economic Growth*, McGraw Hill, Singapore.

Bhagwati, J. and S. Chakravarty (1969), 'Contributions to Indian Economic Analysis: A Survey', *American Economic Review*, Supplement, September.

Bhagwati, J. and T.N. Srinivasan (1993), *India's Economic Reforms*, Ministry of Finance, Government of India.

Bhattacharya, B.B. (1975), *Short Term Income Determination*, Macmillan, New Delhi.

——(1982), 'The Government Budget, Inflation and Growth in India: A Macroeconometric Policy Analysis' (mimeo), Institute of Economic Growth, Delhi.

——(1984), *Public Expenditure, Inflation and Growth : A Macro- Econometric Analysis For India*, Oxford University Press, New Delhi.

——(1987), 'The Effectiveness of Monetary Policy in Controlling Inflation: The Indian Experience, 1951–85', *Prajnan*, Vol. 16, No. 2.

Bhattacharya, B.B. and C.H.Hanumantha Rao (1986), 'Agriculture–Industry Interrelations: Issues of Relative Growth in the Context of Public Investment' (mimeo.), Institute of Economic Growth, Delhi.

Bhattacharya, B.B. and V. Pandit (1985), 'Alternative Mode of Financing Public Expenditure and the Trade-off Between Inflation and Growth' (mimeo), Institute of Economic Growth, Delhi.

Bhattacharya, B.B. and S. Guha (1992), 'The Behaviour of Public Debt in India : A Macroeconometric Analysis', *Journal of Quantitative Economics*, January.

Bhattacharya, B.B., R.B. Barman, and A.K. Nag (1994), 'Stabilisation Policy options: A Macroeconometric Analysis', Development Research Group Studies No. 8, Reserve Bank of India, Bombay.

Bhattacharya, B.B. and S. Kar (2002a), 'A Macro-Econometric Model of the Indian Economy : Some Theoretical Aspects', Discussion paper, Institute of Economic Growth, Delhi, March.

——(2002b), 'A Macro-Econometric Model of the Indian Economy : Some Empirical Results', Discussion paper, Institute of Economic Growth, Delhi, March.

——(2002c), 'Short and Medium Run Growth and Stability: A Macro-Econometric Analysis and Forecasts for India', Working paper, Institute of Economic Growth, Delhi.

Bodkin, R.G., L.R. Klein, and K. Marwah (1986), *A History of Macroeconometric Model Building*, Edward Elgar, Eldershot, UK.

Chakrabarty, S. K. (1977), *Behaviour of Prices in India*, Macmillan, New Delhi.

Chakrabarty, T.K. (1987), 'Macroeconomic Model of the Indian Economy', RBI Occasional papers, Vol. 8. No. 3.

Chakravarty S. (1979), 'Keynes, Classics and Developing Economies', in C.H. Hanumantha Rao and P.C. Joshi (eds.), *Reflections on Economic Development and Social Change ; Essays in Honour of Professor V.K.R. V. Rao*, Allied Publishers, New Delhi.

Chaudhry, N.K. (1963), 'An Econometric Model of India, 1930–1955', PhD dissertation (unpublished), University of Wisconsin.

Desai, M.J. (1973), 'Macroeconometric Models for India: A Survey', *Sankhya*, Ser. B., Vol. 35, No. 2.

——(1997), Macroeconometric Models for Planning, Parts 1 and 2 (mimeo), Institute of Economic Growth–Planning Commission Seminar, London School of Economics, UK.

Diebold, Francis (1998), 'The Past, Present and Future of Macroeconomic Forecasting', *Journal of Economic Perspectives*, Vol. 12, No. 2.

Dutta, M. (1964), 'A Prototype Model of India's Foreign Sector', *International Economic Review*, January, Vol. 5, No. 1.

Fair, R.C. (1994), *Testing Macroeconometric Models*, Harvard University Press, Cambridge, Mass.

Frisch, Ragnar (1933), 'Propagation Problems and Impulse Problems in Dynamic Economics', in *Economic Essays in Honour of Gustav Cassel, October 20th, 1933*, Frank Cass and Company Limited, London, pp. 171–205.

Ghose, D., A.K. Lahiri, S. Madhur, and P. Roy (1983), 'An outline of a Macroeconometric Model of the Indian Economy: Specifications and Estimated Results' (mimeo), September.

Ghose, D., A. K. Lahiri and W. Wadhwa (1986), 'Quantitative Restrictions and Indian Exports', *Journal of Development Economics*, Vol. 20.

Gupta, G.S. (1973), 'A Monetary Policy Model for India', *Sankhya*, Series B, Vol. 35, No.4.

Jalan, Bimal (1991), *India's Economic Crisis: The Way Ahead*, Oxford University Press, New Delhi.

——(1992), *The Indian Economy: Problems and Prospects*, Penguin Books, India.

Joshi, V. (1994). 'Macroeconomic Policy and Economic Reform in India', Exim Bank Commencement Day, Annual Lecture.

Joshi, V. and I.M.D. Little (1994), *India:Macro-economics and Political Economy, 1964–1991*, Oxford University Press, New Delhi.

Kalecki, Michal (1935), 'A Macrodynamic Theory of Business Cycles', *Econometrica*, Vol. 3, pp. 327–44.

Kannan, R. (1985), 'An Econometric Model of Foreign trade Sector (1956/57–1979/80)', Reserve Bank of India Occasional Papers, Vol. 6, No. 1, June.

Klein L.R. (1950), *Economic Fluctuations in the United States 1921–1941*, Cowles Commission Monograph No. 11, Wiley, New York.

——(1965), 'What kind of Macro Econometric Model for Developing Economics', *Indian Economic Journal*, Econometric Annual.

——(1984), 'Econometric Model, Planning and Developing Countries', Silver Jubilee Lecture, Institute of Economic Growth, Delhi.

——(1986), 'Economic Policy Formulation: Theory and Implementation, Applied Econometrics in the Public Sector', in Z. Griliches and M.D Intrilligator (eds), *Handbook of Econometrics*, Vol. 3, North-Holland, Amsterdam, Chapter 35.

Klein, L.R. and A.S. Goldberger (1955), *An Econometric Model of the United States 1929-52*, North-Holland, Amsterdam.

Kothari, V.N. (1995), *Indian Economy During the Decade of Eighties*, M.S. University of Baroda Press, Vadodara.

Krishnamurty, K. (1964), 'An Econometric Model for India 1948–61', PhD dissertation (unpublished), University of Pennsylvania.

Krishnamurty K. (1984), 'Inflation and Growth: A Model for India', *Indian Economic Review*, January–June, Vol. 19, No. 1.

(1992), 'Status of Macroeconomic Modelling in India' (mimeo), Institute of Economic Growth, Delhi.

Krishnamurty, K. and D.U. Sastry (1975), *Investment and Financing in the Corporate Sector in India*, Tata McGraw Hill, Delhi.

Krishnamurty, K. and V. Pandit (1984), 'Macroeconomic Modelling of the Indian Economy: An overview', *Indian Economic Review*, Vol. 19, No. 1.

——(1985), *Macroeconometric Modelling of the Indian Economy*, Hindustan Publishing, New Delhi.

——(1995), 'India's Trade Flows: Alternative Policy Scenarios, 1995-2000', Working paper, Centre for Development Economics, Delhi School of Economics, Delhi.

——(1996), 'Exchange Rate, Tariffs and Trade Flows: Alternative Policy Scenarios for India', *Indian Economic Review*, Vol. 31, No. 2., reprinted in *Journal of Asian Economics*, Vol. 8, No. 3.

Krishnamurty, K., V. Pandit, and P.D. Sharma (1989), 'Parameters of Growth in a Developing Mixed Economy : The Indian Experience', *Journal of Quantitative Economics*, Vol. 5, No.2.

Krishna, K.L., K. Krishnamurty, V. Pandit, and P.D. Sharma (1991), 'Macroeconometric Modelling in India : A selective Review of Recent Research', *Econometric Modelling and Forecasting in Asia*, Development Papers No. 9, United Nations (ESCAP), Bangkok.

Little, I.M.D., T. Scitovsky, and M.Scott (1970), *Industry and Trade in Some Developing Countries: A Comparative Study*, Oxford University Press, London.

Madhur. S. (1987), 'Forecasts and Policy Evaluations Using a Macroeconometric Model for India' (mimeo).

Mammen, T. (1967), 'An Econometric study of Money Market in India', PhD dissertation (unpublished), University of Pennsylvania.

——(1973), 'Indian Money Market: An Econometric Study', *International Economic Review*, Vol. 14, No. 1.

——(1999), *India's Economic Prospects: A Macroeconomic and Econometric Analysis*, World Scientific Publishing, Singapore.

Marwah, K. (1963), 'An Econometric Model of Price Behaviour in India', PhD dissertation (unpublished), University of Pennsylvania.

——(1972), 'An Econometric Model of India, Estimating Prices, Their Role and Sources of Change', *Indian Economic Review* (New Series), Vol. 7, April, pp. 53–91.

Marwah, K. (1987), 'On Managing the Exchange Rate of the Indian Rupee: Modelling Post-Bretton Woods Experience, *Journal of Quantitative Economics*, Vol. 3, No. 1.

Mehta, R. and N. Sinha (1991), 'External Trade, Public Sector and the Indian Economy', *Development Papers No.9*, Econometric Modelling and Forecasting in Asia, ESCAP, UN.

Naastepad, C.W.M. (1999), *The Budget Deficit and Macroeconomic Performance : A Real-Financial Computable GEM for India*, Oxford University Press, New Delhi.

Narasimham, N.V.A. (1956), *A Short-Term Planning Model for India*, North-Holland Amsterdam.

Pandit, B.L. (1983), 'A Note on Inflation and Corporate Investment', *Indian Economic Review*, Vol. 18, No. 2.

Pandit V. (1973), 'National Income and the Price Level in India, 1950–51 to 1965–66', *Sankhya*, Ser. B, December.

——(1977), 'Multiplier, Velocity and underdevelopment', *The Manchester School*, Vol. 45, No. 2.

——(1978), 'An Analysis of Inflation in India, 1950-1975', *Indian Economic Review*, Vol.23, No.2.

——(1984), 'Macroeconomic Adjustments in a Developing Economy' *Indian Economic Review*, Vol. 19, No. 1.

——(1985a), 'Macroeconomic Adjustments in a Developing Economy : A Medium Term Model of Outputs and Prices in India', in Krishnamurty and Pandit (eds), *Macro-econometric modeling of the Indian economy*, Hindustan Publishing Corporation, New Delhi.

——(1985b), 'Macroeconomic Structure and Policy in a Less Developed Economy', *Journal of Quantitative Economics*, January, Vol. 1, No. 1.

——(1985c), *Supply, Demand and Monetary Policy in an LDC: An Empirical Analysis of India* (mimeo), Delhi School of Economics, April.

——(1985d), *Monetary Policy, Growth and Stability*, report prepared for the Reserve Bank of India, Committee to Review Working of the Monetary System in India (Chakravarty Committee).

——(1986a), 'Price Adjustments and India's Trade Performance : A Macroeconomic Analysis', paper presented at a meeting of Project Link, Bangkok.

——(1986b), 'A Note on the Structural Macroeconomic Model of India' (mimeo), Delhi School of Economics, January.

Pandit, V. (1986c), 'Growth Performance of the Indian Economy, Supply or Demand?' (mimeo), Working Paper No. 277, Delhi School of Economics, March.

——(1989), 'Macroeconomic Character of the Indian Economy: Theories, Facts and Fancies', mimeo, Delhi School of Economics, September.

——(1995), 'Macroeconomic Character of the Indian Economy: Theories, Facts, and Fancies', in P. Patnaik (ed.), *Macroeconomics*, Oxford University Press, New Delhi.

Pandit, V. and B.B. Bhattacharya (1987), 'Resource Mobilisation, Growth and Inflation : A Trade-off Analysis for India', in M. Datta (ed.), *Asia Pacific Economics : Promises and Challenges*, Jai Press, New York.

Pani, P.K. (1977), *A Macoreconomic Model of the Indian Economy*, Macmillan, New Delhi.

——(1984), 'A Macro Model of Indian Economy with Special Reference to Output, Demand and Prices (1969–70 to 1981–82), *Reserve Bank of India Occasional Papers*, Vol. 5, No. 2, December.

Panchamkhi, V.R. and Rajesh Mehta (1991), 'Modelling of Trade Flows', Development Papers No.9, Econometric Modelling and Forecasting in Asia, ESCAP, UN.

Pradhan, B. K., D. K. Ratha, and A. Sharma (1990), 'Complementarity Between Public and Private Investment in India', *Journal of Development Economics*, Vol. 33.

Quesnay, F. (1972), *Quesnay's Tableau Economique* [1759], M. Kuczynski and R.L. Meck (eds), Macmillan, London.

Rakshit, M.K. (1982), *The Labour Surplus Economy*, Macmillan, Delhi.

Raj, K.N.(1966), 'Price Behaviour in India, 1949–66 : An Explanatory Hypothesis', *Indian Economic Review*, N.S., Vol. I, No. 2.

Rangarajan, C. and Anoop Singh (1984), 'Reserve Money : Concepts and Policy Implications for India', *Reserve Bank of India Occasional Papers,* Vol. 5, No. 1, June.

Rangarajan, C., A. Basu, and N. Jadhav (1989), 'Dynamics of Interaction Between Government Deficit and Domestic Debt in India', RBI Occasional Papers, September.

Rangarajan C. and R.R. Arif (1990), 'Money Output and Prices, A Macroeconometric Model', *Economic and Political Weekly*, Vol. 25, No. 16.

Rastogi, Anupam (1991), A Rational Expectations Model of the Indian Economy (mimeo), Working Paper No. 91/02, Liverpool Research Group in Macro Economics.

Research Team (1996), 'Macroeconomic Modelling for India', *Theory, Methodology and Model,* Vol. 1, Institute of Economic Growth and Delhi School of Economics.

Pandit, V. (1997), 'Seminar on Macroeconomic Modelling for India', Background papers, September 27, Institute of Economic Growth and Delhi School of Economics.

Sarkar, H. and M. Panda (1992), 'A Short term Structural Macroeconomic Model for India : Applications to Policy Analysis', *Econometric Modelling and Forecasting in Asia*, Development Papers No. 9, United Nations (ESCAP), Bangkok.

Sen, A. (1997), 'On Economic Opennes and Industrialization' in D. Nayyar (ed.) *Trade and Industrilization*, Oxford University Press, Delhi.

Sreenivas, M.A. (1974), *Price Behaviour in India, 1948–49 to 1965–66 : A Comparative Study of Three Macro Approaches*', Bangalore.

Swamy, D.S. and V.G. Rao(1975), 'The Flow of Funds in the Indian Manufacturing Sector', *Sankhya,* Series C, Vol. 37, No. 4.

Taylor, L. (1983), *Structuralist Macroeconomics: Applicable Models for the Third World,* Basic Books, New York.

Tinbergen, J. (1939), *Statistical Testing of Business Cycle Theories*, League of Nations, Geneva.

Tobin, J. (1980), *Asset Accumulation and Economic Activity,* Yrjo Jahnsson Lectures, Basil Blackwell, Oxford.

United Nations Conference on Trade and Development (UNCTAD) (1968), 'Trade Projections for India', *Trade Prospects and Capital Needs of Developing Countries,* United Nations, New York, pp. 298–317.

Virmani, A. (1991), 'Demand and Supply Factors in India's Trade', *Economic and Political Weekly,* February.

Walras, L. (1874), *Elements D'economie Politique Pure,* L. Corbaz, Lausanne.

Weintraub, S. (1965), *Growth Without Inflation*, National Council of Applied Economic Research, New Delhi.

INDEX